Anglo-American relations in the twentieth century

Since 1904, Britain's defence plans have ceased to take into account the possibility of war with the USA. History since that date, however, attests that there were in fact times when the possibility was at least raised. In 1928 Churchill declared that war with the USA was not 'unthinkable'. From its outset the difficulties and disputes that the two countries have had to surmount in order to maintain their special relationship have been many.

Anglo-American Relations in the Twentieth Century traces the growth of friendship which developed from 1895 and led to their special relationship. It looks at the Second World War and the Cold War, both of which cemented the alliance, and reveals more interdependence than has been recognised in the past. The author also unveils the conflicts which jeopardised the harmony and the ways in which they were overcome. He examines the effect the disputes had on the strength of the relationship and discusses what the future of Anglo-American relations may hold.

Alan P. Dobson is a Senior Lecturer in Politics at the University of Wales, Swansea. He has written extensively on the subject of Anglo-American relations and the diplomacy of civil aviation. His most recent book, *Flying in the Face of Competition*, was published in 1995.

Anglo-American relations in the twentieth century

Of friendship, conflict and the rise and decline of superpowers

Alan P. Dobson

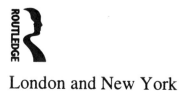

London and New York

First published 1995
by Routledge
2 Park Square, Milton Park, Abingdon, Oxon, OX14 4RN

Simultaneously published in the USA and Canada
by Routledge
270 Madison Ave, New York NY 10016

Transferred to Digital Printing 2005

© 1995 Alan P. Dobson

Typeset in Times by LaserScript, Mitcham, Surrey

British Library Cataloguing in Publication Data
A catalogue record for this book is available from the British Library

Library of Congress Cataloguing in Publication Data
A catalogue record for this book has been requested

ISBN 0–415–11942–1
ISBN 0–415–11943–X (pbk)

Contents

Acknowledgements

The nature of this work has made it necessary for me to delve into numerous archives and to seek financial help to do so. In the course of my research I received help from the following: the United States Embassy, London £350; the Harry S. Truman Foundation $2,000; the Franklin D. Roosevelt Foundation $2,000; and the British Academy £1,842. I am deeply grateful to them all.

I would also like to thank all the librarians and archivists who helped, in particular the staff of the Truman and Roosevelt Libraries. I have also received encouragement from my colleague in Swansea, Mike Simpson, and from my long-standing American friend Warren Kimball of Rutgers University: both of them read parts of the manuscript and made helpful comments.

Bev and my three daughters, Naomi, Jessica and Becky, have been loving and supportive throughout.

Alan Dobson
University of Wales, Swansea, June 1994

1 The lion and the eagle: of twisted tails and plucked feathers

We are at the opening verse of the
opening page of endless possibilities.
(Rudyard Kipling)

It has been nearly a hundred years since either Britain or the USA held the citizens of the other as prisoners of war. The fact that either has done so this century probably comes as a surprise to most readers who know that Britain and the USA have not been at war since the Peace of Ghent in December 1814 and that the two have had a famous special relationship.[1] Indeed, the uniqueness of their relationship in an era of mayhem and total war can be captured by the phrase 'friendly superpowers'. Peace between them has survived even during the transition period when the USA took over from Britain as the world's richest and most potent nation state. In the story that follows the ups and downs of this relationship will be traced through the twentieth century, for, although Britain and the USA have been friendly superpowers, they have also had bitter disagreements and suffered intense diplomatic and political friction. But, before embarking upon the narrative, a few remarks about the nature of the enterprise are in order.

A BRIEF DIGRESSION ON METHOD

Exploring relationships, of whatever kind, always has difficulties. Einstein demonstrated that things never stay still long enough to be captured in thought in the way that classical philosophers had tried to do. We come to know people, things and relationships through the way that they change. But a tendency persists to think in static terms of that which is to be explained. To counter that, it is not necessary to advocate a radical form of relativism. It is not suggested that Anglo-American relations can only be explained in as many ways as there are people who take an interest, all of whom have different perspectives. Change is never absolute, and human knowledge would cease to be knowledge if it were subject to extreme atomisation as a result of radical relativism. In a very strong sense we know people because of what they do and say – types of change as understood in the present argument – and because they are still recognisable as the person they were before saying and doing what they have just said and done. There has to be both continuity and change for knowledge to accumulate and some consensus on how it is produced.

Knowledge for the historian is limited by the evidence that exists for what has gone on in the past. However, trying to explain a relationship that lasts over a lengthy period of time and appears to have some constant elements running through it can tempt one into over-simple generalisations. Before we realise it we fall into the classic trap of trying to conceive of things in static or essentialist terms. Instead of teasing out generalisations from a detailed historical narrative to help us grasp how Britain and the USA have related to each other, there is a danger of using preconceived concepts of how they have interacted to mould the evidence into artificial patterns that are not true to the way the historical actors perceived of the way things were at the time.

One such concept is the so-called 'special relationship'. At a one-day conference at the University of Durham in the mid-1970s, an American official was asked what he thought about it. His answer nicely illustrated the danger of using that concept to explain or characterise Anglo-American relations. He said: 'The question reminds me of occasions when I'm asked how my wife is. I always respond: In relation to what?' As the man suggested, we need to know what was special, when, and in connection with what aspect of the relationship.

Clearly, in a short introduction to twentieth-century Anglo-American relations one, perforce, has to be highly selective of material and resort to shorthand generalisations in order both to give a plausible perspective on the relationship and, more importantly, to stimulate thought and further questions about how things came to pass. The greatest compliment scholars can receive is that they stimulate thought in people who then go on to improve on the work that they have done. Much of what is said here is derived from more detailed research published elsewhere by both myself and many others. The aim of the book is ambitious, because it tries to do three things: first, to provide an adequate picture of Anglo-American relations for those with a general interest in these matters; second, to stimulate thoughts about the relationship, which should result in a more critical awareness of the policies of the two countries, that can only be satisfied by further reading; and third, to engage the interest and raise some questions in minds that will then feel the need to embark on their own research.

IDENTIFYING THE CONTOURS OF THE RELATIONSHIP

One of the most striking things in the literature on Anglo-American relations is the tendency for radically different views to be expressed on the role the various components of the relationship have played. Language and culture, economics, politics and diplomacy, personal and ethnic relations, and strategic and military concerns are seen by some as contributing to constructive and friendly relations and by others as factors which have caused tension, conflict and economic exploitation. It is not possible to give a clear line of interpretation on these contending views without looking in more detail at the events in question, but an overview of the general landscape might help to establish a context in which the problems involved in understanding and coming to know about the relationship may be addressed more easily.[2]

Oscar Wilde once quipped something to the effect that the British and the Americans were divided by a common language. And, indeed, linguistic vagaries do lend themselves to amusing possibilities. An American asking for potato chips in a British pub might be surprised at being presented with a plate of french fries when what he really expected was a packet of crisps. But it is not just at the mundane and trivial level that language has been seen as a problem. In 1928, at a time when there were serious differences between Britain and the USA, Robert Craigie, of the American Department of the British Foreign Office (FO), wrote that the causes of the difficulties included 'the clash of differing national characteristics emphasised by the existence of a common language; the growing discrepancies of speech and style within that 'common' language . . .'.[3] Rather ironically, language was blamed for problems in Anglo-American relations because of both its common and its different usage.

At other times language has been accorded eminence in explaining good relations. H.V. Hodson in the inaugural lecture of the Ditchley Foundation, established near Oxford in 1962 to promote mutual Anglo-American understanding, asserted: 'Our common language does, after all, remove or minimise one great obstacle to understanding between our peoples.'[4] In the nineteenth century, the great German Chancellor Otto von Bismarck, thought that the single most important fact of the twentieth century would be that the British and the Americans spoke the same language, and indeed the ease with which diplomats, the military and politicians from Britain and the USA can converse with each other has been a factor in close co-operation on many occasions. Anglo-American language and culture were seen as so important by the British statesman Joseph Chamberlain that he professed that he could not think of Americans as anything other than blood relatives. In more recent times, James Callaghan, British Prime Minister 1976–9, has spoken of the ease and informality of his relationship with both Gerald Ford and Jimmy Carter, US Presidents 1974–7 and 1977–81 respectively. With the latter there was an agreement that they could pick up the telephone and discuss things that were of concern at any time. On more than one occasion they did just that.[5] Thus from one vantage-point language has promoted and from another undermined good relations between the two states.

Culture has had a similar impact. Early America, while unable to deny its cultural heritage from Britain, came to resent it in many ways and gradually developed a kind of practical Yankee disdain for the effete trappings of high culture. The American good life emerged as a rather contradictory amalgam of plain no-nonsense living and material affluence. To the upper-class Briton, and to the new but quickly assimilated (through public schools,* Oxbridge and the feudal honours system of creating knights and lords) rich commercial and industrial class, Americans appeared rather incompatibly as brash and sanctimonious. For many in Britain the archetypal American was the cowboy, the gangster, the film starlet and later the over-paid, over-sexed and over-here GI. To the American mind the British were either class-ridden or riddled with socialism. Imperialists, haughty, arrogant and diplomatically too smart to be dealt with with anything other than apprehension: these were views that lingered well into the latter part of the twentieth century. It would appear that on the level of the collective, Americans and Britons had little affection for each other. Fortunately, on the personal level there were often warmer relationships, and it must be said that as the twentieth century progressed, things improved, though not in a consistent and linear pattern. With more travel and with Britain exporting more of its singing and dramatic talents to the USA from the 1960s onwards, stereotypical images began to fade and a more accurate mutual appreciation began to emerge.

Britain and the USA have had strong economic ties since the colonial era. In the nineteenth century it was largely British capital that developed America's railways and other vital parts of her industrial and agricultural economy, and British money that bought American exports. The dominance of British economic power was much resented, and viewed as another unpalatable taste of her imperialism. But, beginning in the 1850s, the USA

---

* British public schools are, of course, private: this is another confusing vagary of English usage.

began to invest and develop production in Britain. By the twentieth century the average standard of living in the USA had overtaken Britain's, and its gross national product (GNP) was the greatest in the world. The house of J.P. Morgan had to be called on to raise money for the British war efforts against, first, the Boers in South Africa and then later the Central Powers – Germany and the Austro-Hungarian Empire – in Europe. After the Great War, 1914–18, Britain was indebted to the USA to the tune of $3.7 billion. In the Second World War, 1939–45, money debts were avoided, for the most part because of an arrangement known as Lend-Lease, but costs were involved in terms of the kind of peacetime economic policies Britain agreed to pursue at America's behest. Because of this, some saw Britain as economically subject to an imperial capitalist hegemon – the USA. Others who disagree with that have pointed to her recalcitrance in refusing American demands that she should work within Europe for integration during the 1940s and 1950s. In a similar vein, there was her refusal to abandon the sterling monetary area and British imperial trade preferences, which were forms of discriminatory monetary and trade relations with the Empire, the Commonwealth and client states. Such policies were seen as evidence of her continuing independence and of the relationship with the USA in the economic realm as one of competitive co-operation and mutual benefit.[6] So, did Britain exploit the USA in the early twentieth century? Were roles reversed after 1918? Was the USA an imperial economic hegemon after the Second World War? If relationships of an imperial kind existed between the two, where was there room for a special relationship?

Whatever conclusions one might come to in answer to these questions some facts that cannot be interpreted away have to be taken into account. First, there was an enormous reversal of relative economic fortunes between 1880 and 1980; in the industrial world in which we live, this set the limits of possible international political and military power. In 1880 Britain's manufacturing output was approximatley one-third as big again as that of the USA: in 1980 her GNP was barely one-sixth of that of the USA. Second, Britain's descent from premier superpower status to being a middle-range power, and the USA's ascent from the lower rungs of world affairs to premier superpower status, occurred without any belligerent conflict between the two. There has never been any other comparable peaceful transformation of power roles in the history of the world, a phenomenon that demands consideration as the course of their economic relations is assessed.

In the realms of politics and diplomacy, there appears to be as much that divides as brings together the two countries. In the nineteenth century, the dominant tradition in the diplomacy of the USA fed off a number of moral convictions and prudential precepts that separated her from practices prevalent in Britain and created grounds for possible friction. America was called the New World and was seen by the Americans of the USA as the redeemer of the state of fallen man in Europe:

Give me your tired, your poor,
Your huddled masses yearning to breathe free,
The wretched refuse of your teeming shore.
Send these, the homeless, tempest tost to me,
I lift my lamp beside the golden door!

The parallel between St. Peter at the doors of heaven and this extract from the inscription at the base of the Statue of Liberty hardly needs to be pointed out. And just as a distance needs to be maintained between the earthly and the heavenly, so there had to be an isolation of the New World from the Old to prevent contamination and corruption. Eventually, as the power of the New prospered and grew, there came a time for a crusade, at first, beyond the dominant influence of Europe, and then, as confidence grew, the time was ripe for a second coming: the New World would meet with the Old on its own ground and attempt a conversion from corruption and evil to democracy, liberty and moral conduct. President Woodrow Wilson tried, but failed, to achieve this after World War I.

In addition to this pious view of the world role of the USA, there was a more pragmatic one expressed by George Washington in September 1796 in his farewell address as President, which also contributed to isolationism. Because Europe's interests were not related to the concerns of the USA (and, though this was unspoken, because European states were so much more powerful than the USA) 'it must be unwise in us to implicate ourselves by artificial ties in the ordinary vicissitudes of her politics or the ordinary combinations and collisions of her friendships or enmities'.[7] Extend America's commercial activities abroad by all means, but keep out of Europe's dynastic and immoral squabbles.

From these perspectives on American foreign relations three important characteristics emerged. First, there was the policy of isolationism. The usefulness of this term has been challenged by various scholars; here it is taken to mean isolationism from European political and miltary matters – though by the beginning of the twentieth century that has to be qualified by saying that the USA became concerned with naval power and the defence of the Western hemisphere in such a way that it could no longer maintain its aloofness consistently. The main international plank upon which isolationism rested in the nineteenth century was the Monroe Doctrine of 1823, which proclaimed that any European intervention in the Western hemisphere would be regarded as an unfriendly disposition towards the USA.[8] By a fortunate coincidence of interests it suited Britain to approve of the Monroe Doctrine: it cut down possible European competition for commercial dominance in Latin America and would allow free trade with that area. As no power could challenge the dominance of the Royal Navy on the high seas between the battles of Trafalgar in 1805 and Jutland in 1916, American idealism, backed by the reality of British power, meant that the Monroe Doctrine would be effective.

Second, isolationism led logically to a neutrality policy during European conflicts and that, combined with America's expansion of trade and commerce, resulted in the USA adopting a strong line on neutral rights to trade. This was to provide the longest-lasting and the most difficult bone of contention between Britain and the USA from the Napoleonic Wars in the early nineteenth century to America's entry into World War I in 1917, and beyond to the 1927 Geneva Naval Conference.[9]

Third, the moralising involved in isolationism developed strongly in the nineteenth century, but along lines perhaps not entirely foreseen in the moralising of the Founding Fathers. As America's self-confidence and power grew, so did her vision of her role in world history. Americans began to talk of 'Manifest Destiny', and, ironically, that position subsumed the isolationist sense of America's unique quality of morality in its public, private and political life – sometimes referred to as American exceptionalism. That 'unique quality' contributed to a crusading spirit that would lead to interventionism in order to spread the American way of doing things abroad. The values inherent in isolationism required aloofness from the Old World, but could be used to justify intervention elsewhere to advance America's mission to civilise the world. The legacy received down the years has been a tendency to moralise, sometimes in ways that have oversimplified situations. Of course, this is nowhere near the whole story: pragmatism, *realpolitik*, mistakes, circumstances outside America's control, and the need to mobilise US public opinion (to mention but a few) have also played their part in affecting US foreign policy, but signs of moralising in the manner just drawn often make an appearance.

British conduct in foreign affairs was in marked contrast to the professed principles of the USA in its main traditions, though there were traits that corresponded to attitudes in the USA. Perfidious Albion got her name largely because of what theorists would call a realist approach to foreign policy. This involves a state-centred view in which power is the medium through which affairs are conducted in a world where there is no Leviathan to maintain order and legality. In the nineteenth-century, because of her imperial and commercial preoccupations, the mainstay of British strategic policy was to neutralise the impact of European affairs on British matters by upholding a balance of power in Europe in order to prevent the emergence of a dominant state that could threaten her security. As one of the great nineteenth-century Foreign Secretaries, Lord Palmerston, put it, Britain had no permanent friends and no permanent enemies, only permanent interests. To implement this view of national interest Britain had to be pragmatic and bolster the power of any state or group of states in danger of being overcome by a more powerful state in Europe. British determination to prevent the emergence of an hegemonic military power meant that she had to support states that threatened to disturb the balance of power by becoming relatively too weak. That support had to be rendered irrespective of the morality of the immediate tactical issues at stake, for the sake of British grand strategy. In many American eyes this epitomised the unprincipled nature of European power games and was a clear symptom of the evils of self-seeking imperialistic aggrandisement.

Another major characteristic of British foreign policy, one that caused difficulties with the USA, was naval strategy in wartime. Britain ruled supreme over the oceans of the world, but never had a large army establishment until the Great War of 1914-18. British war strategy thus centred on the use of naval power, and as industrialisation made materials and equipment ever more important for the successful waging of war so Britain took a harder and harder line to deny materials and equipment to her enemies. This led to a long-standing problem with the USA because of her assertion of extensive neutral rights to trade in wartime: the one exception to that in the nineteenth century was US policy during the Civil War, 1861–5.

However, while the USA and Britain seemed to be at odds with each other in terms of their overall styles of diplomacy, there were also similarities. The American sense of moral superiority, perhaps best expressed in its belief in Manifest Destiny, had a counterpart in Britain with the imperialist notion of the White Man's Burden and the belief in the superiority of British culture and political and legal institutions, championed by men such as Cecil Rhodes and Rudyard Kipling. Towards the end of the nineteenth century these ideas came together in the minds of those who advocated a form of Anglo-Saxonism. At the same time there was some convergence between America's predominantly moralistic style and Britain's pragmatic realism. At the end of the nineteenth century there was a flurry of aggressive imperial activity on the part of the USA which brought her nearer to the realism of British policy. In particular, the Corollary to the Monroe Doctrine, pronounced by Theodore Roosevelt in 1904, that unlawful behaviour in the Western hemisphere could be justification, in exceptional circumstances, for US intervention to restore order in foreign countries, seemed based on calculation of US interests, namely the need to safeguard US investments and commerce, more than on anything else.[10] At the end of the nineteenth century atrocities by Turkey, to whom Britain often rendered support in order to contain Russia, and then later the Boer War, 1899–1902, helped to revive moral concerns in Britain about foreign policy. Cold calculation of national self-interest, irrespective of the immediate effects in moral terms, was becoming less acceptable. In the long term these shifts in outlook in Britain and America were to lead to a kind of role reversal, which requires a little more elucidation.

Britain's international role came under scrutiny at the end of the nineteenth century. This was partly prompted by the perception of Britain's relative decline, by new ideas about the Empire, in particular the possibility of a federation of the white dominions, and by various moral concerns. During this volatile mixture of developments, the thoughts of radical Liberals and of the members of the rapidly growing Labour Party began a long-term shift of opinion which directed attention away from international to domestic affairs. Even the Conservative champions of empire contributed to this with their attempts to move away from internationalist free trade and revive protectionism for the sake of Britain's increasingly uncompetitive manufacturing industries. But, the bulwarks of Britain's internationalism – the continuing responsibilities of empire; the city banking, insurance and shipping institutions; her commercialism; her overseas investments; and her trade – ensured its continuation as an important characteristic of British policy, at least until the 1970s.[11] For its part, the USA's isolationism came under threat because of developments to do with her burgeoning industry and trade which began to create a form of internationalism. This was reinforced both by the crusading zeal emanating from belief in US Manifest Destiny and a realisation that the USA was becoming vulnerable through developments in modern warfare. It is true that this latter consideration also led to movements at various times for a fortress America, but time and technological advances were on the side of the internationalists. In retrospect the supporters of fortress America may be seen clearly for what they were: the vestiges of an isolationist creed which the modern world has rendered obsolete. Thus during the twentieth century, as Britain's power declined and as her Empire was granted self-rule and independence, she became more and more inward-looking and Europe-centred. In the USA the situation was reversed. Isolationism gradually gave way to internationalism. In this process Britain found herself urging America to play a more important role in world affairs in the early part of the century: in later years the USA found herself urging Britain to uphold her defence and international commitments rather than retreat into European parochialism.

Politically the two countries share a kernel of truths that have proved resilient through peace and war and in the long term have helped to mould similar attitudes to the major problems that have confronted the world in the twentieth century: the need for a healthy world economy with an amount of freedom compatible with stability; the need to resist German militarism; the need to oppose national socialism, fascism and Japanese militarism; and the priority of containing communism. These constituted a common political morality based on a theory of individual rights and involving limited power for government and its need both to respond to and to be accountable to the people. However, such principles should not disguise the fact that there are also many differences in the political structures of the two countries, some of which have counted in their relationship. The USA is a federal state, with power dispersed between the states and the federal government with its three separate branches – the executive, the judiciary and the legislature. It has a written constitution and a judiciary that participates in government extensively through its power of judicial review, with which it can strike down laws and castigate the actions of the executive on the grounds of unconstitutionality. This is not an easy system to operate. For foreign policy in particular there can be difficulties because of the Senate's power to refuse to ratify treaties, and Congressional reluctance to vote money for the execution of policies. If Britain was perfidious Albion, then the USA gained a reputation in the twentieth century as unreliable Uncle Sam because presidential policy could be uncertain, unpredictable and changeable. American failure to ratify the Versailles Treaty and the Covenant of the League of Nations created a poor view of her in Europe.

The structure of the British political system is very different. It is a unitary state with a unified power structure. The fulcrum of legislative, executive and, to a lesser extent, judicial power is the Cabinet. The Cabinet in turn dominates the main body of Parliament, the House of Commons, through the party system, and Parliament is constitutionally supreme. In theory it can pass whatever laws it likes; in practice it is controlled by the longest tradition of representative government in the world, a free press, a legal system derived from Common Law and statute, and a highly adversarial type of party politics.

During the twentieth century party politics became something of an issue in Anglo-American relations. Unlike the variants on liberal capitalism that predominated in US politics in the form of the Republican and Democratic Parties, in Britain there were clearer ideological divides, not so much between the Liberals and the Conservatives in the early part of the century, but certainly between Labour and Conservative in the 1930s and

1940s and from the 1980s onwards. So far as relations with the USA were concerned the imperial elements in the Liberal and Conservative Parties and the socialism of the Labour Party were causes of friction. For Britain the problems that arose with US political parties were largely bipartisan: isolationism, resentment of British economic power, a dislike of socialism and imperialism, and Anglophobia were all to be found in both parties.

Anglophobia was most prevalent in certain ethnic groups, in particular the Irish, but it was also strong in the Midwest and on the Pacific coast. It was outweighed by Anglophilia among those of British descent who made up the dominant white, Anglo-Saxon, Protestant (WASP) elite, largely based on the eastern seaboard, that generally ran the political affairs of the USA. Furthermore, at the end of the nineteenth century there was a spate of nuptials between American money and British aristocracy that added to the growing ties that drew the two countries closer. The most famous products of these liaisons were Winston Churchill and Harold Macmillan. In fact, at the personal as opposed to the more general level of ethnic relations, there was a steady stream of important friendships that furthered the cause of good Anglo-American relations and fruitful co-operation. But that is not to say that there were not also problems at the personal level, for example, the notoriously bad relationship in the 1950s between US Secretary of State John Foster Dulles and Anthony Eden, successively British Foreign Secretary and Prime Minister.

Finally, we come to military and strategic matters. First appearances suggest considerable problems for Britain and the USA. There was the war of 1812 and the problems to do with neutral shipping rights which had caused it and which had still not been resolved by 1900. Neutral rights to trade were still a highly charged problem in Anglo-American relations in the twentieth century, and in the minds of some very influential people the one issue that could have caused hostilities between the two. There were also unhappy memories of British help for the Confederacy in the US Civil War and troublesome matters over the US–Canadian border that still needed resolving. There had been an ugly incident over a boundary dispute between British Guiana and Venezuela in 1895, when President Cleveland and Secretary of State Olney told Britain in no uncertain terms that she should not interfere in the the Western Hemisphere. And in 1902 Britain held, though it was to be the last time, American citizens as prisoners of war. The prisoners were US volunteers who had fought against Britain in Africa on the side of the Boers, of the Transvaal and Orange Free State, led by Paul Kruger. The Boer War, 1899–1902, was the result of a complex constellation of factors involving the discovery of gold in the Transvaal, racial tension between the Boers and the English, and the designs of British imperial extremists, but in the end it came down to a struggle by the two Boer republics to remain independent from Britain. They failed, but in the meantime Americans fighting on their behalf, and their capture by the British, caused considerable diplomatic activity. Matters were not resolved until October 1902, when a letter from Lord Lansdowne, the British Foreign Secretary, informed US Secretary of State John Hay that the Americans would be repatriated on the first packet boat available.[12]

In addition to all these episodes there was a potentially much more damaging development: the rise of American naval power. In retrospect one can draw a picture of the ineluctable projection of US military power. First came the expansion of US overseas trade, commerce and investment and a natural desire to provide adequate protection for them. At the same time the development of modern armaments caused a shrinkage of the globe in strategic terms, and the USA began to feel vulnerable to powers across both the Atlantic and the Pacific Ocean. Relying as she did on the navy for her main defence, the USA began to see the great advantage of an isthmian canal to enable it to counter threats to either of its coastlines by moving its battle fleet quickly from one ocean to the other. But valuable as the Panama Canal became, it was also a hostage to fortune and required an expansion of America's immediate sphere of defence: the logic of the need for more defence was acquiring a dynamic of its own. The second great factor involved in changing US naval defence policy was the imperial drive for expansion that found its greatest expression in the war against Spain in 1898. That was a success, but again there were more hostages to fortune: the most difficult of all to deal with were the Philippine Islands. The expansionist mentality of the USA in the late nineteenth century was fostered by Social Darwinism, economic dynamics, a sense of racial superiority and Manifest Destiny, and found expression in missionary work, the commercial penetration of more and more foreign countries and expanding trade. The result was an ever-expanding spiral of interests and the need to defend them. How to defend them was a question answered by the great American naval strategist Alfred Mahan.

Mahan believed that America's power and prosperity depended in the future upon her trade and commerce. To ensure that the American merchant fleet would always be able to operate he argued that it was necessary to build a large navy. And as America's interests were now being defined within a necessarily expansive geographical context, a fleet capable of defending America's coast and coastal shipping was no longer adequate. The USA must have a large ocean-going battle fleet in order to be able to engage the enemy wherever it might be. This was the only sure way of protecting American sea-borne commerce.[13] Such a strategy inevitably came to challenge Britain's naval supremacy and her policy, set by the British Naval Defence Act of 1889, of maintaining a navy equal to any other two combined. Under normal conditions of *realpolitik*, which generally governed British naval policy, a challenge such as was eventually mounted by the USA could not be tolerated. In the world of the realist one always has to assume the worst. Today's friend could be tomorrow's enemy, therefore always be prepared and never willingly give up an advantage. A good example of this thinking in British government circles was expressed by Prime Minister Stanley Baldwin in the House of Commons in June 1925 on the matter of air power: 'British air power must include a Home Defence Force of sufficient strength adequately to protect us against air attack by the strongest Air Force within striking distance of this country.'[14] At the time that country was France, supposedly Britain's friend. However, as we shall see, although the USA gradually produced a navy to match and later outstrip the Royal Navy, similar thinking to that expressed by Baldwin was not applied to the USA in the same way as it was to other countries, though that is not to say that there were not difficulties.

Naturally enough, all those things that can contribute towards producing good and friendly relations between states are also exactly the kind of things which can give rise to arguments and disagreements. It should come as no surprise when criminologists tell us that the majority of violent crimes occur within the circle of family, close friends and acquaintances. Matters between states are somewhat different, but states which do not experience any mutual intercourse will have few grounds for friendship or enmity. Quite clearly, Britain and the USA were not like that. They had a whole host of points of connection – language and culture; diplomatic and foreign relations; economic links; similar political values, but different practices and institutions; many personal and ethnic ties; interrelated strategic and military concerns, and for much of the time down to the end of the nineteenth century – those things seemed to hold more potential for souring relations than for anything else. As late as 1940, in a book specifically designed to help nurture good relations, an eminent British politician, Viscount Samuel, wrote about the historical context of Anglo-American relations in an attempt to put the difficulties and prejudices that sometimes undermined things into perspective:

> For them [the Americans] the history that matters begins with the Pilgrim Fathers and those that followed them, setting out to face every peril and hardship for conscience sake; seeking liberty of thought and liberty of worship across the ocean; casting off the yoke of oppressive, tyrannous government – the government of England.

Those first experiences were followed by the War of Independence, the war of 1812, the Civil War, in which the British governing classes 'sympathised with the wrong side', and British maltreatment of Ireland and mass emigration to the USA, creating there 'in the electorate a bitter resentful, anti-British block, enduring for generations'. This is an impressive catalogue of sources of enmity. As Samuel concludes: 'It is a painful story to tell. But it has to be told.'[15]

In fact by the turn of the century the impact of many of these matters was diminishing with the passage of time, but there were still contentious issues: economic rivalry; ill-feeling towards Britain from a number of ethnic groups; a dislike of British imperialism and her class system; continuing friction over neutral rights in war; British disdain for American commercialism and lack of culture; and potential for severe naval rivalry. At the same time, as the historian Coral Bell has observed, the quality of the relationship between Britain and the USA already had something special about it before the close of the nineteenth century.[16]

As noted above, both Britain and the USA began to become concerned about their security and their traditional policies towards the close of the nineteenth century. Britain was concerned with possible threats to her imperial possessions from France and Russia and worried by the rise of Germany on the continent. The USA was also worried about the possibility of a projection of German power into the Western hemisphere through its growing navy and possible liaisons with Latin American countries. There was also the problem of the emergence of Japan, complicated by the exposed outpost of the USA in the Philippines. Bearing these worries in mind, the two countries had to consider what might happen between them if their relations ran into trouble. In any conflict with the USA there were bound to be two serious vulnerabilities for Britain: the difficulty of defending Canada – and later the danger of alienating her – in a conflict with the USA; and the possible loss of a massive amount of British trade and investment. For much of the nineteenth and twentieth centuries, the USA has been the largest or second largest market for British exports. For America, there was the growing need for access to overseas markets and raw materials and the fear of being excluded by European imperialists. There might be rivalry with Britain over markets, but of all the imperial powers Britain was undeniably the most liberal trader, and therefore the USA had an interest in supporting her. Both countries had to contend with the thought that if there were war between them they would be able to harm each other, but how could one actually win? The most likely outcome would be a mutually damaging stalemate. Thus it is not altogether surprising, though the above factors are not offered as an exhaustive explanation of why this came about, that Britain and the USA developed a habit of referring disputes between them to arbitration. As the twentieth century progressed, disputes that had any potential for open conflict faded away, whereas challenges from third parties repeatedly brought the two powers together to resist what they both perceived as aggression and as threats to their increasingly similar democratic liberalism.

At the start of the new century there was a developing convergence of several British and American policies and beliefs. Both countries in fact had experienced versions of isolationism in the nineteenth century: the USA most strongly so, but the British also in that they had fought shy of entangling alliances in Europe. In the early twentieth century, however, both countries began to feel exposed and threatened because of their policies of voluntary solitude, and started to change their outlook. In the process of doing that it gradually emerged that Britain and the USA had more interests in common than observers in the previous century might have realised.

Neither country was a militaristic state in the sense that the continental European powers were. Britain and the USA at the turn of the century were first and foremost naval powers which preferred compromise and accommodation, and the application of limited force rather than all-out war. Under different circumstances their respective naval power could have been reason not to have friendly relations, but as things turned out their common naval experiences – though causing friction – in the end contributed to the bonding-together of the two. In the more threatening world of the twentieth century, Britain and the USA had to reappraise their interests and the likelihood of conflict. As they did so, the things that they shared began to take on new importance, and the problems that would arise if they were to come to blows with each other were seen to outweigh any possible advantages. Their respective diplomatic and foreign policies began to perceive the expansive authoritarian powers such as Japan and Germany as threatening, not just militarily but also economically with their penchant for exclusive control of markets. Their styles of diplomacy began to draw together, with Britain accepting more moral and idealistic values into her debates on foreign policy and admitting the importance of public opinion on certain high-profile matters. At the same time, in the USA there was a shift to a more realist and pragmatic approach as American interests spread across the Western hemisphere and the Pacific. Politically, Britain underwent various reforms that made her more democratic and diluted the importance of birth and status. Such changes brought her closer to the more egalitarian American system. Family connections, especially between the elites of the two societies, flourished and grew in the 1890s, and the influence of Social Darwinism, Manifest Destiny and the White Man's Burden created a sense of mission for Anglo-Saxonism among a considerable number of leaders on both sides of the Atlantic. Both countries were essentially 'have' societies and feared the debilitating effects that a major war might have. Between themselves it became more and more noticeable as the twentieth century progressed that there was an unwillingness on both sides, but particularly Britain's, to follow the normal rules of power politics in their relations with each other. To some extent, as Bell has suggested, this was already so before 1900, but it became a more distinctive characteristic as the century advanced. Thus if readers are looking for a story of war and mayhem between the two main actors they will look in vain, though there is plenty to be said about their joint efforts against others in warfare, both hot and cold. This is not to say that there have not been many disputes and controversies between Britain and the USA in the twentieth century, but a much more significant point is that these two powers, both superpowers at different times in the same century, have undergone a transformation in their relationship with the USA becoming the world's leading superpower in Britain's stead, but without any blood-letting between the two. This, therefore, is essentially a story of plucked feathers and twisted tails for the eagle and the lion: there is thankfully nothing more painful than that to relate of the twentieth century.

2 Assertion and response 1900–19

Let him who desires peace prepare for war.

(Vegetius)

Vegetius' maxim of *realpolitik* was not applied by Britain to the USA in the twentieth century.

Between the first and the second Venezuelan crises of 1895 and 1902–3, there came about a sea change in Anglo-American relations. The most dramatic evidence of this was a 1904 decision by the British government that preparations for a war with the USA would no longer be part of its defence plans. This came at a time when the USA had embarked upon a naval expansion programme, which led the authoritative annual *Jane's Fighting Ships* to rank her second after Britain in 1906, and when the USA had asserted her ascendancy in the Western hemisphere over Britain in the first Venezuelan crisis. For a great power to abandon war plans with regard to such a nation was contrary to the canons of *realpolitik* and must be unique in the annals of international relations.

Simultaneously, there were a number of unsettling problems that were resolved amicably, though some were more intractable than others and persisted beyond the 1914–18 war. Indeed, the issue of neutral rights at sea was to prove most troublesome and severely tested relations during that conflict. Underpinning all, however, were two important factors: the first was a growing sense that the political and strategic interests of the USA and Britain could be mutually supportive and beneficial and that policy should recognise that, at least at an informal level (respective isolationist traditions still forbade anything formal). Strengthening this was the sense, shared by influential people on both sides of the Atlantic, of an Anglo-Saxon mission to civilise and order the world.

The second factor was more complex and was to do with economics. Rivalry increased between the two for investment, banking and financial opportunities, for markets and for sources of raw materials. Economic rivalry would always be likely to cause some friction, but at the turn of the century, and later, a number of conditions exacerbated that tendency. The most important, paralleling the rise and decline of their respective naval power, was the rise and decline of economic power, though in the latter there was less inhibition about taking provocative action to defend perceived interests. As became very evident in America's experience as a neutral between 1914 and 1917, there is a great deal of difference between economic suffering (real or imagined) and losing lives. From the late nineteenth century onwards Britain was concerned about her relative decline and the challenge from the USA. Until 1914 it was largely business as usual, with free trade still in the ascendancy. The types of friction involved in Anglo-American relations were of a kind one might expect with the USA gradually expanding its activity and competing more with Britain. The Great War, however, brought a number of different problems to the forefront.

Finally, in this period, there were the widespread effects of the war itself, which raised economic problems to do with debts and reparations and the competitive standing of Britain. It accelerated US naval expansion, raised questions about the character of the postwar world, and created a whole new series of security and peace-keeping problems which often involved incompatible British and American policies.

Thus, I contend that the relationship developed largely by virtue of four discernible themes. First, there was a readjustment to the changing power equation in the world. Second, and something that will be dealt with in conjunction with the first, was the settlement of various political and strategic points of dispute between the two countries by peaceful means. Third, there was a growing element of friction and aggressive rivalry in the economic realm. And, finally, there was the war itself and its wide-ranging impact.

RESOLVING DIFFERENCES AND CHANGING DEFENCE POLICIES

The Spanish American War, 1898, and the Boer War affected the USA and Britain in fundamental ways by changing their attitudes towards both each other and their respective places in the world order. At the end of the nineteenth century Britain was confronted with a series of problems, all of which were underpinned by her relative economic decline and her growing inability to meet the challenge of defending her far-flung interests. Challenges came from France and Russia in the form of direct threats to her empire in India and Africa and to her economic interests in the Far East.

From Germany the threat was both closer to home and more far-reaching. The expansion of its naval forces, especially with Admiral Alfred von Tirpitz's Navy Bill of 1898, threatened Britain's naval supremacy in the sea lanes approaching her ports. In the effort to meet that challenge a second problem arose. The Royal Navy's battle fleet had to be concentrated in home waters, but then Britain had to find means to compensate for this and safeguard far-away places that still remained precious to her against predatory action by others. In addition to all this, there was another problem caused by Germany. With the emergence of its military might the traditional balance of power in Europe began to break down. Consequently, Britain's policy of 'no entangling alliances' was defeated because, no matter where her power was directed, it could no longer achieve balance. Britain's isolationism now afforded her no viable policy and left her exposed and vulnerable with no powerful friends and with powerful, jealous and rather spiteful potential enemies in Europe.

A final, and what would have amounted to a catastrophic, problem for Britain would have been the development of animosity with the USA. From the 1890 Naval Act onwards the USA became a challenger to the naval powers of the world. Furthermore, the USA, as we have already noted in relation to the first Venezuelan crisis, became much more assertive of its interests in the Western hemisphere. Both of these developments could have caused very serious problems if the USA had been conceived of as a major threat to British interests, and there are obvious reasons why the British might have construed things in just that way. In fact they did not and, unlike many in Europe, were quick to assess the impact of the change in international relations wrought by the emergence of the USA as a great power. This adjustment by Britain, while not easy, was one of the most diplomatically important in modern times, and it will be helpful, even if it means delving back into the end of the nineteenth century, to have more understanding as to how it came about.[1]

The first Venezuelan crisis was a minor matter in itself and was to do with a boundary dispute between that country and British Guiana. In the end the affair was resolved, on the insistence of the USA, by arbitration. The result was favourable to Britain, though it lost the entry to the Orinoco River, which Washington had wanted to keep out of British hands all along because of its economic value. However, it was more the manner than the outcome of arbitration that was important. When the problem erupted, President Grover Cleveland took a very assertive line, warning Britain not to interfere in matters in the Western hemisphere. When Prime Minister Lord Salisbury ignored this because of his preoccupation with European threats to British interests, Secretary of State Richard Olney was ordered to reiterate, in no uncertain terms, the US warning. Olney did so, claiming that: 'today the United States is practically sovereign on this continent, and its fiat is law upon the subjects to which it confines its interposition'.[2]

The incident aroused much public debate, and for a short time there was a war scare, though that was soon replaced with a more measured view of things. The claim by the USA that Britain could not resolve the matter of her own accord was rather insulting, but Britain had both general and specific problems that caused her to give way to American wishes. Britain was isolated and strategically vulnerable, and fearful that any entanglement outside Europe could be taken advantage of by France or Russia or Germany. And in December 1895 the infamous Jameson Raid* against the Boers had provided the Kaiser with the pretext for taking a more overtly anti-British stance. His letter of support to Paul Kruger, President of the Transvaal, worried the British government and convinced it that it could not afford to be distracted by a minor boundary dispute or risk offending the USA. Britain, through the astute judgement of Salisbury, in effect deferred to the new realities of American power, recognised her own relative decline and agreed to arbitration.

The course taken in the Venezuelan boundary dispute helped to set the pattern for resolving differences between the USA and Britain in the years that followed. The USA continued to be assertive and at times made belligerent noises; Britain tended to respond flexibly and with a willingness to make concessions. In the end most of the outcomes were reasonable (though the Canadians did not always think so) and often achieved by some form of arbitration. In most cases Britain conceded more than the USA, but such concessions were prudent given the USA's predominance in the Western hemisphere and Britain's need for friendly relations with her. The need to be conciliatory, however, was by no means confined to Britain. After the Spanish–American War of 1898, the USA began to appreciate the problems of far-flung interests itself and both countries perceived the benefits of friendly relations, if not of active co-operation, and of at least parallel and mutually supportive action.

On the eve of war with Spain, Britain approached the USA regarding the ambitions of the continental European powers to establish exclusive zones in China, which threatened both its integrity and British, Japanese and American trading and commercial interests there. This was the so-called

---

* Dr Leander S. Jameson, an Empire extremist, led an irregular military force against the Boer Republic of Natal in December 1895/January 1896 in the hope of both toppling the Kruger government with the help of non-Boer residents in Natal and expanding British rule. The raid was a fiasco, and Jameson's force was easily defeated, but the incident caused an outcry against Britain, notably in Germany.

China open-door issue. The USA refused to be drawn into joint action with Britain for a variety of reasons, including suspicion that the USA might be manipulated to protect British interests, and the problem of imminent war with Spain. However, a year later, Secretary of State John Hay issued the first of two Open-Door Notes: the second was issued in July the following year as the European powers, Japan and the USA put down the Boxer Uprising, which was inspired by a form of nationalism and directed against the presence of European and other foreign enclaves in China. The Notes embodied the same aims as Britain had, namely to keep China intact and open to trade.

At the same time as some coincidence of Anglo-American interests emerged in the way the great powers related to each other over China, British goodwill was also in evidence and much appreciated by the USA in the Spanish–American War. The causes of the war are still difficult to untangle, but included US zeal for expansion, and revolutionary unrest in Cuba, which challenged the politically bankrupt Spanish imperial regime and also threatened US economic interests. Both favourable British public opinion and benevolent neutrality towards the USA were in marked contrast to the critical attitude of the rest of Europe. One incident in particular became part of the folklore of friendly Anglo-American relations. During the naval action in Manila Bay in the Philippines, while Admiral George Dewey put paid to the Spanish naval forces there, British and German ships stood off-shore. At one point the British manoeuvred in between the Americans and the Germans. This was widely interpreted as a friendly act to shield Dewey, though a variety of other reasons have been given, including that the British simply moved to get a better view of things.

The Americans won the war against Spain without great difficulty: the main problems came with the results of that. The Sprouts, in their classic account of the rise of US naval power, commented that the war 'profoundly altered the situation of the United States, transforming us from a geographically isolated continental Power into a scattered empire with a strategic problem virtually insoluble without recourse to alliances absolutely incompatible with the traditions of American foreign policy'.[3] The most important consequences of the war were a greater US presence in the Caribbean and the Pacific, US suzerainty over the Philippines, and the problem of how to defend those islands in the light of the expansion of Japanese naval power. The last problem later caused difficulties with Britain because of an alliance she formed with Japan in 1902. It also caused renewed American interest in the building of an isthmian canal between the Pacific and Atlantic Oceans, and that quickly led them into awkward negotiations with the British.

In fact, following the Spanish American War there were a number of significant negotiations between Britain and the USA that continued the process of removing possible bones of contention from their relationship. However, the process was far from smooth. The first Venezuelan crisis had demonstrated that friendship could very easily be replaced by hostility and xenophobic jingoism. Between 1898 and 1902, there were a number of occasions when such eventualities again threatened to disrupt things. Not everything can be considered here – for example, long-running disputes over fishing rights, alien labour laws, mining rights, naval vessels on the Great Lakes, etc. – but the Alaskan boundary dispute, the revision of the 1850 Anglo-American Bulwer–Clayton treaty concerning the building of an isthmian canal, arbitration, the Boer War and the second Venezuelan crisis all need to be mentioned. In doing so, however, two things need to be borne in mind. First, in 1898 the Germans embarked decisively on a major naval expansion programme that posed an imminent threat to Britain, and it also increasingly worried the Americans, especially Theodore Roosevelt when he was President, 1901–9. The thought of naval threats to the USA in both the Pacific and the Atlantic made an isthmian canal a top priority for the USA. Second, although public opinion on both sides flared up, charged with jingoism and animosity towards each other, at various times, there were influential men on either side who were convinced of the need for a strong and friendly relationship. Arthur Balfour, a leading figure in government in London, was well disposed to the USA and in July 1902 took over as Prime Minister from the more isolationist Lord Salisbury. Foreign Secretary under both these prime ministers, Lord Lansdowne, was also well disposed to America and aware of the importance of sustaining friendly relations. An illustration of that may be found in his attitude in May 1901 during the rather unrealistic talks about an Anglo-German alliance. They were unrealistic because of naval rivalry, political incompatibilities and recent friction over the Boer War. The talks were eventually ended by Salisbury, who insisted on maintaining an isolationist policy in the face of German demands for British commitments not just to Germany but to Austro-Hungary and Italy as well, and by Lansdowne, who also eventually balked at those prospects. But, there was another aspect to Lansdowne's position: 'The risk of entangling ourselves in a policy which might be hostile to America. With our knowledge of the German Emperor's view in regard to the United States, this is to my mind a formidable obstacle.'[4] On the American side there were similarly well-disposed leaders. In particular Secretary of State John Hay, who, while pursuing America's national interest vigorously and sometimes at Britain's expense, managed to craft a friendly government policy towards Britain during the Boer War when

American public opinion was strongly critical and pro-Boer. At one point Hay professed: 'As long as I stay here no action shall be taken contrary to my conviction that the one indispensable feature of our foreign policy should be a friendly understanding with England. But an alliance must remain in the present state of things, an unattainable dream.'[5] Thus a desire for friendship among a number of key people, and a growing fear of German ambitions, underscored much of what went on between the two countries in the aftermath of the Spanish–American War.

The first Venezuelan crisis had frightened many who believed that friendly relations between Britain and the USA were really a normal state of affairs and that the unpleasantness and conflicts that had gone on from the War of Independence down to the Civil War were aberrations. The 1895 war scare rather undermined that viewpoint. Determined to provide safeguards against similar disruptions to this vision of natural Anglo-American harmony, leaders from both sides strove to extend the use of arbitration. In the spring of 1898 they set up a High Commission to help resolve problems. However, it was not long before difficulties were encountered over the Alaskan–Canadian boundary and the revision of the Bulwer–Clayton Treaty.

Salisbury tried to bring the two problems together in one set of negotiations. He did this because the Bulwer–Clayton Treaty gave Britain a strong hand, with a legal claim to a say equal to America's on an isthmian canal, which provided a good bargaining position and one that might be helpful for resolving the Alaskan boundary question. The latter posed difficulties for the British both because it was directly in the sphere of American power and because Britain did not wish to upset the Canadians by conceding too much and too readily to US demands. Although the Bulwer–Clayton Treaty provided Salisbury with a strong position on paper, it was really a reflection of the power positions of Britain and the USA in 1850. In the intervening years their relative power and the importance of such a waterway to the two countries had changed dramatically. This was especially so in the light of US gains from the Spanish–American War, the growth of Japanese naval power, and Mahan's ideas on naval strategy. Not surprisingly, then, Salisbury's tactic did not bear fruit: the USA refused to deal with the two issues together and adopted an inflexible line on Alaska.

British hopes of getting a fair settlement of the boundary were jeopardised by America's refusal to accept arbitration and by the exigencies of the Boer War. The fact that the USA had forced Britain to accept arbitration in the first Venezuelan crisis seemed of little moral consequence to the Americans, who gaily ignored the precedent and applied the canons of *realpolitik*. Reverses for Britain in December 1899 at the hands of the Boers forced the British to be conciliatory. Soon the isthmian canal and the

Alaskan issue were separated, and Britain lost any hope of using leverage from one to benefit the outcome of the other. Britain felt obliged to accept the American suggestion for adjudication by three US, two Canadian and one British jurist. Just to make US determination to get a favourable outcome quite clear, President Roosevelt moved troops into Alaska in 1902, thus indicating that if the adjudication were not to America's liking there were other ways of resolving things. In 1903, with the British judge siding with the Americans, the Canadians found themselves outmanoeuvred and sold short for the overarching need for good Anglo-American relations: the USA got the boundary it wanted.

Long before that was settled the British and the Americans had agreed on a new canal treaty, and again the need to cultivate good relations, acknowledge America's dominance of the Western hemisphere and the exigencies of the Boer War were all in evidence in determining the outcome. Salisbury's bid to connect the canal and boundary issues was an early indication that Britain was ready to concede ground on the canal in return for a *quid pro quo* in Alaska. Things did not work out like that, but concessions were squeezed out anyway, including a controversial one by the US Senate. The first version of the new treaty was signed on 5 February 1900 by John Hay and British ambassador Sir Julian Pauncefote. It gave the USA more or less what it wanted, and in particular the right to proceed alone in the construction of the canal. The following December it was ratified by the US Senate, but only after amendments which granted the right to construct fortifications. That was contrary to British hopes of keeping it a neutral waterway, and Lansdowne rejected the revision and protested to Hay. Hay himself was angry with the Senate, and in the following months a face-saving formulation was drafted whereby the USA was allowed to police the canal on condition that it should be open in time of peace or of war to all merchant ships and warships without discrimination or inequality of tolls.

Much of what happened between Britain and the USA in the Alaskan boundary and canal negotiations seemed to be a one-way street. Britain repeatedly gave way to American diplomatic demands and political blustering. In the great order of Britain's imperial concerns, it is true to say that the things involved were all pretty minor, though Canada's resentment over losing a slice of what it considered to be its own land had important ramifications at a time when Britain was beginning to nurture the idea of closer union with the dominions. Nevertheless, Britain's sacrifices of her own interests, and her decision not to stand upon the niceties of honour as other nations might have done, were to benefit her position in the long run. Furthermore, some years later, in another episode involving Britain and the

Panama Canal, the USA discovered the virtue of a conciliatory attitude, partly out of a sense of justice and partly because of prudential concerns about its own wide-ranging interests.

In 1913 President William Taft, in readiness for the opening of the canal the following year, signed into law measures that gave American coastal shipping preferential tolls. British Ambassador James Bryce protested, writing that his government 'conceives that international law or usage does not support the doctrine that the passing of a Statute in contravention of a treaty right affords no ground of complaint for the infraction of that right'.[6] So far as the British were concerned the US law was clearly contrary to the provision that all tolls had to be levied equally.

Taft's successor, the moralistic liberal Woodrow Wilson, inclined to the British way of seeing things, but there were other, more self-interested reasons for repealing the Taft law. In 1914, revolution in Mexico threatened to result in widespread anarchy. As the situation deteriorated Britain strove to protect her economic interests, especially in the oil industry, and ended up somewhat inadvertently supporting a different faction to the Americans. Things were not helped by Britain's appointment of a highly anti-American ambassador, Sir Lionel Carden, a 'handsome, perfectly groomed, tall, fresh complexioned, white moustached, unmistakable Briton'.[7] Again, in the end, Britain deferred to US policy, but not before there had been some give on the US side in relation to the canal tolls. Colonel House, Wilson's adviser and confidant, agreed with Wilson that 'it was better to make concessions in regard to Panama rather than lose the support of England in our Mexican, Central and South American policy'.[8] The USA was starting to follow Britain out of isolationism and to realise that it could no longer stand aloof from European political and strategic concerns. It, too, needed friends. In 1914 the Taft law was repealed by Congress.

Relating the story of the problems arising from Mexico and the canal tolls has anticipated our story a little, but it illustrates well the growing entanglement both of the USA in international affairs and of the USA with Britain.

The Alaskan boundary dispute did not stop the policy of trying to establish wide-ranging powers for arbitration within an appropriate institutional framework. The First Hague Conference, called by Russian Czar Nicholas II to convene in May 1899, managed to set up a Permanent Court of Arbitration, and at the Second Hague Conference in 1907 further progress was made; but severe problems remained and arbitration failed to solve the power conflicts in the world of the twentieth century. Even Britain and the USA failed to put into operation the bilateral arbitration treaty they signed in 1904: the US Senate amended it in part, and it was then abandoned by the Executive. Attempts at arbitration, such as the Root–Bryce Treaty of 1908, continued, but with only very limited success. So far as Britain and the USA were concerned, by 1904 there were few issues left where serious problems could arise. Most difficulties had been solved: the one remaining issue of consequence was that of neutral shipping rights and that was not put to rest until the Second World War. Many regretted that a general arbitration treaty between Britain and the USA was not implemented, but events in the second Venezuelan crisis of 1902 demonstrated just how well Britain had adjusted to the new-found power of the USA: it also illustrated the need for caution regarding Germany.

During 1902–3 Britain and Germany took naval action in an attempt to collect debts from Venezuela. This was condoned by the International Court of Justice at the Hague, but Theodore Roosevelt took a dim view of European and particularly German interference in the Western hemisphere and exerted pressure for arbitration. The British quickly fell into line. Not so the Germans: they persisted in their naval action for some time before finally backing down. Among other things this incident later helped prompt the Roosevelt Corollary to the Monroe Doctrine, but a more immediate result was the way Britain and Germany had behaved and how the incident helped to confirm American suspicions of the latter. Over the following years Anglo-American relations continued to improve, and although America's Red War Plan, designed to cope with a war against the British Empire, remained in place, Britain withdrew militarily from the Western hemisphere and radically changed its defence stance *vis-à-vis* the USA. Meanwhile, Roosevelt's fear of possible German intervention grew:

> The specter of German aggression in the Caribbean or elsewhere in Latin America, became a veritable nightmare with him. He was absolutely convinced that the Kaiser would one day start trouble. . . . Ignoring or belittling the all but insuperable strategic, technical, and political obstacles in the way of such aggression, Roosevelt harped on this theme until it became almost an obsession.[9]

By the end of the second Venezuelan crisis in 1903, a pattern had emerged in the Anglo-American relationship. In response both to the emergence of the USA as a great power and its assertion of dominance in the Western hemisphere, Britain acknowledged these things and deferred to the USA in that part of the world. Both countries had got into the habit of fostering good relations and guiding their affairs peacefully through disputes, even in the face of difficulties with jingoistic public opinion, and chauvinistic actions by the US Senate. Diplomacy, judicial committees, arbitration: these were the main weapons in the confrontations that took place in

1895–1904 and beyond. Furthermore, Germany, not Britain, was now seen by the USA as the main European threat, especially after the expansionist German Navy Bill of 1900 and tension in the second Venezuelan crisis.

By 1904, under the tutelege of Lansdowne, Britain's strategic plans had been transformed, not just in relation to the Western hemisphere, but in the Far East and in the Mediterranean as well. We may recall that Britain was posed with the problem of countering German naval power in the North Sea and as a result sought to concentrate its battle fleet there, even though this denuded much of the Empire of effective defence. It was this problem that forced Britain, led by Lansdowne, into abandoning its traditional isolationist policy and engaging in treaties and understandings with other countries.

The first of these was to do with the Pacific and Britain's most far-flung interests. For years Britain had worried over and tried to contain Russian expansion. In 1902, with that in mind as well as the volatile situation in China and the need to slim down its naval presence in the Pacific, Britain entered into an alliance with Japan. This was not entirely unwelcome to the USA in the early days, though with the outbreak of the Russo-Japanese War in 1904 and Japan's impressive success the USA became concerned that the balance in the Far East should not be overturned in Japan's favour completely so as to result in her regional supremacy. Those fears grew as time went by and Japan grew more powerful. Relations became more strained because of racialist restrictions on Japanese immigration and discriminatory laws passed by the Californian legislature. Britain soon found that there were costs to be paid for her alliance with Japan, and she had to go out of her way to reassure the USA – in the end to the extent of curtailing the liaison with Japan. But at the time the alliance was of great benefit to Britain. It bolstered her position in the Pacific, while allowing her to reduce her forces there, and the Japanese victory over Russia put an end to Czarist plans for expansion at the cost of the British Empire.

The second major change in 1904 was the establishment of the *entente cordiale* with France, which among other things allowed for an arrangement for some reciprocal protection of each other's maritime interests and thus enabled Britain to cut back on its naval presence in the Mediterranean. These developments constituted a revolution in Britain's traditional strategic and diplomatic policies. They seemed to answer the main problem of how to match the threat from Germany at sea and, indeed, on the continent, because in 1907 there was also a *rapprochement* with Russia. There now came into being a triple *entente* between Britain, France and Russia which seemed to even up the scales of power. Unfortunately, Germany did not see it that way. Instead of an evening-up, it saw encirclement and threat. The *status quo* powers were hemming in Germany. At sea they had unquestionably succeeded, but on land events were to prove different.

Finally, on strategic matters, we come back to the Anglo-American relationship because the story has not yet been completed there. Indeed, it could not be until an overview had been given of the problems with and changes to British strategy that Lansdowne crafted elsewhere between 1900 and 1905. It is in the context of response to threats from Europe and the need for major changes to British policies that the radical re-adjustment to the USA that is about to be explained must be seen.

In 1904 and in subsequent debates within the British government and in particular in the newly created Committee of Imperial Defence (the CID first met in 1902), the idea that there could not be war between Britain and the USA took on a whole new meaning, a meaning that set the tone of the relationship for the rest of the century. During the period 1904–10 there were numerous discussions involving interested departments in London, but centred mainly in the CID, about the eventuality of a war with the USA and the problem of defending Canada. In 1904 the British took the view that war with the USA was so remote and that the problems involved were so great that in effect they might as well abandon planning for such a contingency. That was by no means the end of the debate, but it was the end of any practical defence planning for the Western hemisphere. In a Colonial Office Defence Committee paper of 1909 the following assessment was given:

> In view of the remoteness of the contingency of a war with the United States, and of the extreme difficulty of providing local defences adequate to deal with the formidable scale of attacks they could bring to bear, it has been decided by the Committee of Imperial Defence that attack by the United States need not be taken into consideration in determining the standard of defences of ports of the Western Atlantic.[10]

By 1904 there was still no hope of any kind of formal alliance between Britain and the USA. Indeed, the US Senate would not even accept the sort of entanglement involved in an effective arbitration treaty. However, there was something different in the relationship that the two countries enjoyed compared with ties between other countries. The decision of the CID to discount the possibility of war with the USA and to leave it out of British war planning was partly a contribution to this difference and partly a symptom of it. The habit of peacefully resolving differences through arbitration and other means, along with Britain's quick adjustment to the emergence of the USA as a major world power, the sense of friendship and of common interests felt by a number of leading figures in both countries, and the obstacles to the waging of a successful war all contributed to the unusual quality of their relationship, which became even more discernible after 1904. It is difficult to rank factors according to importance without going into great detail, but the outcome is clear: by 1914 Britain and the USA found it difficult to conceive of a real likelihood of war between themselves. There were still many difficulties remaining: neutral rights at sea were to cause no end of problems in the Great War, and there was also friction in their economic relations, but war was no longer a realistic prospect.

ECONOMIC RIVALRY

A recent study of the decline of the British Empire characterises its experience with the USA in terms of economic challenge and response. Clearly, there are many other important facets to the relationship in the twentieth century, but the central role of economic power should not be understated.

> The pressure [on Britain] came largely from the unparalleled economic dynamism of the republic spilling out dramatically into the world in the shape of trade and finance, and undermining the British position just as surely as Britain's own market power had once undermined the economic foundation of the international power of Portugal, The Netherlands, Spain and France. So, although there were tense moments of naval rivalry, the central battle was between economies, Treasuries, central banks and stock markets rather than between armies and navies.[11]

Many of the disagreements with Britain between 1895 and 1914 had an economic aspect to them and involved an assertion of American economic prerogatives in the Western hemisphere. Indeed, American diplomacy in this area and in this period involved so many interventions to safeguard American commercial interests or to expand their scope that it is often referred to as 'dollar diplomacy'. As we have seen, Theodore Roosevelt publicly justified this type of interference in the affairs of other sovereign states in 1904 in the Corollary to the Monroe Doctrine.[12]

The rise of US economic self-confidence and the challenge that her manufacturing prowess, along with that of Germany's, posed to Britain caused great concern even before the war, and some questioning of the efficacy of free trade for Britain under the new circumstances. From 1914 onwards the opposition to free trade grew rapidly. Government controls and intervention to organise war production created a model of *dirigisme* that some believed ought to be emulated in peacetime. In the war an alliance of imperialists, Liberal Unionists (who joined the Conservative Party in 1914), Conservatives and industrialists swung opinion against free trade for a time in favour of protection and a drive for imperial unity. At the international level these ideas were given some substance in the Paris Economic Conference of 1916. At that meeting, the allies envisaged a postwar system embodying state direction, preferences and tariffs, government-funded research and development (R&D), import and export controls, and direct government participation in the development of foreign markets. At the national level British policy followed this line in the 1919 Budget and the Empire Settlement Act of 1922, though, as we shall see, these developments proved to be false dawns for the empire consolidators and the economic protectionists.

Nevertheless, these developments at the time did not augur well so far as US economic ambitions were concerned. They posed threats to the USA, which had grown economically very powerful in the war and which looked to the international economy to sustain her new industrial power and wealth. By contrast, Britain suffered greatly and her rate of relative decline was accelerated. In particular *vis-à-vis* the USA, she was greatly weakened, becoming dependent upon American loans and war supplies and ending the war with huge debts. But as Britain became economically defensive and sought to engage the power of the state in order to protect her interests more, so the USA became more expansionist and also looked to government to facilitate the growth of American overseas trade, investment and banking, and the international use of the dollar. In the postwar period much of this expansionary zeal was to be orchestrated by Herbert Hoover as Secretary of the Department of Commerce, but before anything like that would be possible the USA had to alter its antitrust laws to enable co-operative ventures abroad by US enterprise. In 1916, the 1913 Federal Reserve Act was amended in order to allow US banks to co-operate abroad, and in 1914 and 1918 respectively the Clayton Antitrust Act and the Webb–Pomerene Act permitted US companies to collude in dividing foreign markets for the sake of their development. However, while this penetration of overseas markets was proceeding apace, the USA had high protective tariffs and continued to strengthen them even further from time to time until 1934. This anomaly did not ostensibly trouble US policymakers, who defended tariffs, demanded open markets and free trade and targeted preferences as the bogey of the international economy because they were 'political' and discriminatory.[13]

The contrasting economic fortunes of Britain and the USA, and what appeared in the years 1916–22 to be their increasingly diverging international economic policies, were a recipe for increased Anglo-American economic friction. Further complications were added to this by the respective images that each side held of the other's economic policies.

On both sides of the Atlantic there have always been populist pictures of the deleterious effects of the other country's economic power or policies – from the British tax on American tea to the mass import of American films into the UK from the 1920s and 1930s onwards. Such things had impact on policy-making through public opinion and because they interacted with the prejudices and dislikes of sections of the British and American elites. In the USA in the twentieth century, the focus was on Britain's imperial affluence and her control, or at least potential control if free trade gave way to a more mercantilist philosophy, of so much of the world's markets and raw materials. In Britain the picture was of America gradually buying out the British economic inheritance and taking over British industry. This image was conjured up at various times in the press and in populist histories such as *The American Invaders* and *The American Take-over of Britain*. Written sixty-six years apart both these books give out the same paranoid message and in a remarkably similar way. They contain roll calls of familiar items bought in Britain made by American companies. In one of them there is a 'Mrs John Bull's Diary', which catalogues some ninety items that Mrs Bull and her husband use in the course of an ordinary day in their English home and which are all made by American firms. This type of fear was symptomatic of a deeper sense of resentment born out of the broad challenge that the USA posed to Great Britain. Interestingly, by 1987 Britain's holdings in US property and industry were almost double US holdings in Britain, £79.5 billion to £44 billion, and were more than twice the amount Japan held in the USA. One heard little of US resentment of Britain but a great deal about the threat from Japan. Just as in the earlier relationship between Britain and the USA, the fear came not of the investment level alone, but from a broader and deeper and more paranoid fear of the challenger in general. These attitudes, derived mainly from populist writings and public opinion, had an effect on relations between the two countries at the level of high policy-making.[14]

THE IMPACT OF WAR

The First World War was an enormous trauma for Europe and it inevitably impacted on Anglo-American relations in a wide-ranging way. It exacerbated tensions in their economic dealings; brought into question the reliability of the USA as a long-term friend; posed difficult questions about the future world order; brought Anglo-American naval rivalry into sharper focus; and, most immediately of all, placed the issue of maritime neutral rights at the forefront of their diplomatic activity.

The war, despite its name, was essentially a European conflict. The

British Empire and its European allies lost about 4.25 million killed in combat (including Russian losses up to the German–Soviet Peace Treaty of Brest-Litovsk, 3 March 1918); the USA lost over 53,000 through battle deaths and another 63,000 from other causes. Britain, with less than half the population of the USA, suffered proportionately nearly fifteen times as badly in terms of deaths and ten times as badly with her 2 million wounded. This unspeakable carnage that more than decimated a whole generation of young Britons caused a revulsion against war and a distaste for direct involvement in continental European affairs which had serious consequences in the 1920s and 1930s. Of more concern to Anglo-American relations, it also caused resentment of the way the USA grew economically stronger because of the war and of its arrogance in wanting to remould the world in its own image even at the expense of the main combatants, Britain and France. The war embittered Britain and made her adopt, at least initially, a more punitive attitude to Germany than the USA held, which was also to be a source of difficulty. But the most immediate problem was Wilson's hectoring attitude and his stand on neutral maritime rights. This problem almost broke relations between Britain and the USA during the war and it emerged at the peace to complicate matters yet again:

> if it is intended to affirm that a neutral ship may take on a contraband cargo ostensibly for a neutral port, but destined in reality for a belligerent port, either by the same ship or by another, without becoming liable, from the commencement to the end of the voyage, to seizure, in order to the confiscation of the cargo, we do not agree to it.[15]

It was this type of policy and extensions to it that caused so much distress in Anglo-American relations between 1914 and 1917. The British were purely and simply following the logic of total war. If the whole of society is mobilised in the war effort, it becomes impossible to justify trade *courant normale*, which had been part of British naval policy in the past, or to draw a distinction between contraband and non-contraband goods except in certain humanitarian cases. But even the argument for this lost purchase with the adoption of a strategy of starving a people into submission. America's moralistic insistence on neutral rights to trade, and her indignant protests at the way the Royal Navy implemented the blockade, galled the British, who were fighting for survival and suffering terrible losses on the Western Front. There was also irony involved in all this. President Wilson had not hesitated to intervene militarily on several occasions in Latin America with very dubious legal right. In 1916 General John J. Pershing forayed into Mexico, which Wilson described as 'measures short of war'. The British now aped the Wilsonian formulation and described their control of shipping on the high seas as 'measures short of blockade'. Furthermore, the lengthy quotation given above, which in effect describes the doctrine of continuous voyage, and on which much of the British blockade policy was based, was not promulgated by Britain. The words, in fact, are those of US Chief Justice Salmon P. Chase in the *Bermuda* Supreme Court case of December 1865. It was a policy devised under the pressures of the Civil War and with the aim of denying the Confederacy supplies. Britain was following and developing a precedent set by the USA.

British actions were provocative to the USA, but that was a danger that had to be risked. The FO was aware of the danger and tried to ensure, often by restraining the Navy, that America would not be provoked too far. As the Foreign Secretary, Lord Grey, recorded in his memoirs: 'The object of diplomacy, therefore, was to secure the maximum blockade that could be enforced without a rupture with the United States.'[16] That rupture nearly came in 1916, not solely because of the blockade policy, though that was certainly a major factor. For, although Britain was following US precedents, it also developed the blockade in novel and extreme ways.

Britain expanded the list of contraband goods and of conditional contraband, i.e. goods that should be quantitatively controlled; she applied the principle of continuous voyage to conditional contraband; she redefined continuous voyage to cover those cases where the second leg of the journey was overland; because modern cargo ships were so large, the Royal Navy ordered them into port for search and that often caused long and very irritating delays; and, finally, companies found to be trading in contraband with the enemy were put on a blacklist and prohibited from trading with any part of the British Empire. By 1916 Wilson was finding all this unbearable. In July he wrote to his assistant, Colonel Edward M. House:

> I am . . . about the end of my patience with Great Britain and the Allies . . . I am seriously considering asking Congress to authorise me to prohibit loans and restrict exportations to the Allies. . . . Can we any longer endure this intolerable course?[17]

Fortunately for the Allies, America soon saw that it was far preferable to suffer indignities at the hands of the Royal Navy than lose lives at the hands of German U-boats.

Rather strangely, while the furore went on more or less unabated over America's right as a neutral to trade unmolested, economic intercourse with Britain mushroomed, and financial ties became a transatlantic umbilical cord that fed the British war machine and allowed the Allies to continue. By 1915, Britain was troubled by a shortage of dollars to pay for crucial war supplies because while her exports declined her imports rose massively.

Between 1914 and 1916 US exports to France and Britain rose nearly fourfold: to Germany they dwindled to virtually nothing. To pay for the massive increase in imports Britain raised loans in the USA and it did so through the offices of the Anglophile Morgan Banking House. By the end of the war Britain had borrowed $3.7 billion. Thus while the blockade caused the USA some headaches, at the same time the war resulted in a massive expansion of her export markets and shifted much of the financial power of the world from London to New York. These developments had important consequences in terms of how the USA viewed its place in the world and how it perceived of its interests.

As early as May 1914 Walter Hines Page, the strongly pro-British US ambassador in London, wrote to Wilson: 'The future of the world belongs to us. The English are spending their capital. . . . Now, what are we going to do with the leadership of the world presently when it clearly falls into our hands? And how can we use the British for the highest uses of democracy?'[18] The economic consequences of the war created much opportunity for the USA. Nevertheless, there were also factors that circumscribed US action. Thus by the crisis year of 1916, although Wilson was indignant at British blockade policies and angered by lack of Allied enthusiasm for the proposals for peace orchestrated by Colonel House's peace mission to Europe in 1916, the USA would have found it very costly economically to turn against the Allies. America had effectively invested in Allied victory.[19]

America's entry into the war was not motivated mainly by calculation of economic self-interest, but that must have played some part, and certainly in the months that followed Wilson clearly thought that holding the economic ace cards would allow him to exert a lot of leverage on Britain and France. In July 1917 he wrote to House: 'England and France have not the same view with regard to peace that we have by any means. When the war is over we can force them to our way of thinking, because by that time they will, among other things, be financially in our hands.'[20] In fact, things were not as straightforward as that.

The build-up to the crisis in Anglo-American relations in 1916 has to be seen in the context that has been sketched above: expanding economic intercourse; a British policy that recognised that the USA must not be provoked too far; and German policies that went far beyond economic hurt to cause death in the U-boat campaign against Allied and neutral shipping. There was also the now rather familiar sense of underlying friendship in Anglo-American relations and ethnic ties. In early 1915 Secretary Franklin Lane wrote to House:

There isn't a man in the Cabinet who has a drop of German blood in his veins, I guess. Two of us were born under the British flag. I have two cousins in the British army, and Mrs. Lane has three. The most of us are Scotch in our ancestry, and yet each day we meet we boil over somewhat, at the foolish manner in which England acts.[21]

Lane was referring to the blockade policy, but there were other troublesome factors in 1916. The suppression in Dublin of the Irish Easter Uprising against British rule, lack of positive Allied moves on Colonel House's peace proposals, and anger at British economic warfare collectively resulted in a cooling towards Britain and a warming of attitudes towards Germany. It must be added, however, that all this was relative. Overwhelmingly, public opinion was against Germany. Its violation of Belgian neutrality at the outset of the war, alleged atrocities – many unfounded but made much of by effective British propaganda – and the sinking of the cruise liner *Lusitania* with loss of American lives during the first period of unrestricted U-boat warfare all helped add to the fear and dislike of Germany that was prevalent in many sections of US society before the war. But if the day had been in need of saving for the Allies in 1917, then German actions would have done it. At the end of January they renewed unrestricted U-boat warfare. A month later British intelligence intercepted a telegram to Mexico from German Foreign Minister Arthur Zimmermann, offering to help regain territory lost to the USA in the past in return for an alliance in the event of war between America and Germany. Perhaps Theodore Roosevelt's fears of German intervention in the Western hemisphere were not so fanciful after all. Two months later, after US merchant ships had been sunk by German U-boats, the US Congress, at Wilson's request, declared that a state of war existed between the USA and Germany. The fate of Germany and the success of the Allied powers and their Associate the USA were now assured, providing Britain could survive the U-boat onslaught upon merchant shipping bringing in vital food and supplies. In the end she did, but only by a narrow margin. The way the USA assured an allied victory was, in itself, important to the Anglo-American relationship, but there were a number of other things that emerged that also had important consequences for their future.

ASSOCIATED BUT NOT ALLIED

The Anglo-American experience from 1917 to 1919 will be considered under three informal headings: naval and military affairs; economics and supplies; and the debate about the peace and postwar security. While dealing with each of these there will also be some comment about the character of the main actors and how they affected the quality of the relationship.

The British sent no fewer than three missions to the USA. Arguably the most successful was the one led by Arthur Balfour, who was the first British minister to visit the USA while in office: the rest of the century was to see many more follow in his path. Balfour was personally successful with the Americans and helped co-ordinate the flow of supplies: in this one might see the origins of the work done by the combined boards of the Second World War. On the financial front it again became easier to obtain loans after some official US discouragement in 1916. So the supplies flowed and the loans were forthcoming, but the prospect of being saddled with enormous debts at the end of what was now a commom war effort cast a shadow of deep concern in the British Cabinet. War debts and reparations were to cause much difficulty in Anglo-American relations in the years to follow. An incident in 1918 revealed that the British were also concerned about their export markets and their competitive standing *vis-à-vis* the Americans, who had not only increased their exports to the Allies in the war but had made significant inroads into markets previously the preserve of the British. US share of total world exports rose from 13.5% in 1913 to 25% in 1920. In the face of this advance the British were seriously considering defensive economic policies and in the late days of the war actually diverted shipping back to commercial use and away from transport duties, which slowed down the US troop build-up in France.[22]

In the theatres of war there was a rather surprising contrast between the way that the armies and the navies of the two countries got on together. The build-up of the US army was painfully slow so far as British and French perceptions were concerned. Much of that pain was felt as a result of absorbing the last major German onslaught in the spring and summer of 1918 without any significant American help. When US troops arrived on the Western Front they were commanded by General Pershing, who had clear ideas about how they were to be used, and, in fact, their first large scale operation was not until 12 September, when they removed the German bulge in the Allied lines at Saint Mihiel. Pershing had taken the associate status of the USA seriously. The US army in France was conceived of as an independent national force to be used at the discretion of the USA. There was little here that could be built on for future Anglo-American co-operation. Even at the recreational level the interaction was limited because, unlike GIs in the next war, US doughboys did not stay, but only passed through Britain in transit to France.

In 1916 President Wilson accepted recommendations of the Navy Board and campaigned for a Navy Bill which had the intent of ultimately creating a navy 'second to none': in August after much controversy the Congress passed it. The danger of conflict with Britain over naval leadership was thus accentuated even more. However, despite both British resentment at the prospect of their supremacy being eroded and some difficult personal relationships, naval co-operation turned out to be highly successful.

The success or failure of Anglo-American naval co-operation was determined by Admirals Lewis Bayly and William S. Sims of the Royal and US Navies respectively. They were not a guaranteed recipe for success. Bayly was a crusty and difficult man, but Sims, fortunately, had charm and determination and was an Anglophile – so much so, that in 1910 President Taft had reprimanded him for speaking publicly of an Anglo-American alliance. As things turned out, Sims and Bayly soon came to respect and admire each other, and the rest flowed from that. The war against the U-boats was finally turned in favour of the allies with the introduction of convoying and with the help of US destroyers, which Sims had vigorously requested from Washington. Bayly and Sims got on so well that the former allowed the latter to take command at the Queenstown naval base for a short time. American and British ships were co-ordinated in their operations, and invaluable experience was gained in allied co-operation.[23]

This naval togetherness was not built on in the following years, and naval rivalry became a touchy subject for the British. But the success of Bayly and Sims does provide an illustration of how a common language, similar traditions and values, and a common enemy, could make it easy for Americans and British to work together in the defence sphere. During the latter half of the twentieth century there arose many cases of close and friendly co-operation between British and American forces. There were also notorious cases of difficult and disliked personnel – General 'Vinegar' Joe Stillwell, Lord Louis Mountbatten, General George Patton, Field Marshal Bernard Montgomery, Admiral Ernest J. King, and so on, but on balance military co-operation has been unprecedented in its closeness and level of success.

While economic and naval problems lay ahead, trying to formulate the conditions for peace and the character of the postwar world drew Britain and the USA into more immediate difficulties. The agenda that caused many of the problems was unilaterally promulgated by President Wilson in January 1918: it became known as the Fourteen Points. Wilson sought to end American isolationism by recreating the world anew in the image of the USA. This was the second coming: the Old World was to be redeemed by the New. Wilson called for free trade; the right to the self-determination of peoples; freedom of commercial waterways and of the high seas; and open diplomacy that would be subject to democratic scrutiny and held accountable to the people. The peace was to be just and charitable to the losers: there should be no reparations.[24] This was the way forward, Wilson asserted: the response of the Europeans was less than enthusiastic and they eventually modified the President's vision.

Britain and France had lost vast quantitiies of men and money and had been forced to make agreements during the course of the war that Wilson could not happily reconcile with his principles. The European states wanted some recompense financially and territorially for their efforts, could not afford to be as disinterested as the Americans, and had difficulties with the idea of self-determination, both because of deals struck during the war and because of their colonial holdings; and Britain also had to take account of dominion calls (especially Australia's and South Africa's) for the right to strengthen and safeguard their own positions by taking over colonial territory from Germany. Finally, there was the problem of keeping the peace between France and Germany. For a short time it looked as though collective security through the League of Nations and specific guarantees to France from Britain and the USA would solve that problem, but the situation soon changed.

Sadly for Wilson and his vision of a Europe created anew along the lines of his Fourteen Points, two major things went wrong. First, Germany collapsed and the war ended more speedily than people had thought possible. Wilson's hopes that, among other things, Britain and France would be in American hands financially did not materialise to the extent he had hoped. The French and the British were both more recalcitrant than he had thought possible. Second, in the 1918 mid-term elections the Republicans had a major electoral victory and now controlled the Senate. The new chairman of the Senate Foreign Relations Committee was Henry Cabot Lodge, a powerful man and one who disliked the cavalier attitude of Wilson towards the Senate and who held numerous reservations about the negotiations in Paris.

Wilson's insistence that peace should be sought with Germnay on the basis of his Fourteen Points irritated the Allies. In Britain there might have been more sympathy with Wilsonian liberalism before the war, but now the prevailing dispensation was more conservative. Not least of the reasons for this was popular opinion in the khaki election of December 1918 which looked for a more punitive peace and more reparations than Prime Minister David Lloyd George wanted, but he bent with the prevailing political wind. There was impact from democratic sources on all three main participants in Paris, and generally speaking that made it more difficult to reach agreement. As the conference assembled there were widely different aims held by Britain, France and the USA. Britain wanted a revival of her economic welfare, secure communications with her Empire, and stability in Europe. France wanted to restore her honour and security. The USA, or rather Wilson, wanted to implement the vision embodied in the Fourteen Points; however, he was out-manoeuvred by Lloyd George and the French leader Georges Clemenceau in Paris, and undermined in Washington by political opponents.

Wilson got a foretaste of the problems to come when Lloyd George explained to him that no British minister could accept freedom of the seas and remain in office if it meant that the Royal Navy would be unable to take measures such as it had in the war. Reluctantly Wilson acknowledged that Britain would not agree to this principle prior to negotiation: the first compromise was made, and it was the first of many. But perhaps the most telling compromises arose from the political situation in Washington.

Wilson found in Washington, during a month's break from the talks in Paris, that he had to concede to Republican demands that the Western hemisphere be treated differently by article 10 of the League Covenant from other areas of the world. Article 10 was at the heart of the idea of a new world order: it was to substitute collective security for traditional power politics. All members of the League had to 'respect and preserve as against external aggression the territorial integrity and existing political independence of all Members of the League'. Confronted with Republican threats that they would reject the Covenant unless the Western hemisphere was treated as a special case, Wilson, on arriving back in Paris, sought to defuse domestic US opposition by asking the British and the French for a compromise. The irony of that did not go unnoticed and soon the Europeans started to make capital out of the situation.

That they made such headway was largely due to the characters of the three protagonists: Wilson, Clemenceau and Lloyd George. John Maynard Keynes, the celebrated economist, who acted as a Treasury adviser to the British delegation, provided judgements on these three in his famous critique 'The Economic Consequences of the Peace'. They give much insight into the reasons for Wilson's failure to realise his vision of salvation. First Wilson: according to Keynes, 'He had no plan, no scheme, no constructive ideas whatever for clothing with the flesh of life the commandments which he had thundered from the White House.' 'There can seldom have been a statesman of the first rank more incompetent than the President in the agilities of the council chamber.' Most damning of all, Wilson was not aware of his own shortcomings. The American council of advisers, brought together to study the problems of the peace, might have saved him from some of his tribulations in Paris (even though they were only of mediocre talent), but the first and last time he convened them before the treaties were signed was on the voyage across the Atlantic for the opening of talks. 'What chance', Keynes scornfully asked, 'could such a man have against Mr Lloyd George's unerring, almost medium-like, sensibility to everyone immediately round him?' And, lastly, with his moralistic idealism, Wilson found it equally impossible to match or meet respectively Clemenceau's analytical intelligence and his worldly realism. 'One could not despise Clemenceau or dislike him', opined Keynes,' 'but only take a different view as to the nature of civilised man, or indulge, at least, a different hope.' 'He felt about France what Pericles felt of Athens – unique value in her, nothing else mattered; but his theory of politics was Bismarck's. He had one illusion – France; and one disillusion – mankind.'[25] The story that followed from this has been well documented, and told before on many occasions: all that is necessary here is to give the general contours of the agreements reached and in particular of those that had a future bearing on Anglo-American relations.

Matters outside of the immediate European sphere were settled much to Britain's benefit. The question of freedom of the seas went unresolved and left Britain with the freedom of action that she desired. The thorny question of ex-enemy colonial possessions seized by the Allies in the war was solved by the South African statesman General Jan Christian Smuts. He produced a face-saving formulation to appease the Americans, one based on different categories of mandates. In Europe much had to be done to appease the French and ensure that the peace would not pass beyond punishment to vindictiveness. Reparations of $33 billion were agreed and German trade was to be restricted for a period. France gained the right to occupy the Rhineland for fifteen years, and a modified version of article 10 of the Covenant was accepted, but most surprisingly of all Britain and the USA agreed to give France interdependent security commitments: Britain's guarantee was dependent upon the USA giving the same commitment, and *vice versa*. For a time it looked as if the New World had entangled itself with the Old in order to redress its imbalance.

In fact, all that had been so painfully woven together in Paris unravelled in the US Senate. Neither the Irreconcileables led by Senators William Borah and Hiram Johnson nor the Reservationists led by Henry Cabot Lodge would accept the treaties or the Covenant. Much of the problem was Wilson himself, his arrogance and refusal to compromise. Other reasons for the failure in the Senate were to do with fears of the USA being dragged into the dynastic squabbles of Europe by article 10 of the Covenant or by the security commitment to France. There was also a moralistic element to the opposition. The constitution of the USA granted Congress the power to declare war. Under article 10 that prerogative was undermined through a general commitment to collective security. The wiles of the Old World were undermining the integrity of the US Constitution. This was a major concern and one that did not die with the Senate rejection of the League: it recurred, though more from fears of internal corruption and the development of war-making powers by the presidential office than from treaty obligations. The rejection of the Covenant and the Peace Treaty meant that the world's most powerful nation would not be part of the new collective security system and that the Anglo-American guarantees to France were nullified.

In 1921 the Republicans returned to the White House. Anglo-American relations were about to embark upon a difficult period. The USA was turning inwards in security terms, but ever outward in its economic expansion. The two countries had naval and debt problems to sort out and in the background to all this were concerns about instability in Europe arising from economic disruption and the fear of Bolshevism spreading westward; a sense of injustice in Germany; and feelings of insecurity in France because of an ineffective League and no guarantees from Britain and the USA. There were also the growing power of Japan in the Far East and the debilitating consequences of economic recession. All these things were to test Anglo-American relations between 1919 and 1939, but the relationship that had emerged between 1895 and 1904 proved strong enough to survive in such a way that revival and renewal were possible.

3 Stability and change 1919–39

In England the outward aspect of life does
not yet teach us to feel or realise in the least
that an age is over.
                    (John Maynard Keynes)[1]

Only two conditions of humankind really count, war and peace – the latter
in its fullest sense: may peace be with you. The great failures of Britain and
the USA in the 1920s and 1930s were their inability both to absorb the
changes wrought by the last war and to prevent the next. One of their great
achievements was that peace was kept in their own relationship to an extent
that made their world-saving co-operation possible between 1940 and
1945. The reasons for their failure and their success are not unconnected, as
the context for their relationship in the inter-war period will show.

The great powers, the erstwhile great powers, and those soon to be great
again had different attitudes towards stability and change in the world order
between 1919 and 1939. Because of the complexity of the world and
humankind's limited ability to control affairs, none got its own way for
long and it proved impossible to reach an understanding that might have
avoided war. On the extremes were France, which sought security through
upholding the Versailles Settlement, and Germany – later joined by Italy –
which wanted to modify and eventually overthrow not only Versailles but
ultimately, with their accomplice Japan, the whole system of liberal capitalism, international law, and human decency. The Soviet Union had
somewhat similar aims but brooded, a pariah on the sidelines of world
events, for much of this period. Britain and the USA took the middle
ground. Both concluded that Versailles should not be upheld. They thought
it was economically punitive and politically harsh and feared eventual
German retaliation. They also believed that a revival of Europe depended
upon Germany's economy. If Europe did not stabilise, this would affect

British and American economic fortunes adversely and might also create favourable conditions for the westward spread of Bolshevism. Britain and the USA therefore sought peace and stability through revision of Versailles. Both had vested economic interests that would be damaged by war, and British leaders believed that war would cause further decline of British power and wealth. The pursuit of stability did not, however, result in harmony between Britain and the USA. They had different ideas about peaceful change, about the roles they should each play, and about an acceptable structure of stability. Britain was committed to, and a leading member of, the League of Nations: the USA remained outside. They argued over war debts, trade and monetary policy. They had trouble with naval matters and neutral rights and they also operated from different circumstances.

Britain had world-wide political responsibilities without the economic wherewithal to cope with them, which caused her endless worry and inhibited her from making European commitments. Her defence priorities were: the British Isles; her trade routes; the Empire; and, lastly, the interests of friends and allies. However, Britain could hardly defend even its first priority. A need for economy, revulsion against war, and ill-founded optimism led the British to adopt the Ten-Year Rule in 1919: planning was to assume that there would be no major war for ten years. Inevitably that impacted on British military capabilities.

The USA had economic power but shunned international political and official economic responsibility. American priorities were: prosperity and US economic expansion in an open and liberal world economy; security through that and naval power; and, finally, that the USA should have a free hand, untrammelled by political or defence commitments in either Europe or Asia.

Anglo-American relations were thus far from smooth, and in fact they rollercoastered in the inter-war period. They sank after the war in the Paris peace talks and because of war debts, the troubles in Ireland, diverging economic policies and naval rivalry. They revived in the early 1920s with the creation of the Republic of Ireland, and as Britain and the USA came to a common policy on reparations, negotiated both a debt and a naval agreement and reached compromises on such difficult issues as oil rights and cable and radio communications. But in 1927–8 difficulties arose again. The worst of these was the breakdown of the 1927 Geneva Three-Power Naval Conference. This nadir in their inter-war relationship prompted a wide-ranging discussion among British officials and ministers. Partly because of the results of that, but also owing to his own disposition, Prime Minister Ramsay MacDonald managed to mend Anglo-American fences in 1929 during talks with President Herbert Hoover. Sadly, the renewal was not long-lived. The Great Depression and the rise of totalitarianism muddied the waters of their new-found understanding. Instead of bringing Britain and the USA close together, depression and totalitarianism did much the opposite. Their economic policies diverged again and on the eve of war in 1939 Anglo-American relations were still strained, though there were last-minute improvements.

President Franklin Delano Roosevelt recognised the threat from the dictators and the benefits of some degree of solidarity with the European democracies. In 1938 the two countries signed a new trade pact, and Britain mounted an effective propaganda show in 1939 with the first royal visit to the USA. Despite these improvements, they still remained suspicious of each other's intentions and laid part of the blame for the world's descent into war at each other's door. Yet, shortly, Winston Churchill coined the term 'special relationship': whatever ups and downs there were between 1920 and 1940, the rollercoaster relationship was not derailed.

There was a strong desire in both Britain and the USA to return in the 1920s to what was referred to as 'normalcy'. That ugly word is Gamalielese: a form of bastardised English used by President Warren Gamaliel Harding. He proposed that there should be a return to economic normality after wartime *dirigisme*, but it is a mistake to suggest that there is a normality in economic or, for that matter, in any other kind of world affair. Something of the past can often be retrieved, but the more extensive and violent the change the more difficult and less fruitful is the effort. In their respective ways, Britain and the USA tried to recapture a normality drawn from the past and in doing so were driven by ambitions for the future and a shared revulsion against war.

Britain rapidly drew back from the model of a more directed economy that it had toyed with during the war. Gentlemanly capitalism, as it has been termed by Cain and Hopkins, re-asserted itself on the basis of the power of the city banking and commercial institutions and their confidently iterated canons of free-market principles: competition, free trade, a balanced budget and a stable currency. Many believed that banking and commerce were more important than manufacturing and there were strong grounds for that: in 1914 invisibles earned 44% of the total cost of imports. The protectionist coalition of imperial consolidators, conservatives and industrialists was not coherent or strong enough to resist effectively. In December 1923 the Conservatives tried the politics of protection in the General Election and were soundly defeated, but even so it was not a complete return to the minimalist watchman state: both social and, later, defence spending were to prevent that. Although it was not a complete return in substance, in spirit it was an attempt to regain Britain's pivotal role in a free-market world economy, which it feared was slipping-away into American hands. The slipping-away involved a lot of pulling by the USA, as we shall see, and caused much unrest and resentment in London.

Americans were more unanimous and adamant than the British about a free-market world economy and expended much energy in trying to create it. However, their ideological commitment to this vision was tempered by the pursuit of US national economic interests and by a form of corporatism that involved government encouragement of industrial co-operation in the international sphere to try to maximise efficiency, profits and output. The USA thus erected the highest protective tariff in its history; and government, in the guises of the Commerce and Treasury Departments, helped mastermind US penetration of markets and monitored US loans abroad. The spirit of all this was identical to that which controlled British policy, namely, the desire to dominate the world economy. Not surprisingly, this resulted in conflict, but also a certain amount of co-operation as the British adjusted to the new-found economic strength of the USA and admitted her into areas previously their preserve. This was done, in part, because of British perception of the wider need for at least tolerable, if not good, Anglo-American relations.[2]

In the defence field the two countries yearned for similar things. There was a common reaction against war and its horrors, and strong peace and pacifist movements developed. This was in marked contrast to the glorification of war by fascists, national socialists and Japanese militarists. In high policy, the peace movement influenced the rapid move to demobilise and slash defence spending. Complementing this, both nations placed faith in the maintenance of peace through the just resolution of conflicts by the League or through arbitration, by the creation of a prosperous world and, so far as the USA was concerned, by the setting of a moral example. The other way of ensuring security in the official minds of both was through naval supremacy combined with isolation from Europe's political and strategic problems for the USA, and through the avoidance of specific defence commitments in continental Europe for Britain. So, once again, it is possible to see parallels in British and US policy. In the matter of naval supremacy this would generate friction between them since only one could, in fact, be supreme – though, for a while, an arrangement was made that conveniently camouflaged that reality.

Foreign policy-making changed in both countries as a result of World War I. In Britain the FO lost some of its prestige and Prime Ministers generally tended to take more direct involvement in policy formulation. Economics played a more important role, and Treasury parsimony and Britain's economic performance in the inter-war period limited the possibilities and ambitions of the FO and the defence establishment. The revulsion against war, peace movements and public opinion all had impact on policy-makers, and, while public opinion was welcomed by many as an extension of the domain of democratic practice, it was by no means always beneficial. As one historian has observed: 'the problem with "public opinion" after 1919 was that many sections of it did *not* match that fond Gladstonian and Wilsonian vision of a liberal, educated, fair minded populace, imbued with internationalist ideas, utopian assumptions and respect for the rule of law'.[3] Britain was also influenced by the dominions and India. Notwithstanding the Empire Settlement Act of 1922 and moves in the 1930s to consolidate the Empire and dominions into a more organic political and economic entity, the reality of the situation was that in successive imperial conferences the dominions sought and achieved more independence from the mother country. The relationship became much more one of give and take, and one thing the dominions strongly opposed was any British commitment in Europe that might drag the Empire into another war.

In the USA, peace movements were stronger than in Britain and combined with other indigenous social and political strands to strengthen isolationism – that is to say, a rejection of European security and political ties: there was no isolationism in terms of US economic, tourist and cultural interest in Europe. Public opinion was also stronger and made more manifest by Congress at governmental level than was the case in Britain. In the actual conduct of foreign policy, the USA's experience in the 1920s and for much of the 1930s was quite unique. In the former decade, in particular, the USA relied greatly upon unofficial representatives at European conferences and engaged the service of businessmen and bankers to help solve the world's problems, which were mainly defined in economic terms. The State Department had effective leadership from time to time, notably under Charles Evans Hughes, and tried through the Rogers Act of 1925 to increase its professionalism, but its bureaucracy was small, lacked expertise, experience and self-confidence and had to accept incursions into foreign affairs from the Commerce Department and into policies of high politics from Presidents such as Hoover and Roosevelt. And it had to cope with foreign uncertainty about the worth of US policy after the Senate rejection of the League Covenant and the Peace Treaty. Later actions by Congress in the economic field also posed questions as to just how much in control of foreign policy any US administration could be.

These factors in Britain and the USA had the effect of making foreign policy more complex and difficult to handle and inclined both governments to seek economic prosperity in a free market and pursue peace through disarmament and negotiation, but without firm commitments to restraining totalitarianism. The great failing of both, in retrospect, was that they consistently defined their national interest in a narrow way, which excluded the possibility of taking action against the radical expansionist states until it was too late to deter them. The two countries fell into similar patterns of behaviour. The Americans refused to take a stand against Japan in the Pacific, and Britain went a step further and actively sought to appease Germany in Europe. Underlying much of the thinking in both Washington and London was a common liberal notion that all humankind is rational and amenable to reason: the error was that Hitler, Mussolini and Tojo were not. Once a cycle of appeasement is entered, it is very difficult to say no and get the other side to understand that that is what is meant. The only course then open to honourable men, however peace-loving, rational and liberal they may be, is war, and that is sadly what it all led to in 1939.

While British and US diplomacy failed to arrest the descent into world war, the two countries were not without successes in the inter-war period. Perhaps most vital of all was the fact that their relations, though storm-tossed and damaged in the 1920s and 1930s, did survive intact in such a way as to be able to be amply renewed from 1940 onwards. But just how close they came to irreparable rupture we must now examine.[4]

DEBTS, NAVIES AND ECONOMIC POLICIES 1920–5

The two great issues which dominated Anglo-American relations between 1920 and 1925 were debts and naval power, both of which had direct bearing on wider economic policy.

The war-debt problem involved a complex mixture of self-interest, altruism and hypocrisy. Britain ended the war with more owed to her than she owed to the USA. The problem was that much of it would not be forthcoming, either because loans to Czarist Russia had been repudiated by the Bolsheviks, or because Britain's debtors in Europe were not in a position to repay. Britain was thus in a dilemma. It wanted to avoid offending the USA by defaulting and, with her ambition of regaining the world leadership in banking and commerce, she could not afford the stigma of bad debtor. But, neither could she afford to pay in full because it would damage her economy and undermine her ability to compete with the USA and regain markets lost in the war. The British thus tried to tie reparations to debts and get their reduction or cancellation. Their overriding aim was not to have to pay out substantially more than they received.

The USA was inconsistent. It urged a policy of no, or at least only light, reparations, but Treasury Secretary William McAdoo insisted in November 1918 that debtors must negotiate bilaterally with the USA the full repayment of their loans with interest. The USA rightly feared that heavy reparations would stymie economic recovery in Europe, but why debt repayments should not have a similar effect on the wider world economy Americans never adequately explained. The US position hardened even further as disillusion with her wartime associates grew in the peace talks. The Americans refused to accept the idea of 'from each according to means to each according to needs', which is what Britain and France essentially argued. The latter two had been most damaged in what ended up as a joint war effort against the Central Powers, and the USA had the greatest ability to be generous in the early 1920s. However, the USA, far from feeling any obligation to be generous, insisted on payment in full. It was critical of the policy of the Allies which expanded their empires under the guise of the mandate system, imposed reparations contrary to the wishes of the USA, and undermined US principles in the peace talks. And, in any case, Washington was determined to use its economic power to create an open-door international economy which would benefit the USA and the world in general. This complex constellation of factors and reasoning is in evidence in a letter from US Treasury Secretary David Houston to Austen Chamberlain, Chancellor of the Exchequer, in March 1920:

> This nation has neither sought nor received substantial benefit from war. On the other hand Allies, although having suffered greatly in loss of life and property, have, under terms of treaty of peace and otherwise, acquired very considerable accessions of territories, populations, economic and other advantages. It would therefore seem that if a full account were taken of these and of whole situation there would be no desire or reason to call upon Government of this country for further contributions.[5]

The British felt that this was harsh, especially as the debt problem could not be isolated from other concerns that they had to deal with. It would be difficult to craft a coherent economic policy until debt repayments were settled, and there was also the problem of naval rivalry. The USA was still committed to a navy second to none, and their building programme would take them ahead of the Royal Navy unless a costly naval building programme were undertaken in Britain. How politicians in London could justify such action, in conditions of peace and economic difficulty, with a strong antiwar sentiment in the country and when the re-armament would be directed against a friendly state, was a question that could not easily be answered. Knowing that it had leverage, the USA pressed Britain to settle her debts. In November 1920 American views were sent to Chamberlain through private channels and received caustic comment:

if the funding is done at once it 'will do more to strengthen the friendly relations between America and Great Britain than any other course of dealing with the same' . . . on the other hand, if it is not done at once, then, 'in the present state of opinion here there is likely to develop an unfortunate misunderstanding'. The statement concludes with an eminently characteristic paragraph which may be intended to convey a threat and is carefully worded so as to convey no shadow of a promise.[6]

Chamberlain was furious, but thought that there was no alternative to undertaking funding negotiations: 'The American Government and people are living in a different continent – I might say in a different world. It is useless and worse than useless to criticise their insularity, blindness and selfishness and it is not compatible with our dignity to appear as suitors pressing for a consideration which is not willingly given.'[7]

Action on the debt was urgently needed. Britain was more concerned than ever about the economic challenge from the USA, but was finding it difficult to craft an alternative to co-operation with her. Lloyd George had thoughts of bolstering Britain's position through the development of an economic system in Europe linked to sterling, which Maynard Keynes had drawn up, but whether or not that could come to fruition remained to be seen. In the meantime, the debt to the USA and uncertainty about how it was to be dealt with weakened Britain's hand. Britain needed co-operation from the USA if debts were to be settled satisfactorily and if friction was to be avoided in naval matters. But debts, naval matters, the outcome of the peace negotiations and 'unwarrantable interference' in Anglo-Irish affairs by the USA all seemed to be creating the very kind of atmosphere most calculated to result in a harsh funding agreement. Then, an opportunity arose to approach things from a slightly different angle and with hope of better results.[8]

After some Anglo-American exchanges, President Harding issued invitations to attend a conference to deal with naval armaments and matters relating to the Pacific. The USA had three main concerns: the potential naval threat from Japan, the Anglo-Japanese Alliance, and the Congress's unwillingness to fund further expansion of the US fleet. As early as May 1920, the USA had begun moves to cope with these worries.

First, the USA tried to handle Japan. It struck a deal, which was typical of the free-market diplomacy of the 1920s, in which Japanese acceptance of an open-door policy for China was exchanged for access to the New York money market. The USA hoped to influence and check Japanese policy through economic leverage, but it also sought a way of making Japan more vulnerable by persuading Britain to abandon, or at least modify, its alliance with her. On 10 May, US Ambassador John Davis was instructed to tell the British that the US wanted modifications which would both explicitly acknowledge the open door in China and indicate that the Alliance could not be used against the USA.[9]

The question of the Japanese Alliance became complicated for Britain because of general naval disarmament considerations, war debts, the cost of new ships, the need for economy, and her relations with the dominions and the USA. With regard to the latter, without a withdrawal from the Japanese Alliance, there looked to be little likelihood of a naval agreement, and thus Britain would be saddled with large armament costs in an attempt to keep abreast of the US Navy. In addition, there would remain grounds for disagreement with the USA when good relations were necessary in order to deal with other questions, most notably war debts. In May 1921, First Lord of the Admiralty Lord Lee of Fareham wrote a lengthy appraisal for the Cabinet, which raised many of these points.

> fear of Japan, and dislike of the Anglo-Japanese Alliance, is the real driving force behind the 1916 and subsequent [US] Navy Bills, and there is, I am convinced, no prospect of any agreement on Armaments unless and until these disturbing factors can be got out of the way.

> . . . the Japanese Alliance makes us suspect, and we have no alternative but to stagger along under our financial burdens in the effort, which is an obligation, to keep pace with American naval expansion. It is a vicious circle of ever widening evil, from which there seems no escape unless statesmanship comes to the rescue.[10]

Lee was friendly with Theodore Roosevelt Jr, US Assistant Secretary of the Navy, and favoured close ties with the USA, but he was not blind to the disadvantages of dissolving the alliance with Japan which had helped to protect British interests. His ideal solution was to draw in the USA and form a tripartite alliance, but US statesmanship would not extend itself to that and Britain also found that Canada bitterly opposed any relationship with Japan that might damage ties with the USA. In the end, the British had so many needs that militated against a continuation of their alliance with Japan that they felt constrained to let it go. At its funeral – the Washington Conference – a face-saving arrangement was devised in order to let the Japanese down gently, but there was no avoiding the conclusion that Japan was being isolated by the two great Anglo-Saxon powers. Later, Japanese resentment was aggravated by the 1924 US Immigration Law, which racially discriminated against them. Here was material for nationalist Japanese propaganda that was used to fuel the country's expansionist ambitions.

Furthermore, while the lapse of the Anglo-Japanese Alliance removed a source of friction in Anglo-American relations, that was no substitute for help to protect British interests in the Far East. The USA would make no alliance that would tie it to the defence of an ally. Restrictions on naval power adopted at the Washington Conference were fine, but there were no enforcement provisions. Ultimately, they depended upon the signatories' willingness to abide by them, and by 1935 Japan would no longer do that.

The Washington Conference of 1921–2, masterminded by Secretary of State Charles Evans Hughes, was regarded as a great success at the time. Hughes led the American delegation, and Lord President Arthur Balfour the British. Hughes opened the conference with a dramatic flourish, proposing major naval cuts and a ratio by which the great powers' naval armaments should be related to each other. The main difficulty involved for Britain was acceptance of naval parity with the USA. Well before the war, the British two-navy standard – the Royal Navy should be as powerful as any other two combined – had been modified and by 1910 the order of the day was a 60% superiority over the next largest navy. In June 1921, at the Imperial Conference in London, the British had agreed to abandon even this for a one-power naval standard, but there were still difficulties. Although acceptance of parity might look like the kind of statesmanship that Lee of Fareham had spoken of, it was not agreeable to most of the navy chiefs. Nevertheless, accepted it was for a number of compelling reasons. A committee on government expenditure – the Geddes Committee – was urging further economies and cuts in defence spending in the light of Britain's economic problems. There was the fear of an expensive naval race and of the adverse way that a failure to reach agreement with the USA would affect a number of other issues of common concern, and all this added up to a price too expensive to pay. The Four-Power Agreement between France, Japan, Britain and the USA substituted for the Anglo-Japanese Alliance well-meaning platitudes about respect for each other's possessions in the Pacific and commitments to negotiate if difficulties arose. The Nine-Power Treaty, which included the four powers plus China, Italy, Belgium, The Netherlands and Portugal, produced a multilateral commitment to the open door in China. And the Five Power Naval Agreement limited capital ships to ratios for the USA, Britain, Japan, Italy and France of 5:5:3:1.5:1.5 respectively, and introduced a ten-year building holiday for capital ships.[11]

In the end all this became meaningless, but at the time it went down well with public opinion as it cut back on armaments and saved money. For Britain and the USA it solved the problem of naval friction between them for the time being and allowed relations in general to improve. In a broader perspective, it was further evidence of British realism in adjusting to the rise of US naval power while maintaining friendly relations with her. Not all were happy in London by any means, and some thought that the USA had achieved a very favourable agreement from a hand that held few cards. A naval race with the USA, much feared in Britain for economic reasons, might never have materialised because Congress was unwilling to vote the money for a construction programme. But in fact, as we have seen, there were many other cards that the USA held which led Britain into agreeing to US proposals. The alternative would have been increased difficulties in a whole range of areas (even if the naval situation had not deteriorated), and the government was not prepared to allow that. The first of those issues to be taken up was the settlement of war debts.

Britain's position on the debt to the USA came to be dominated by her attempt to regain leadership of world commerce and banking and maintain good relations with the USA: to achieve both she had to honour debts. Given that Britain could not avoid settling her debt, the question then to be answered was how it could best be done. In searching for answers, the government adopted two strategies. The first was to try to persuade the Americans of the equity of cancelling debts and reducing reparations; the second was to try to strengthen Britain's economic position to enhance her bargaining position. Both these strategies failed. Lloyd George's attempts to implement Keynes's plan to extend the use of sterling into Europe and bolster the importance of the City of London came to nought at the Genoa Conference in April–May 1922, largely because of American opposition. With Britain's economy still performing poorly and with the gentlemanly capitalists gaining ascendancy, a hard settlement of the debt with the Americans became inevitable. In the light of the US protective Fordney–McCumber Tariff of 1922, it was also going to be increasingly difficult to earn export money to pay back dollars owed to the USA. Already by 1922 the interest on the loans was mounting rapidly and a funding agreement and a schedule of repayment were urgently needed.

In 1921 Secretary of the US Treasury Andrew Mellon had failed to get broad executive powers from the legislature to negotiate war-debt terms. Instead, in February 1922 Congress set up the World War Foreign Debt Commission, with little discretion allowed for settlements. Mellon was appointed Chairman by President Harding, with Hughes, Hoover and two Congressmen as members. With a strait-jacket imposed from Congress and with midterm congressional elections due in November, the room to man-oeuvre for the administration was limited. Nevertheless, the British felt that if they could not get a good settlement, at least they could make their position public and point the finger at the USA as the one responsible for what was about to occur.

On 1 August the British government released the famous Balfour Note; it was considered by the Cabinet on 25 July and sent to the relevant governments after minor amendments:

> The policy favoured by His Majesty's Government is . . . that of writing off, through one great transaction, the whole body of inter-allied indebtedness. But if this be found impossible of accomplishment, we wish it to be understood that we do not in any event desire to make a profit out of any less satisfactory arrangement. In no circumstances do we propose to ask more from our debtors than is necessary to pay our creditors. And, while we do not ask for more, all will admit that we can hardly be content with less.[12]

Furthermore, if a general solution for war indebtedness were found, Britain would be willing to relinquish her claims to reparations. There were two weaknesses in this position. First, the USA was unwilling to regard the debts as anything other than a commercial transaction. As Calvin Coolidge put it after succeeding to the Presidency after Harding's untimely death, 'They hired the money, didn't they?' Americans would not regard the war against the Central Powers as one in which all pooled their resources in a common effort according to their abilities. The second weakness was that, high-minded as the Balfour Note sounded, the Americans knew that the proposal involved Britain wiping out what were largely bad debts in return for the US wiping out good ones.

In the end, after the fall of Lloyd George's coalition government and the return to power of the Conservatives under Bonar Law, the new Chancellor of the Exchequer, Stanley Baldwin, committed himself to repaying the debt in its entirety and set sail on the *Majestic* for the USA in December 1922. As he did so, negotiations about reparations from Germany, now economically devastated by the war, the peace and inflation (escalating into hyperinflation), broke down and Germany was declared to be in default. Stability in Europe appeared elusive and the USA, apart from humanitarian aid masterminded by Hoover, stood aloof and demanded the repayment of debts. It was partly to try to help bring some stability and a more positive US attitude towards Europe's problems that Britain had finally agreed that her debt to the USA now had to be funded.

Baldwin was accompanied by Montagu Norman, the highly influential Governor of the Bank of England and the leading light of the gentlemanly capitalists and their free-market orthodoxy. The negotiations with the Debt Commission were tough, but Baldwin talked to them in their own language. 'Our wish is to approach discussion as businessmen seeking a business solution of what is fundamentally a business problem.'[13] Baldwin and

Norman managed to get the Americans to soften the terms of repayment somewhat, but the annual bill was still staggering: $161 million for ten years and then $184 million thereafter for fifty-two years. When Baldwin returned to London with this, Bonar Law balked at the prospect of making such payments, but after further persuasion from colleagues he reluctantly agreed. Britain and America, at least, had managed to stabilise their relations even if they had done so in a way that heavily burdened the British and led to resentment later.

Elsewhere, things became more fraught. After the German reparation default, France invaded the Ruhr, as she was entitled to do under the Peace Settlement, but there followed even worse economic consequences for both France and Germany. Ironically, this provided the opportunity that the USA had been waiting for to bring about a more sensible economic settlement in Europe and create opportunities for American economic expansion. The British also now favoured a scaling-down of reparations for the sake of German recovery and stability in Europe and so they and the Americans were able to co-operate in finding a solution. Charles G. Dawes arrived in Europe from the USA to head a commission to revise the reparations Germany owed to the victors and to try to bring stability to Europe's economy. The commission, in the short term, succeeded beyond people's wildest expectations. Reparations were revised down drastically from the $33 billion imposed in 1919, and the French withdrew from the Ruhr. European states were set on the path back to the gold standard, abandoned during the war. Germany was given a dollar loan to help revive its economy, and the mark was linked to the dollar and hence to gold. There then followed an enormous influx of US investment into Germany, and its economy blossomed.

The long-awaited recovery had arrived. And for a while all was well with the world. America's prestige was high and Americanisation held allure for many. It had metaphorically and literally come up with the goods. America and Americanism seemed to be the model for the future. As Frank Costigliola has put it:

> Americanism meant a pragmatic, optimistic outlook on life; a peaceful, rational compromise of political differences; an efficient, modern way of organizing work that emphasised mass assembly production; rising standards of living with declining class antagonisms; scientific use of statistics and other information; and the predominance of mass society (this meant democratic politics, widespread consumption, and popular entertainment).[14]

The Americans and the impact of the American way had certainly achieved much in the early 1920s. The world economy revived. There was a greater sense of security, with the League coming into operation, naval armaments limitations, and US promotion of international arbitration. The prospects for peace, prosperity and stability looked good, and Britain and the USA had mended their relations. Looking back a few years later, a FO memorandum commented that between 1920 and 1923 'a series of events occurred which had a profoundly beneficial effect on those [Anglo-American] relations; the Mesopotamian oil question was settled, the Irish Free State was created, the Washington Naval Treaty was signed, the Anglo-Japanese Alliance was abrogated and the debt settlement took place'.[15] The effect of all that in the USA, especially the debt settlement, was to 'place the name of Britain higher in the esteem and regard of the American people than at any previous time within living memory'. And while Britain resented the harshness of the settlement, it could console herself that 'British prestige . . . gained immeasurably from the settlement.'[16] However, everything was not right and soon problems again afflicted international relations and the bilateral relations between Britain and the USA.

SECURITY AND ECONOMIC DEPRESSION 1925–34

The mid-decade got off to a good start. The Dawes Plan helped revive the European economy and created an atmosphere in which security could be enhanced. At the Locarno Conference in October agreement was reached, most significantly between France and Germany, about the existing borders in Western Europe, and Britain agreed to be one of the guarantors. The way was now paved for German entry into the League. However, Britain never went beyond Locarno, and even the commitments given in 1925 were vague and difficult to invoke. Any idea that Britain was prepared to be the mainstay of a security guarantee system in Europe was exposed as false in its position on the Geneva Protocol.

France needed security. When British and US guarantees of French security expired because of the US Senate's rejection of the peace treaties, France was left to confront the eventuality of a German revival alone, knowing that its manpower and industrial potential far exceeded her own. French security aims now centred on the League, and the Protocol for the Pacific Settlement of International Disputes presented her with a possible lifeline. The Protocol envisaged compulsory arbitration of any international dispute with sanctions for enforcement of the League Council's writ. The Protocol was unanimously accepted by representatives of the forty-eight member nations, including Britain, but needed ratification by their governments.

The British government at the time was the first Labour administration led by Ramsay MacDonald, which had a strong commitment to peace and disarmament. Unfortunately for the Protocol, the government was defeated in Parliament over its refusal to prosecute the *Workers' Weekly*. The matter involved anti-communist hysteria, and that problem was later compounded by the scandal of the Zinoviev Letter, purportedly from the Soviet Union, inciting British workers to revolution. The outcome of all this was a Labour defeat in the General Election. Stanley Baldwin now formed a Conservative government with Austen Chamberlain as Foreign Secretary: his view of the protocol was not favourable. Chamberlain's instinct was to avoid the possibility of entanglements in Europe, and that was reinforced by his assessment of US attitudes towards the Protocol in January 1925, two conclusions of which were important. First, 'if the protocol went through as it stands, it is no exaggeration to say that they [the Americans] could hardly help considering that body [the League] a potential enemy. It is, of course, the compulsory arbitration and the sanctions provisions which inspire this feeling.' Chamberlain speculated that the USA might move to protect the Panama Canal or uphold neutral rights in wartime and fall foul of the League. Thus he came to his second conclusion: 'In short, if His Majesty's Government ratify the protocol, they will be running a serious risk of grave trouble with the United States in the future.'[17] The Protocol was rejected by Britain on 24 March 1925. It never came into operation, and the hope for collective security was lost. France was left exposed to cope with the danger of Germany as best she could. Neither Britain nor the USA would guarantee French security either bilaterally or through the League. At the same time, the USA, with British collusion, had undermined the authority of the Versailles Settlement by revising it through the Dawes Plan. Already by 1925 there was an implicit acknowledgement that the Versailles Settlement, to which France looked to uphold its security against Germany, was unjust and probably unworkable.

The USA still offered arbitration as a solution to international conflict, but problems of enforcement and the insistence of the Congress that it should have the final say in whether or not a matter should be submitted for arbitration negated any usefulness such treaties might have had. The epitome of this form of attempt to deal with conflict came with the 1928 Pact of Paris. It is better known as the Kellogg–Briand Pact: it was an agreement open to universal participation that purported to outlaw war. No enforcement sanctions were involved: it was simply an expression of moral condemnation of war before the event and a cry for the peaceful resolution of disputes. So far as US–UK relations were concerned, the pact complicated matters to do with a US proposal for a bilateral US–UK arbitration treaty. As we shall see shortly, for reasons to do with belligerent rights, Britain avoided committing herself.

While Britain, with the exception of the likes of the great disarmament proponent and idealist Robert Cecil, had little time for, or faith in, the Kellogg–Briand type of moral preventative of war, it offered little else instead. Like the USA, Britain was not prepared to commit herself to action beforehand to save others from aggression, for fear of being drawn into a situation against her will for a cause she might not agree with. Thus when the Geneva General Disarmament Conference was convened in 1932, the government decided that it could not commit itself in Europe beyond Locarno. As one study has put it, that sank the conference before it even started. If Britain would not guarantee French security, then the French would never feel secure enough to recognise what Germany was calling for, namely, equality of status with other sovereign states and the right to re-arm to a level commensurate with other countries. Whether a British commitment to France would have made any difference is difficult to say. The circumstances were not propitious. The Depression was at its height and undermined the capabilities of the democracies to take effective action. The image, and in particular the moral suasion, of the USA had collapsed with Wall Street. Japan went on the rampage in the Far East in January, and Hitler came to power in Germany in 1933. In these circumstances, and given the puny defence capability Britain could put into France, it is doubtful if the course of history would have been substantially altered if Britain had given a commitment to her.[18]

When Japan contrived through the Mukden Incident to make war in China in 1931, Britain felt that she could not take action. Foreign Secretary John Simon refused to join with the USA in invoking the Nine Power Treaty, which ended any illusion of an Anglo-American front in the Pacific. Instead, Simon insisted on going through the League: a course of action which proved totally ineffective. Later, in 1934, the Treasury argued that the cost of action in the Pacific would be prohibitive. There were fears that hostilities, or even increased defence expenditure, could destroy the economy and in any case Britain alone could not hope to defeat Japan if war erupted between them. A war in the Far East would also leave Britain dreadfully exposed to the danger of blackmail and possible aggression from Germany or Italy. A similar logic prevailed a year later when it was argued that Britain could not take action against Italian aggression in Abyssinia for fear of being over-stretched in the event of a war in the Far East: until about 1937, Japan was considered the main defence problem by planners in London. In the USA, President Hoover thought that it would be impossible to take a hard stand against Japan because public opinion would not see it as a matter of vital US interest. The Americans thus consoled their consciences with a doctrine of non-recognition of gains by armed force in China. The only fighting was over who authored the doctrine: Hoover or Henry Stimson, his Secretary of State. History has awarded Stimson the prize.

For the present account, perhaps the most notable things about these great and general problems of world peace were the lack of Anglo-American co-operation and the similarity of approach that they both adopted. Their policies ultimately failed. They made it obvious that they thought that Germany had been ill-treated and that Versailles should be revised, but failed to give adequate reassurance to France. Britain participated in the League but refused to make it a force for collective security. The USA adopted righteous and moral stances whose only force lay in America's world prestige, but after the collapse of Wall Street that prestige withered away. The other US strategy was economic leverage, but the power of that also waned with the depression and in any case was a two-edged sword. One could argue that Japan chose war rather than to submit to the possibility, likely or not, of economic strangulation by the USA. The net result of American and British policies was an ongoing charade of disarmament proposals and talks, punctuated by moral pronouncements which together gave a false sense of security and obscured the dangers emerging in Japan, Germany and Italy. In retrospect, it is so easy to be hard on Britain and the USA, but their policies were popular at the time. Much of the substance arose out of well-intentioned ideas and, particularly so far as Britain was concerned, scope for action was severely limited by economic constraints.

Areas where Britain did have more interaction with the USA proved to be fraught with difficulties in the mid-1920s and nowhere more so than in economic affairs. Although Americans decided to keep out of the political and security affairs of Europe, their leaders recognised the need for economic stability there and for the cultivation of opportunities for US business and investment. A safe way to do this was through a type of semi-offical intervention in Europe such as the Dawes Plan, and assistance from the Commerce and Treasury Departments for US business to exploit the market in Europe. America could thus have the best of all worlds: economic power and prosperity without political responsibilities and entanglement in Europe. Public opinion for much of this was orchestrated by the newly founded US Council on Foreign Relations and other similarly august bodies. America aimed to create a stable world economy through the re-creation of a widely used gold standard that would encourage trade and international investment. The USA would take advantage of this to the benefit of all, but mostly the USA, with the export of industrial products from a well-protected home manufacturing base and the free import of raw materials: this trade policy was largely the brainchild of William Culbertson, the US Tariff Commissioner. There were two prerequisites for the success of this policy: the revival of the German economy, and the return of Britain to the gold standard. In 1925 the latter move was made, though with some trepidation felt by certain British politicians, most notably the Chancellor of the Exchequer himself, Winston Churchill. But pressure from the USA and the ambitions of Governor Norman and other gentlemanly capitalists proved persuasive in the end. There was also a fear that some of the dominions might move away from sterling and fall into the orb of what in effect would be a competitive and stronger dollar area. As one historian has aptly put it, 'The return to gold at $4.86 signified the fulfilment of a long held British policy goal. But the return must also be understood as part of Britain's effort to reinforce imperial ties, regain position as center of the world economy, and meet the American challenge.'[19]

Meeting the challenge proved difficult. The war had allowed the USA to take the initiative in a number of markets previously dominated by Britain, and by 1930 the USA had wrested the lead as an exporter from Britain in Japan, China, South America and Canada. It now had 16% of the world's export market compared to Britain's 12%. This was partly because of Britain's internal economic problems: the General Strike of 1926; an over-valued pound, which made exporting difficult; and deflationary domestic policies, which hurt manufacturing industries already suffering from low productivity. A lot of this had to do with trying to return to a normality that she was not suited for in 1925, and there were added complications arising from US policies. Repayment of war debts in full was one obvious factor: others include the import protection afforded by the Fordney-McCumber tariff, and aggressive US policies to undermine British economic advantages in oil concessions in the Middle East, in cable and radio communications and in rubber production. The oil problem had arisen in the early 1920s with regard to Mesopotamia and was resolved by a cartel agreement between the oil companies, with the British government leaning toward appeasement in order to keep friendly with the USA. When difficulties arose again towards the end of the decade, a so-called Red Line Agreement was drawn up marking out areas in the Middle East respectively for the Europeans and for the USA. However, this was not the end of the matter, as we shall see in a later chapter. In cable and radio communications similar compromises were worked out which demonstrate that there was a degree of co-operation, albeit rather reluctant from the British, between the two countries even in areas where there were initially disputes. But the most contentious issue was rubber and it gives some insight into British and

American attitudes which were to play against each other for many years to come.

The facts of the rubber saga are straightforward enough. By 1922 over-production had caused a slump in price. Colonial Secretary Winston Churchill became concerned over the fate of the massive British investment in the industry and commissioned a committee led by Sir James Stevenson to investigate matters. Britain controlled over 70% of the world's production, and Stevenson recommended that controls should be imposed to end the glut and raise prices. His plan was adopted and put into effect. Among American tyre-producers, which used the majority of the world's production of rubber, the plan initially had a mixed reception, with some approving of the attempt to stabilise prices. In 1925, however, there were howls of protest as rubber prices rose, even though there was evidence that US manufacturers were making excessive profits. A Congressional investigation showed that they continued to do so even during the Stevenson Plan. In 1925 they paid $88 million more for rubber, but passed a $500 million increase on to consumers.

There was some division of opinion in the USA about the Stevenson Plan and what should be done about it, but Commerce Secretary Hoover, aided by Secretary of State Frank Kellogg, whipped up a storm of protest and arranged a rubber conservation programme, as well as legally dubious collusion between the tyre-makers. The situation between Britain and the USA deteriorated. In talks with Austen Chamberlain, US Ambassador Alanson Houghton rather worryingly observed in July 1925, albeit in sober and measured terms: 'how deplorable it would be if . . . when the state of the world made it more than ever necessary that we should cooperate, a conflict over a trading question made such assistance and cooperation impossible'.[20] At the end of the year Kellogg wrote a strong letter to Houghton bemoaning British interference in the rubber market, which, he lamented, had inevitably led to politicisation of what should be a commercial activity. Four months later, writing on behalf of Chamberlain, Permanent Under Secretary Robert Vansittart pointed to the mote in America's eye: 'High customs tariffs are one of the most important of the phenomena tending, as [HMG] are convinced, to afford perhaps the most powerful support given by governments to price fixing combinations.'[21] Perhaps Vansittart was not aware of the antitrust laws, but there was no denying the advantage – artificial in terms of the free market – reaped by American manufacturers because of the tariff and also, notwithstanding the antitrust laws, that tyre prices in the USA did seem highly inflated (no pun intended).

Despite repeated attacks upon British policy, the Stevenson Plan was maintained until 1928, when it ceased to be a viable strategy because of the massive expansion of Dutch rubber production in the East Indies. The episode unsettled relations and highlighted factors that went beyond the issue of rubber itself. The USA was becoming increasingly concerned about British control of raw materials such as oil and rubber and her potential to close the open door into the Empire. Also, there was conflict between the two, which was to grow worse, over different forms of protection. The USA refused to acknowledge economic nationalism in tariff protection and turned its wrath on discrimination, quotas and production controls. The British for their part could not see what the great evil was in those practices compared with the high tariffs of the USA and its hard creditor policies.

As the rubber controversy rumbled on, serious problems also arose over naval armaments and belligerent rights at sea. Lord Robert Cecil had continued to talk on and off with the Americans about more naval disarmament after the Washington Conference, and in February 1927 Coolidge issued an invitation to take up issues not yet covered by treaty arrangements. This was at a time when the big navy supporters in the USA were making their voices heard once again. In the time of Secretary of State Hughes, they had found it difficult to make headway, but Kellogg was a weaker man, and allegations that Britain had outwitted the USA and prevented her from achieving a navy second to none were becoming commonplace.

The Conference assembled at Geneva and was a disaster. The two delegations did not get on well together and there was a difficult substantive problem. Britain needed numerous small cruisers to protect its trade, whereas the USA needed larger cruisers for the great reaches of the Pacific. So, when they tried to establish controls an impasse developed. The Americans wanted numerical equality: the British wanted the size of ships to be taken into account. Recriminations and anger spread and infected the whole character of Anglo-American relations. The British position was made even more difficult by the resignation of Lord Cecil from the Cabinet in protest at the British failure to reach an agreement.

In London the crisis in Anglo-American relations caused a spate of ministerial memoranda about the general relationship, its place in Britain's overall foreign policy, and specific naval problems, especially the issue of belligerent rights at sea. A hundred and sixteen years after the War of 1812 this problem still bedevilled Anglo-American relations and was seen as the one issue that might still conceivably be a *casus belli*.

Austen Chamberlain thought it was not only conceivable but probable that hostilities would break out between Britain and the USA, if Britain tried to enforce its rights as it had in the Great War. He observed with a touch of melancholy that since then: 'The world position has been altered to our disadvantage.'[22] Churchill expressed a similar view about the possibility of war: 'No doubt it is quite right in the interests of peace to go on talking about war with the United States being "unthinkable" [but] everyone knows that this is not true.'[23] In November 1928 the FO American expert Robert Craigie, at the request of Acting Secretary of State for Foreign Affairs, Lord Cushenden, produced a lengthy analysis of Anglo-American relations, and he too spoke in harmony with Churchill and Chamberlain: 'Except as a figure of speech, war is *not* unthinkable between the two countries. On the contrary, there are present all the factors which in the past have made for wars between states.'[24] The view of Dominions Secretary Leo Amery, who, along with Lord Curzon, was one of the leading lights of British imperialism, thought that no one should lose sight of the right perspective. In fifty years' time the British Empire and its human and material resources could be as far ahead of the USA as the USA is of the British Empire at the moment. The situation in 1978 was not quite as Amery hoped that it would be: US officials had had to caution President Ford a couple of years earlier not to keep referring to the British economic experience as an example of what not to do to avoid precipitous economic and political decline. However, despite his rather fanciful vision, Amery cautioned care under the existing circumstances.[25] In fact, notwithstanding the references to the conceivability of war between Britain and the USA, the overwhelmimg weight of facts and of the desires of ministers indicated the vast chasm between conceivability and probability.

Churchill seemed to be in two minds. He had expressed bitter criticisms of the Americans in the 1920s and resented repeated British concessions to them which had yielded little in return, but he observed: 'After all, the only bad thing that has happened in Anglo-American relations is our not being able to agree about cutting our navy down.'[26] For the time being he was against further talks until they could see what President-elect Herbert Hoover might do. He saw no point in talking to Coolidge who had the 'view-point of a New England backwoodsman . . . [and who] will soon sink back into the obscurity from which only accident extracted him'.[27] The uncharitableness of that jibe was only exceeded by the remark of Dorothy Parker: when told Coolidge was dead, she responded: 'How can they tell?'.[28] Craigie in his memorandum, after vividly portraying America's lead over Britain in power and wealth, concluded: 'Every consideration and common sense seems to dictate that, if ever there is to be a trial of strength between the Empire and the United States, this is not the moment to choose for it.'[29] Comparisons were drawn with the situation between Germany and Britain pre-1914, but there were considerable differences. American public opinion, despite being stirred up after Geneva by the big navy party, was generally well disposed to Britain. Many of the problems between Britain and the USA were, concluded Craigie, soluble by negotiation. Even when the main difference between Germany and the USA was considered, namely that the USA posed a threat to British naval supremacy and Germany never did, it was observed that the USA, unlike Germany, looks out upon the world arrogantly, but is generally well disposed. Furthermore, estrangement from the USA would divide the Empire; British public opinion would turn against the government; and Britain's position in Europe would be weakened. The USA was Britain's best export market and she depended upon her financial support and good offices for her well being.

Many of these realities had been recognised and taken into consideration by both Austen Chamberlain and the CID. In the latter, much was made of the long period since 1904 during which Britain had made no defence preparations for a war with the USA. Chamberlain reiterated that publicly in the House of Commons on 8 February 1928: 'preparation for a war with the United States has never been and never will be the basis of our policy in anything'. In July he elaborated on the problem in the CID:

> He suggested that if America made our attitude on belligerent rights a *casus belli* we should not be able to afford to risk hostilities with her and would have to give way. It would indeed not even be necessary for the United States to take any warlike action against us in protest. They could close markets and financial sources of vital importance to us. Such a situation, he reiterated, was, in his opinion, the only one from which a war with America might arise, but he could not imagine that the British Government would be mad enough to create such a position.[30]

That puts the whole business of the discussion of the 'possibility' of war with the USA into its correct perspective. The anger and irritation of the moment felt by ministers and some advisers did not change British policy: both reality and underlying sentiment prevented that. Craigie believed that the Anglo-American relationship needed careful tending, for he saw a natural propensity for it to deteriorate. Whether or not that judgement was accurate we may be able to tell as the story continues to unfold. Certainly in the mid-1920s things had deteriorated, but far from irretrievably so. In March 1929 Hoover was inaugurated as President, and two months later Labour gained most seats in the General Election and Ramsay MacDonald became Prime Minister. Somewhat to the surprise of observers of Anglo-American relations, the kind of tending Craigie thought was necessary was forthcoming from these two leaders in the autumn of that year. But even before they took office British Ambassador Sir Esme Howard was writing to inform Chamberlain that the rift had clearly worried the Americans as well: 'The fact is that there is now here a real atmosphere of willingness to come to reasonable terms and a desire to be friends.'[31] Hoover invited MacDonald to visit the USA. It would be the first time a British Prime Minister had met an American President on US soil and only the second time that a Prime Minister and a President had met face to face.

The ground for the meeting between Hoover and MacDonald was prepared with care. The situation had become even more complicated after Geneva because the British had concluded an agreement with France, which made it look as if there was an Anglo-French position on cruisers opposed to the one adopted by the USA. Coolidge was so angered by this that a visit to London by Kellogg, as he returned from concluding the Kellogg–Briand Pact, was cancelled. Since then things had mellowed somewhat, but the context and the agenda for the talks were difficult. The agenda consisted of three main items: traffic in narcotics and alcohol; the Kellogg Pact; and freedom of the seas in wartime – which connected with the problem of cruisers.

MacDonald went to the USA knowing that the Cabinet was divided over the crucial issue of belligerent rights. Chamberlain in the previous administration had come to the conclusion that this was at the heart of the matter of disagreement over cruisers. The Belligerent Rights subcommittee of the CID had looked into the problem when considering US proposals for an arbitration treaty, but it resulted in an unreconcilable minority composed of the First Sea Lord, Bridgeman, Dominions Secretary Amery, and Lord Peel, Secretary of State for India (they were also supported by Sir Maurice Hankey, Secretary of the Cabinet), who opposed concessions on Britain's rights.[32] MacDonald's job was thus not easy because belligerent rights were specifically on the agenda, and the Kellogg–Briand Pact and the USA's desire for an arbitration treaty with Britain also raised that problem.

MacDonald was able to play on the priority that Hoover and Henry Stimson, his Secretary of State, had for further naval arms reductions. He gave ground to the Americans on cruisers, but insisted that belligerent rights could not be dealt with because they would complicate things and prevent the reaching of broad agreement on naval disarmament. With great reluctance, Hoover and Stimson complied with MacDonald's wishes. As a result, the London Naval Agreement of 1930 extended the Washington Conference naval controls. On the thorny problem of cruisers, there was a compromise whereby Britain had an advantage in light cruisers in exchange for an American advantage in heavy cruisers.

In his Cabinet report, MacDonald said of Hoover: 'He is not sentimentally pro-British, but rather is desirous, as a practical man, to work for the general good of the world with the country which he thinks he understands the best, and with whose policies he finds himself more often than not in agreement.'[33] MacDonald had struck up a good working relationship. He solved the cruiser problem and avoided the problems involved in an arbitration treaty and in belligerent rights in wartime. The Americans pressed the British from time to time on an arbitration treaty, but the British continued to stall and in any case the US Navy had begun by the end of the 1920s to doubt the wisdom of whittling down belligerent rights. In October 1933 US Ambassador Robert Bingham reported to Secretary of State Cordell Hull that the FO felt its agenda was so full that it would prefer to have the matter of the arbitration treaty set aside for some considerable time. It was, in effect, postponed indefinitely.[34]

The event that transformed all things at the end of the 1920s was the Wall Street Crash of October 1929 and the Great Depression that followed. The great speculative boom on Wall Street ended in disaster for the USA, Europe and the world as a whole. As US loans to Germany dried up, the fragile system of reparation and debt payments also collapsed. In the USA the depression bit deeply: unemployment soared to over 25%, GNP fell by over one-third, and the USA raised its tariff yet again with the 1930 Hawley–Smoot Act: America's debtors would find it even more difficult to export to earn dollars to pay debts. The prestige and the moral example set by the USA were now heavily discounted abroad. The economic restructuring of Europe and the world economy by open-door and free-market policies had not succeeded for anything more than the short term. Hoover tried to salvage something by declaring a one-year moratorium on debt and reparation payments in 1931, but it did little good and was partly motivated by fears of default if the USA did not offer her debtors some palliative. In Europe, Hoover's proposal infuriated the French because of the suggestion to stop reparation payments. In June 1932, reparations were finally put to rest for all practical purposes at the Lausanne Conference, but not before the French got their own back on the Americans: the radical reduction of reparations agreed on was to be contingent on similar action on war debts – something the USA would never accept.

The final act of rejection of political responsibility for the international economic order was left to Hoover's successor, Franklin Delano Roosevelt. Before leaving office, Hoover had helped to arrange the World Economic Conference that met in London in 1933. Its aim was to restore stability in an ever more unstable international exchange system, which had abandoned gold and in which competitive devaluations and discriminatory arrangements were now commonplace. Such conditions had contributed to the collapse of world trade. However, when the conference convened, although Secretary of State Cordell Hull hoped to make a constructive contribution, Roosevelt prevented him by announcing that the USA would not agree to stabilise the dollar and that US energy must be devoted to the rebuilding of the domestic economy. Among other things, Roosevelt did not want to lose the advantage for American exports gained through the US abandonment of the gold standard and the devaluation of the dollar.

While Roosevelt's policy resulted in more overt economic nationalism and less internationalism in the USA, similar responses were also made elsewhere. Most notable of all were drives for economic autarchy in Germany, Japan and Italy (the Soviets had adopted such a course years earlier), but there were also moves in that direction by Britain.

The economic crisis in Britain forced drastic measures upon the government. Towards the end of August 1931, MacDonald resigned and formed the National Government: a coalition that tried to balance the budget. The Labour Party expelled MacDonald, and colleagues who continued to serve with him, for this 'act of betrayal'. Over the following months economy measures provoked riots and a naval mutiny at Invergordon. On 21 September Britain abandoned the gold standard, and a new departure in economic foreign policy was embarked upon. In October a General Election returned the National Government with a massive majority. MacDonald remained as Prime Minister, but Conservatives dominated the Cabinet: Neville Chamberlain was Chancellor of the Exchequer, and John Simon, Foreign Secretary.

The desire for protectionism now became irresistible. The Conservatives mounted a campaign to win over the ex-Labour people and the Liberals to a policy of tariff protection and imperial preference to raise revenue and increase empire trade. This was the resurrection of ideas that had been current during the early 1920s. With the failure of the inter-war economic system inspired by America and British gentlemanly capitalists, a more nationalistic and managed system was now possible. Not all in the Cabinet were won over, but a free vote in the House allowed the National Government to continue and imperial preference to be developed. At the Ottawa Imperial Conference in 1932 a system of Empire preference, whereby members levied lower tariffs on each other than on outsiders, was adopted. This helped revive trade within the Empire, and also strengthened the position of sterling. With the exception of Canada, sterling was the medium through which the trade of this new bloc was conducted.

The actual effect of the Ottawa system was not all that great. It did not create an autarchic economic bloc, and Britain's trade policy was still more free-trade than protectionist. One specialist on Empire economic policy estimated that by 1937 Empire preferences had pushed up British exports and imports to and from the Empire by 5% and 10% respectively.[35] So

Empire preference was significant, but it was nowhere near as protectionist as the US tariff. Nevertheless, this departure down the road of tariff preference was seized upon by the USA, and in particular by Cordell Hull, as a discriminatory evil that must be exorcised from the international economy. When the pattern of trade encouraged by the system of preferences was later strengthened by sterling controls, Hull's criticisms became even more strident. Not only was economic discrimination evil, it also led to political friction and eventually war – according to Hull and his acolytes. And discrimination by Britain was damaging not because of her practices alone, but also because of the potential impact her example would have on others.

By 1934 the whole postwar economic and security system fostered by the USA was unravelling and Anglo-American relations were deteriorating. The international economy was in deep recession; Hitler's arrival in power had finally put paid to the reparations question; and in 1934 Britain along with every other country except Finland, defaulted on war-debt repayments to the USA. Perhaps most damaging of all was that Anglo-American relations diminished in the 1930s in terms of active interaction. There was not much to the relationship during this period. Elsewhere in the world, political and economic initiatives passed into the hands of the totalitarians. Forms of economic autarchy, politically dominated trade deals, and authoritarian politics took the place of discredited capitalism, the free market and liberal doctrine. It was not just Anglo-American relations that had lost their way but liberalism, capitalism and the humanitarian tradition of representative democracy.

THE DICTATES OF SENTIMENT AND THE NEEDS OF SELF-INTEREST 1934–9

Looking back at British and American behaviour in the 1930s, one gets the impression that they were in but not of this world.

After the split in the Labour Party in 1929, the Left were less restrained in their criticisms of government and more vociferous in their pacifism. At the same time, the dangers of war rapidly increased and in 1932 Britain abandoned the Ten-Year Rule. However, there followed little of practical consequence for several years. The General Disarmament Conference dragged on until 1934 and kept hope alive in the hearts of optimists, and even after its failure re-armament was difficult because of both public opposition and lack of economic strength.

In the USA things were similar. The Roosevelt New Deal was preoccupied with alleviating the dreadful domestic situation, and when attention was directed to foreign affairs it was generally in order to be critical of international involvement. In 1934–5, the famous report by Senator Gerald Nye's Committee, set up to investigate America's entry into World War I, concluded that it had much to do with bankers and arms-exporters who made profits from the involvement. That strengthened the beliefs of those who thought that the USA should steer clear of European entanglements and gave further ammunition for those who believed that America had been led into the First World War by the wiles of Europeans for the sake of their own imperial interests. In the face both of this swell of public and official opinion and of the outbreak of violence in the international arena, the solution to the problems of the world adopted by the USA was a succession of neutrality laws. America was not going to be drawn into another war because of trade as she had been in World War I. The neutrality policy changed incrementally through the 1930s, but essentially after 1937 American goods had to be bought for cash and carried away in foreign ships. At first armament sales were prohibited, but after Roosevelt came to appreciate the threat of totalitarianism he tussled with Congress, and the arms embargo was repealed on 3 November 1939. This helped the Allies because, with their naval dominance of the Atlantic, they could get US supplies while denying them to Germany, but the repeal only came after a long debate in Congress, and, of course, the Second World War had already been under way by then for two months.

By 1934 the pattern of British and American response to the actions of the totalitarians had been set. Neither country was prepared to underwrite the security of Europe, or take effective action in the Far East. The result was runaway expansion by Japan, Italy and Germany.

In 1933 the League accepted the findings of the Lytton Report, which was the outcome of an investigative commission of the same name that it had set up to examine Japanese actions (aggression) in Manchuria. Japan had agreed to the commission but now rejected the report, and its findings were seized on as a pretext to leave the League. Two years later, Japan refused anything less than naval parity with the USA and Britain and embarked upon naval expansion. In China the war became more widespread and vicious. In December 1937 the Japanese took yet another major Chinese city: estimates vary, but about 5,000 women were raped and 150,000 Chinese soldiers and civilians killed. However, these figures are for fatalities *after* the fall of the city: it is known as the Rape of Nanking.[36] The character of the Japanese war machine was becoming clear, but still no effective action was taken. The Americans were caught in a dilemma. If they pushed the Japanese too far there was always a danger of full-scale war, and that would lead to immediate losses for the USA in the western Pacific, namely the Philippines. To justify strong action, therefore, US leaders had to be able to convince themselves and public opinion that vital US interests were under direct threat from Japan, and throughout the 1930s they could not do that convincing.

In Europe, 1935 was a pivotal year. It started well with the Stressa Front: Britain, France and Italy condemned German re-armament and reaffirmed the *status quo* in Europe. But, soon after, Anglo-French differences arose. Britain was critical of the Franco-Soviet Pact concluded in May. It feared that Europe was splitting into blocs reminiscent of 1914 and that Germany would again feel threatened. Partly to offset those fears, and also to safeguard Britain's main strategic concern, in June London signed an Anglo-German naval agreement, which restricted the German surface fleet to 35% of the Royal Navy's and its submarine fleet to 45%. This upset the French and was an acknowledgement that the Versailles naval restrictions on Germany were dead. At the end of the year Anglo-French diplomacy did come together, but only for an attempted act of appeasement of Italian aggression in Abyssinia. The Hoare-Laval proposals, however, shocked public opinion, and British Foreign Secretary Samuel Hoare resigned, but nothing effective was done in the aftermath.

With the Western democracies in disarray, Hitler made his move. In 1936 he re-militarised the Rhineland, and neither France nor Britain did anything about it: this was the final nail in the coffin for both Locarno and the Versailles Treaty. There now followed the saga of appeasement. Britain looked for reasons to accept Germany's revision of her condition in Europe, in the hope that Hitler would become content before a full-scale war became necessary. Germany expanded in quick succession into Austria through *anschluss* and into Czechoslovakia through the pretext of protecting the German Sudetens from Czech harassment. Once the Sudetenland had been sacrificed by the Munich Agreement, negotiated by British Prime Minister Neville Chamberlain in 1938, Hitler moved shortly thereafter to digest the rest of Czechoslovakia. His next move was on Poland in 1939, but that elicited a different response from Britain and France.

While the world situation deteriorated Anglo-American relations remained, for the most part, distant and tepid. The generally pro-American Vansittart was angry that British concessions in the 1920s had not resulted in a more positive and co-operative line on world events from the USA. In September 1934 he wrote to Ambassador in Washington Ronald Lindsay: 'In ageing I have lost my wind for running after the United States government. It is a futile paper-chase.'[37] There was no co-operation to stem the rising tide of violence in the affairs of humankind. The Stimson Doctrine and the neutrality laws had made it clear that the USA would not be drawn into attempts to stand up to the dictators for the sake of other nations' interests. John Simon's refusal to invoke the Nine Power Treaty with the USA, and the development of appeasement policies, made the same effective statement about British policy.

Most of their exchanges were to do with more mundane matters such as trade. Hull had managed to edge Roosevelt back to a modicum of internationalism in 1934 with the passage of the Reciprocal Trade Agreements Act (RTAA), which gave the President discretion to negotiate reciprocal tariff reductions of a considerable size in bilateral talks with other states. Hull's main target was to get the British to mend their ways, and straightaway there were conversations with them about the possibility of a new trade agreement. By February 1936 things were developing and Ambassador Lindsay was harangued at least twice within two weeks by Cordell Hull about the evils of the discriminatory imperial preference system.[38]

In 1938 Hull's ambition was partially realised, though the reasons for the concluding of a new agreement with Britain have more to say about their relationship in general than about trade matters themselves. By 1938 the British were aware that trouble was brewing with Hitler. Appeasement by this time was as much a matter of sacrificing other nation's interests for the sake of Britain and her need for time to re-arm, as of any hope of Hitler becoming satiated. By that year British defence spending was 38% of total government expenditure – three years earlier it had only been 15% – and from January there were naval co-operation talks with the USA. Prime Minister Neville Chamberlain had a pretty low opinion of America and on a number of occasions expressed the view that its friendship and commitments were not worth much. Nevertheless, he agreed to the conclusion of what was a rather unsatisfactory trade agreement for Britain in order to bring the two countries closer together and to counter the Rome-Berlin Axis formed in talks between Count Ciano, Benito Mussolini's Foreign Minister, and Hitler in November 1936.[39]

As the fateful year 1939 ran its course Anglo-American relations did improve, not least because of the visit to America of King George VI. Underlying sentiment was still friendly and those in America who thought about foreign policy saw much to fear from the military regimes of Germany, Italy and Japan and much in common between herself and the liberal democracies of France and Britain. In London, while British leaders might be scornful about the worth of American commitments and friendship, rather ironically there was a consistent acknowledgement that without help from the USA Britain could not fight a long war. Both interest and sentiment would push the British towards closer links with the USA. As time went by the USA came to realise that much of her sentiment was in sympathy with the plight of Britain, and rapidly on the heels of that realisation came the conviction that American interests could also be best served by closer co-operation with London. The special relationship was about to flourish as it never had before or was to again.

4 In war and Cold War 1939–51

We must be the great arsenal of democracy.
(Franklin D. Roosevelt, 29 Dec. 1940)

Give us the tools, and we will finish the job.
(Winston S. Churchill, 9 Feb. 1941)

Roosevelt was right, Churchill only half right. The USA had to become the great arsenal of democracy, but Britain, while needing tools, could not finish the job alone. Britain's dependence on US supplies, and the need for the USA to play a more decisive and larger role than Britain in the defeat of the Axis powers, did much to mould Anglo-American relations and elevate the USA to a pre-eminence some have regarded as hegemonic in relation not just to Britain but to the postwar Western Alliance as a whole. However, just as Britain was unable to finish the job alone in the Second World War, so the USA discovered that it could not consummate the Cold War alone. That had impact on US policy and its relations with Britain, and brings into question its purported hegemony.

Britain's economic sovereignty was infringed by the USA because of the exigencies of the war as early as 1941, and from late 1943 onwards, as the massive mobilisation of US manpower and resources bore fruit, Britain's voice in strategic and postwar security planning began to diminish as America's became more powerful. From then it was clear that Britain had become a junior partner in the relationship. Nevertheless, despite the asymmetry of power, many believe as Lord Callaghan has put it: 'The Second World War was the apogee of the special relationship.'[1]

Even prior to the Japanese attack on Pearl Harbor, 7 December 1941, the Americans moved steadily from neutrality to become a non-belligerent helper of Britain's war effort. There were problems for Roosevelt along the way, with vocal domestic opposition to involvement in the European conflict, legal restraints and a cautious Congress. However, beginning with the repeal of the arms embargo in late 1939, the USA then proceeded to supply more and more help to Britain. On 2 September 1940, after Britain's determination to resist was demonstrated in the Battle of Britain between the RAF and the Luftwaffe, the USA agreed to give Britain US destroyers, to help protect vital naval supply-lines from U-boat attack, in exchange for the 99-year lease of bases on British islands in the Caribbean and in Newfoundland. On 29 December 1940 there was a Presidential 'fireside chat' radio broadcast, which proposed that American material assistance should be lent to Britain. In the spring of 1941 legislation was passed enabling Lend-Lease to come into operation. In August 1941 Roosevelt and Churchill met for their first summit, the Atlantic Conference at Placentia Bay, Newfoundland. There they issued the Atlantic Charter, a set of broad principles that mounted a democratic counter-attack against the philosophy of totalitarianism: it also questioned the morality of colonialism, but, while this was to be an important area of disagreement between Britain and the USA in the course of the war, for the moment the British played down the issue. Meanwhile the USA was moving towards more help for Britain in convoying in the Atlantic, and in the denial of strategic material to Germany. By the summer of 1941 the USA was neutral neither in thought nor in deed.[2]

This moving-together was only a foretaste of what was to come after Pearl Harbor. From the Combined Chiefs of Staff (CCS) to intelligence co-operation; from collaboration to produce the atom bomb to US and British generals commanding each other's troops; from co-ordinated economic warfare to the system of combined boards to help direct war production; from Britain's dependence on Lend-Lease supplies to joint Anglo-American planning for the peace; from the friendship of Churchill and Roosevelt to the socialising that went on with thousands of GIs stationed in Britain; it is clear from all these things that the Anglo-American experience was broad, deep and intimate. In September 1943, Churchill referred to a special relationship: it expressed both a desire on his part but also, at the time, a reality. From all this, it is clear that volumes could be written about their wartime co-operation, but here we must resort to selected themes for the sake of brevity. Matters will be considered under the headings of intelligence, atomic and military co-operation; personal relations; postwar security plans; and economic relations.

INTELLIGENCE, ATOMIC AND MILITARY CO-OPERATION 1941-5

At the start of the Second World War the USA had virtually no foreign intelligence service. By contrast, Britain had highly sophisticated intelligence-gathering and cryptographic analysis systems and a wealth of experience. Before the war was very old, Britain began to share her know-how with the USA. This was partly through the efforts of William Stephenson, code-named 'A Man Called Intrepid'. Stephenson had access to and the favour of Churchill and was appointed head of British Security Co-ordination in New York in May 1940. He quickly made contact with Roosevelt's favoured intelligence man William 'Wild Bill' Donovan and arranged for him to visit London in July later that year.

Donovan was given privileged insights into intelligence operations and fed with views about Britain's will to fight on against Hitler in order to counter some of the defeatist reports going to Washington from US Ambassador Joseph Kennedy in the wake of the British military evacuation from Dunkirk. The British had intercepted messages from the embassy and decoded them with ease, something that Churchill was later to inform Roosevelt about in tactful diplomatic language.[3] Donovan became a pivotal figure in Anglo-American intelligence co-operation. On his return to Washington, he spoke positively to Roosevelt about Britain, and soon after that the 'destroyers for bases' deal came to fruition – though it was not solely a result of Donovan's intervention.

In November 1940 the first of many intelligence agreements between Britain and the USA was signed. Eight months later Donovan was appointed Co-ordinator of Information to head the office which was the precursor of the Office of Strategic Services (OSS) and the Central Intelligence Agency (CIA). The organisation and methods of operation for the new US intelligence agency were drawn up jointly by Stephenson and Donovan. Years later Donovan confessed: 'Bill Stephenson taught us everything we ever knew about foreign intelligence operations.' By July 1941 the inter-dependence of the Anglo-American intelligence network was already remarkable. British Chief of Naval Intelligence, Admiral Godfrey, reported at this time: 'Colonel Donovan has been supplied with memoranda on a great variety of aspects of intelligence and he has been offered any degree of collaboration he may require with British Intelligence Organisations.'[4] Co-operation was given increased standing in 1943, when the two countries signed the BRUSA agreement which formalised the passing of Britain's top secret ULTRA material to the Americans: the British codebreakers at Bletchley Park had cracked the workings of the German ENIGMA code machine. BRUSA also provided for co-operation in signals intelligence and for the exchange of personnel. In the field, there was both division of labour and co-operation between the OSS and Britain's Special Operations Executive, and as the war progressed Canada, Australia and New Zealand also entered into the co-operative system of Anglo-American intelligence work.

The level of sharing in this most sensitive of all fields of governmental operations was unprecedented between nation states. In its infancy it was a very uneven relationship, with the British providing most of the information, the expertise and the practical know-how. As a result they influenced the development of the US foreign intelligence system. That established a legacy of shared experience and friendship that was to be returned by the USA in the postwar period when relations were again very unbalanced, but this time heavily weighted towards the USA. As Richelson and Ball have put it, these were 'The Ties That Bind'.[5]

The British were not as forthcoming in the field of atomic research as in the intelligence sphere. When Sir Henry Tizard and Professor Cockcroft travelled on mission to Washington in the autumn of 1940 to exchange scientific information with the Americans they discovered that Britain was ahead in atomic research. Thus when the Americans suggested collaboration to produce an atomic super-bomb, the British hesitated. Lord Cherwell, Churchill's friend and scientific adviser, strongly advocated an independent British atomic programme. At this point, therefore, the US proposal for a joint effort was not taken up.

By 1942 circumstances had changed. The US had taken a clear lead in atomic research. It was now Britain's turn to propose collaboration, and America's to procrastinate. But, eventually, after various exchanges and talks between Churchill and Roosevelt, the British were allowed to co-operate in the Manhattan (US code word) or the Tube Alloys (British code name) project to produce an atom bomb. Co-operation now, however, did not mean equal partnership. In the Quebec Agreement of 19 August 1943, Britain and the USA agreed: never to use the bomb against each other; not to use it against a third party without mutual consent (i.e. a mutual veto); and not to pass any information about the bomb to another country. These provisions were even-handed, but paragraph 4 stipulated that because most of the burden of the work was being undertaken by the USA, any postwar commercial developments could only be enjoyed by Britain with permission of the President of the USA.

Even though the restriction on postwar commercial exploitation might have been galling, the main goal had been achieved, namely a form of Anglo-American nuclear-weapons partnership. At Roosevelt's home in Hyde Park, New York, in September 1944, Churchill and Roosevelt cemented things more firmly in place. They put their names to an *aide-mémoire* of which item 2 said: 'Full collaboration between the United States and the British government in developing tube alloys for military and commercial purposes should continue after the defeat of Japan unless and until terminated by joint agreement.'[6] There looked to be a sound future for

Anglo-American relations, with their joint monopoly on the most fearful weapon of immediate mass destruction ever devised. However, there were those in the USA, especially in the military, who were reluctant to grant Britain full access to the fruits of nuclear research. At the war's end things did not turn out as the British might have expected on the basis of the Quebec and Hyde Park agreements.

The field of military planning discloses how the USA had come to perceive of Germany and Japan by the summer of 1940 and how important a role Britain had to play in her global strategy. In August, US Generals Emmons and Strong, and Admiral Ghormley had talks in London with their British counterparts and laid the basis for more formal talks in Washington in early 1941 which produced the strategic agreement known as ABC-1. In the event of war with Germany and Japan priority would be given to defeating Germany. Part of the necessary logic of this was that Britain had to act as the springboard from which to mount US operations into Europe (a logic the USA deployed from 1946 onwards with the Soviet Union in mind). Even after Pearl Harbor, Roosevelt courageously held to the Germany-first strategy. Such planning was unprecedented between a neutral and a belligerent and made a stark contrast with Anglo-American relations between 1914 and 1917.

The plans also provided for officers from each country to act as liaison groups in London and Washington. Once the USA entered the war this developed into the Combined Chiefs of Staff (CCS) system, a closely integrated system of Anglo-American military co-operation. Britain's senior member of the CCS Committee and Head of the British Joint Staff Mission in Washington was Field Marshal Sir John Dill, whose charm helped develop excellent working relations with the Americans until his death in November 1944. The integration at the top was mirrored down through the military structure, for example, with Lord Louis Mountbatten in overall command in south-east Asia and Dwight D. Eisenhower in charge of the 1944 Allied invasion of Europe.

Not everything ran smoothly. There were various difficulties about relations with the French, including a very serious dispute about tactics and the Anglo-American invasion of French North Africa: the US wanted to co-operate with French military leaders such as Admiral Darlan, who had had close links with the Nazis, which pleased neither the British nor the Free French leader General de Gaulle. However, probably the most serious problems arose over matters involving Britain's imperial interests. The Americans suspected that British strategy in the Far East had an eye on renewing colonial control. Throughout the war there were rumblings of discontent in the Roosevelt Administration about British imperial policies and how they both influenced their actions in relation to India, Malaya and Singapore and impacted on strategy in the Chinese theatre of war. Likewise in Europe, the controversy over opening the second military front had much to do with US fears that Britain had ulterior motives. There was bitter argument over the respective merits of thrusting from the Mediterranean against Hitler, through what Churchill called the soft underbelly of Europe, and a cross-Channel invasion. Americans thought that Mediterranean operations would be inconclusive and delay a mass attack into occupied France, and that they were only favoured by the British as a means of reasserting their power in the Mediterranean and of curtailing Soviet advances into central Europe. There was some truth in all this. Britain could see its relative power declining and grasped at opportunities to shore up its international position. The USA on the other hand could appear more disinterested because they would have such overwhelming power at the end of the war that they thought that they could get what they wanted whatever the circumstances. The disagreements, however, also stemmed from different military traditions and experiences. Churchill feared that a cross-Channel invasion could be costly on the scale of British losses in the Great War and he was burdened by the memory of his responsibility for the disastrous Gallipoli amphibious landings in 1915 and the ensuing abortive campaign against the Turks. Also, Britain had long practised strategies of attrition with peripheral attacks and naval blockade, and now added to those was aerial bombardment. By contrast, the US tradition since the Civil War had been to pit overwhelming force against the enemy. Until the Cairo and Teheran Conferences of November and December 1943, Britain got much of her own way: for example the invasion of North Africa in 1942 contrary to the wishes of US Chief of Staff General George Marshall. As Kimball has aptly put it, after Pearl Harbor, the 'urgency of the military problems that beset the two leaders created an atmosphere of equality that lasted until mid-1943'.[7] After then the USA began to overtake the UK in terms of its deployed military manpower. When that was added to its economic power the USA found itself in a position that allowed it to overrule British strategic preferences.

Though there were sharp differences over strategic policies, there continued to be close and effective co-operation after 1943 at the organisational, personal and operational levels and much experience was accumulated in Anglo-American military, naval and aerial operations. This proved to be a valuable legacy for the future.

PERSONAL RELATIONS

The most important personal relationship was undoubtedly the one between Churchill and Roosevelt, but it was by no means the only one. In the intelligence sphere there was rapport between Stephenson and Donovan. Dill had friendships with many in Washington, and Eisenhower formed a good relationship with Harold Macmillan while in North Africa that was to pay dividends for Anglo-American relations in the future when they were respectively President and Prime Minister. But the Churchill-Roosevelt link was quite unique, as is disclosed in their voluminous wartime correspondence (1,949 messages in all) and by the fact that they met nine times during the war. They started modern summitry.[8]

Friendship, no matter how strong, could not always prevent controversies arising from different national interests. For much of the war these were muted, by Roosevelt in particular, in order not to distract from the war effort. We shall see a prime example of this in the economic sphere. Nevertheless, several issues caused much tension between Britain and the USA and were reflected in their personal relationship. The crisis in Greece in 1944, with Britain using force to suppress communists (who had previously been fighting the Nazis) in favour of royalists, caused much controversy. The USA was highly critical, and the OSS at times actively opposed British policy. It was not until 1945 that things improved and the USA was drawn in to help financially in Greece by the British.[9] The most heated exchanges between Churchill and Roosevelt came in the field of postwar civil-aviation policy. At the Chicago Conference in 1944, called by the Americans to create a new aviation system that would follow the pattern of open-door trading, the UK organised opposition out of fear of a postwar US monopoly of civil aviation and successfully obstructed American aims. At least they did so temporarily, much to the anger of Roosevelt and other US leaders.[10]

The most worrying development, however, for the wider relationship between Britain and the USA was the way that Roosevelt began to deal with the Soviet Union and treat Churchill as a junior partner within the allied triumvirate. This had a direct bearing on plans for postwar security.

POSTWAR SECURITY PLANS

To deal with postwar security without bearing in mind other aspects of policy would be a serious distortion of what actually happened. There was a widespread assumption in Britain and the USA that peace would be elusive unless security plans were accompanied by economic prosperity, an international forum for all states, and a just postwar settlement. Throughout the war Britain and the USA worked on plans that would bring economic prosperity and exorcise from the international system evils that had caused friction and contributed to the outbreak of war. They were also determined to avoid the mistakes committed after the Great War. There was to be no punitive peace (the Morgenthau Plan for the dismemberment and pastoralisation of Germany adopted for a short time in 1944 was an aberration). There were to be no secret agreements struck for expediency at the expense of equity, and the USA was to be a full participant in the international order. In the Atlantic Charter of 1941, initiated by the USA partly to pre-empt Britain from making secret wartime agreements, Roosevelt and Churchill committed their countries to self-determination (for enemy-occupied countries, not the British Empire – so far as Churchill was concerned) and free government, liberal and open-door economic policies, freedom of the seas, social justice and the abandonment of the use of force, the disarmament of those that threaten force, and the creation of a permanent security system.[11]

This was the first joint indication of what the postwar world should be like. Over the next four years they tried to mould these ideas into more concrete form, but as they did so problems arose. Two central difficulties were: that Britain placed emphasis on the traditional balance of power, while the USA took a more radical and internationalist line; and the Soviet Union. While Britain and the USA might differ about the future of the British Empire and how to implement what were essentially shared views about the postwar economy, social justice and democratic principles, Soviet views were radically different across the board. How to deal with the Soviets was problem enough in itself, but it also exacerbated problems between Britain and the USA.

At the heart of the Soviet matter was Roosevelt's belief that it was imperative to come to some understanding with the Soviets if peace was to be secured, whereas Britain took a more pessimistic view. She believed that there had to be an Anglo-American front to deter the Soviets from aggression. Also, any opportunity should be seized to deal with the Soviets when the Allies had leverage in order to get arrangements that would restrict their expansion of power. The most famous case of this was in late 1944 in the bilateral meeting between Churchill and Stalin in Moscow. Churchill believed that the success of the allied landings in Normandy had strengthened his bargaining hand and so he negotiated a deal with Stalin to divide up central and eastern Europe into spheres of interest. Ideally, Churchill wanted an Anglo-American condominium that would police the world and counterbalance Soviet power, if and when that became necessary. There should be a series of regional groupings, in all of which Britain would conveniently be represented, and the USA would be drawn into the European region in order to ensure the peace there. In the summer of 1943 Foreign Secretary Anthony Eden had put forth these ideas in Washington and he presented them again later, in October, at the Foreign Ministers' Conference in Moscow.

Roosevelt and Secretary of State Hull were both more idealistic and internationalist in their outlook, though Roosevelt had graduated from the full idealism of Wilsonian collective security. He wanted an amalgam of idealism and power-political realism. He believed that any arrangement had to take into account the great powers and their interests. If their co-operation could not be engaged, then no lasting peace could be achieved. At the same time he did not want the more nakedly power-political solution of the British. He feared that simple regionalism might lead the USA back to a form of isolationism where she sought the freedom of unilateral action, as she had in the 1920s. Nor did he want a condominium with the British that would alienate the Soviets, nor for the USA to have a permanent presence in Europe's security arrangements.

Much of this was made clear to Eden during his visit to Washington in March 1943 and at the First Quebec Conference in August later that year. The USA presented the British with a global plan for a United Nations in which the Big Four – the USA, Britain, the Soviet Union and China – would all have an equal and major say. Over the following months there were considerable disagreements over the postwar security plan, but Roosevelt's internationalism was strengthened by the creation of bipartisan US political support through the Republican Party's formal abandonment of isolationism at the Mackinac Conference. Also, this was the year 1943 and the USA had become the more dominant partner in Anglo-American relations: not surprisingly her views prevailed.

At both the 1944 Dumbarton Oaks conference and the inaugural conference of the United Nations (UN) in San Francisco in 1945 amendments and changes continued to be made, but the USA more or less got her own way. There were to be no regional arrangements, except that, rather ironically, the Western hemisphere was to be a special case. The UN would be a global organisation charged with keeping the peace and with helping to achieve economic development and social justice. The General Assembly was an open forum in which all had equal status. The Security Council was different. Here Roosevelt's ideas of great-power co-operation and the need to protect their vital interests were embodied. There were to be five permanent members (the USA, the Soviet Union, Britain, China and France) and the rest of the Council would be made up by a rotation of temporary members. All, however, could veto peace-keeping or any other kind of action by the Council, but not the discussion of issues. In short, no action could ever be taken contrary to the will of a great power.[12]

Britain went along with all this despite much disagreement in the government and disappointment that closer Anglo-American co-operation was not an integral part of the plan for postwar security. Also, the British felt that, in order to bring the Soviets into the UN (and also to get their commitment to go to war with Japan after the defeat of Germany), Roosevelt had given way too far and too often on specific aspects of policy to do with Europe. Too much was dependent on Soviet goodwill. If Roosevelt had not succeeded in bringing the Soviets fully on board, then the UN could not restrain them, and the cost of trying to bring them aboard had given them a strong position in Europe from which to create grave problems for the security both of Britain and of Western Europe as a whole. Roosevelt's response to all this would probably have been: what alternative was there apart from war, which was morally unacceptable and would not have been tolerated by public opinion?

The heart was in the right place, but the guns were not.

ECONOMIC POLICY

In trying to summarise Anglo-American wartime relations, it has been necessary to assert rather than demonstrate the ways in which they co-operated and conflicted over issues and policies. In this final section on the war more detail is given to flesh out the arguments and to give a more effective picture of the complexities of their relationship.

Economic rivalry between Britain and the USA continued in the war, but problems came under joint consideration as they tried to devise a regime for the postwar world. Many matters made discussions difficult. For example, they had adopted different forms of trade protection, and the Americans thought that their tariffs were far more acceptable than British imperial preference, which was discriminatory. But the fundamental reason for difficulty was their traditional rivalry. In October 1943 there was a flash of refreshing candour which cut through the hypocrisy that afflicted both sides as they pursued economic self-interest in the guise of altruism. A Foreign Economic Administration (FEA) official Bernhard Knollenberg, commented on the more favourable Lend-Lease treatment that the FEA accorded to China and the Soviet Union compared with Britain. He wrote to his chief, Leo Crowley, saying that the real and 'deeper' reason for this was that neither the Soviet Union nor China was 'a great traditional competitor of ours in international trade'.[13]

Ironically, rivalry implied that Britain and the USA also had vested interests in ensuring that the world economy flourished. That meant re-forming the pre-war system which had produced exchange-rate chaos and a collapse of international trade. About this, there was no fundamental difference between the prevailing political and economic forces in London and Washington. Both sides valued gains to be had from comparative trade advantages and the overall system of liberal capitalism providing the latter had sufficient management to avoid the inter-war pitfalls. This is not to say that there was not a spectrum of opinion in both countries about reforming the world economy, or that there were not serious differences about how to achieve a largely agreed-upon goal, or that with regard to specific issues there were not violent arguments.

In the UK at one end of the spectrum was an unholy alliance of imperial-ists and left-wing socialists who favoured imperial trade preference and reliance upon a sterling currency area. They saw this as a way of both insulating Britain from the vagaries of international capitalism as suffered in the Great Depression and preventing economic domination by the USA. The imperialists also saw this kind of economic regionalism as a way of continuing Britain's imperial splendour. These two groups led the opposi-tion to American proposals for the postwar economy.

The anti-American group was a minority. The majority thought that co-operation with the USA was vital, though there was concern that stra-tegically important industries such as agriculture and the airlines should be given some degree of protection.[14] There were also timetable concerns. Given the problems of war damage and reconversion to peacetime production, and the need to recover lost export markets, the British wanted a long transition period which would condone economic controls and enable them to get back on their feet and into a position from which they could compete. Finally, there was concern both over striking the right balance of concessions with the USA and over whether the normally protectionist USA would be able to get laws through Congress in order to match British reforms.

On the American side there were similarly diverse views. At one extreme was the Republican Party tradition of high tariffs combined with aggressive economic penetration of overseas markets, but much of that kind of economic nationalism, while still strong in the Congress, was out of favour in the Roosevelt administration. As in Britain, consensus formed round the idea of a managed international economic order that would encourage freer trade and stable exchange rates. There were strong nationalistic elements in that consensus, for many saw such an economic order as in the interests of the USA since it would enjoy comparative trade advantages. By contrast, the British, fearing the loss of many comparative advantages by the war's end, saw international organisations as in their interest because they would prevent America gaining overwhelming control of the world economy.

The Roosevelt administration had different emphases within it. In particular, Hull advocated the elimination of trade discrimination above all else – or almost above all else! His obsession with eliminating discrimination took second place to upholding America's economic interests, as the negotiations about the postwar wheat trade with Britain in 1941–2 demonstrated.[15] In the US Treasury the preoccupation was with currency convertibility and stable exchange rates. Henry Morgenthau and his chief adviser in this area, Harry Dexter White, wanted to impose New Deal ideas of responsibly controlled capitalism on the international monetary system: on the whole they succeeded. For much of the war these different emphases caused bureaucratic tensions, but after Fred Vinson replaced Morgenthau in July 1945, and with William Clayton in charge of State Department economic policy, things improved and agreement emerged that ending monetary rather than trade discrimination was the first priority.

The American consensus on the need for a multilateral liberal economic world order was strengthened by fears that the massive expansion of US industry during the war would result in surplus production in peacetime that would trigger a depression unless overseas markets could be found. These fears were all the more potent then as it was before the postwar consumer society had been conjured up by mass advertising. However, even though the need for multilateral economic liberalism was strongly felt, there were reservations about its benefits for certain industries, and there was also a realisation that America could not go it alone. She would have to persuade other countries, and above all others Britain, that the US vision for the postwar world was one that helped other people as well themselves. The USA's attempts to persuade Britain to partner her in creating a freer world economy immediately after the war caused friction between the two countries and revealed much about the quality of their relationship.[16]

There are a number of things about the Second World war that stand out in people's minds: the Holocaust; the carnage on the eastern front; the destruction of Hiroshima and Nagasaki; and the economic miracle that took place in the USA. A less recognised, but no less momentous, event occurred in Britain. On 7 December 1940, Prime Minister Winston Churchill wrote to President Roosevelt: 'The moment approaches when we shall no longer be able to pay cash for shipping and other supplies.'[17] Fifteen months of war reduced Britain, the world's greatest trading nation and creator of the largest ever empire, to *de facto* international bankruptcy. More than anything else, that dictated the course of Anglo-American economic relations over the following five years.

British bankruptcy was stark evidence of the shift in power in Anglo-American relations. The solution to Britain's economic problem came with Lend-Lease and the combined production boards. These measures allowed Britain to continue her war effort, and the USA, after the State Department took over responsibility from the Treasury for working out consideration for US aid, abandoned any thought of cash payments. As a result Britain received approximately $21 billion net of aid. However, although Britain did not pay cash, costs were involved.[18] Lend-Lease enabled Britain to concentrate on war production and abandon export markets as making things for profit took second place to the needs of war supply. It also made the UK highly dependent upon the USA. Those three things taken together – abandonment of exports, the decimation of peacetime production, and dependence upon the USA – placed Britain in a situation which made it difficult to resist US demands for non-cash payments.

In pursuing their respective economic interests, within a framework of which the Lend-Lease system was an integral part, four important matters arose for Anglo-American relations. The first involved the consideration for Lend-Lease; the second, controls over British exports to ensure that Lend-Lease was not misused; the third the re-growth of Britain's gold and dollar reserves after Lend-Lease averted the danger of bankruptcy; and the fourth a division of labour that was instituted for sound reasons but nevertheless disadvantaged Britain in terms of postwar commercial potential, for example in the nuclear and airline industries. Of these four, the first three are of concern here.

In examining US policy it should be borne in mind that, although the USA had a commanding negotiating position, it was not without constraints. Domestically, Roosevelt had to contend with Congress and, as the war progressed, with business elements within the administration, both of which limited bargaining strategy. In addition, Britain was not without leverage. It controlled or influenced a large part of the world's economy through formal and informal political ties, through the sterling area and imperial preference. Furthermore, the USA needed Britain's co-operation if a multilateral liberal economy was to be created, and Britain would not be willing to undertake such co-operation if her position was so impoverished that it would not be able to compete and gain benefit. Finally, the more avid pursuers of a tightly formulated multilateral postwar economy were restrained by Roosevelt for purely pragmatic reasons. He did not want to disrupt the Alliance by quarrelling over the postwar economy: Britain was too important in the war effort, and the winning of the war was the paramount goal.

Roosevelt's attitude played an important role in the talks for Lend-Lease consideration. The State Department wanted British commitments: to co-operate in fashioning the postwar economy; to reduce tariffs and other barriers to trade; and to eliminate preferences – which would affect Britain much more than the USA. By the time Churchill and Roosevelt met for the Atlantic Conference, the haggling over consideration was well under way.

The Under Secretary of State Sumner Welles tried to get Churchill to commit Britain to the elimination of imperial preference in the Atlantic Charter. The Charter was duly issued, but Churchill had skilfully protected British interests. In the fourth paragraph the two leaders committed themselves to: 'endeavour, with due respect for their existing obligations [read imperial preference], to further enjoyment of all States, great or small, victor or vanquished of access, on equal terms, to the trade and the raw materials of the world'.[19]

Such mealy-mouthed commitments did not please Cordell Hull, who continued to press for something more concrete. By February 1942, after much heated debate, it looked as if he was about to succeed. State Department officials were urging Britain to accept a draft of article 7 of the Mutual Aid Agreement, which specified the consideration for Lend-Lease. The article committed both countries to early talks about substantive economic matters, to the elimination of discrimination in international commerce by agreed action, and to reducing tariffs and other barriers to trade.

The British Cabinet balked at these provisions.[20] There was concern that Britain would throw away its bargaining hand if it committed itself to the abolition of imperial preference before getting the US to reciprocate with commensurate reductions of its tariffs. There was also a growing fear that the USA wanted to move too quickly on liberalisation, when Britain would need a long transition period after the war in order to get back to normality. In the end Roosevelt gave ground in response to appeals from Churchill and in order to get this troublesome matter out of the way now that America was also in the war.

Rather disengenuously, Roosevelt wrote that a trade of imperial preference for Lend-Lease was 'the furthest thing' from his mind, that America was not asking Britain for 'a commitment in advance' of negotiations to abolish imperial preference, and that article 7 'does not contain any such commitment'. With that assurance Churchill was content, and so again, as in the Atlantic Charter, the USA was left with only vague commitments.[21]

In the operation of the mutual-aid programme the Americans managed to get more of their own way. In fact their management of Lend-Lease resulted in an offensive intrusion into UK economic sovereignty. The intrusion had two complementary sides to it: controls over British exports, and a unilateral US attempt to limit the growth of British reserves to $1 billion.

In September 1941, after protracted negotiations with the USA, the British agreed not to apply

> any Lend-Lease materials in such a way as to enable their exporters to enter new markets or to extend their export trade at the expense of the United States. Owing to the need to devote all available capacity and manpower to war production, the United Kingdom export trade is restricted to the irreducible minimum necessary to supply or obtain materials essential to the war effort.[22]

The British accepted these controls with reluctance and hoped that once the USA entered the war they would be abandoned as both countries pooled their resources for the war effort. In fact the Export White Paper, as it was known, remained in force with minor modification until VE (victory in Europe) Day under the auspices of a US policy known as the marginal theory. President of the Board of Trade Hugh Dalton explained to the Lord President's Committee in June 1944 that it prevented receipt of Lend-Lease items unless Britain had 'reduced the civilian population to siege levels and given up all export trade in that particular commodity.'[23]

The Americans insisted on this for several reasons: they did not want Britain to gain commercially from Lend-Lease; there was concern that Congress should not have ammunition to attack wartime aid to Britain; there was a desire to oust Britain from her export markets in Latin America; and it was also seen as a means of keeping Britain vulnerable and thus receptive to US proposals for reconstructing the postwar world economy.[24]

The Export White Paper was the first foray by the USA into Britain's commercial wartime activities. The second was more serious and intrusive into British economic sovereignty. Since the start of Lend-Lease the Americans had had discussions about limiting British gold and dollar reserves, but these talks were held almost exclusively among themselves, and the matter was not raised officially with the British. The American argument was that Lend-Lease had been introduced because Britain had no gold or dollars to pay for American supplies and that its continuation could only be justified on those grounds. In reply the British believed that America's entry into the war and the notion of pooling resources – Britain gave Reciprocal Aid to the USA – changed the circumstances and justified the rebuilding of reserves that had been expended in 1939–40 in what was now a common war effort. In addition, Britain's postwar economic re-conversion to peacetime production and trade would require reserves, in particular, to maintain confidence in sterling in the light of rapidly accumulating debts because of war expenditure. They totalled nearly £3.5 billion in 1945, and the British argued all along that it did not make sense to limit British reserves without taking liabilities into account. The USA, with the exception of the State Department and a pro-British faction within the office of the Lend-Lease Administration (later the FEA), remained unconvinced, or at least unmoved.

In November 1942 there were simultaneous moves by Lend-Lease officials led by Oscar Cox and by the Board of Economic Warfare under the chairmanship of Vice-President Henry Wallace, to bring in unilateral US controls over the level of British reserves. This move had dangerous implications for Britain. Nevertheless, within a few days a US Cabinet Committee was set up with a working group under Harry White. It recommended that British reserves be held between $600 million and $1 billion. Roosevelt approved the recommendation on 11 January.[25]

Over the next two and a half years the USA pursued a policy which upheld the Export White Paper restrictions and actively sought to influence the level of Britain's reserves by withdrawing items from Lend-Lease so that they would have to be bought with dollars, and by trying to persuade Britain to give the USA more Reciprocal Aid. Throughout, the Americans tried to maintain the fiction that these policies were dictated by political and Congressional considerations alone. They denied that the USA had the aim of manipulating things in order to keep British reserves to a unilaterally established and clearly arbitrary limit. On 8 February White told Morgenthau, regarding this matter and the British: 'Our position so far has been that it involves no new policy, that the range [$600 million to $1 billion] is merely a guidepost for the implementation of our present policy.'[26] In spite of reductions in Lend-Lease and increases of Reciprocal Aid, British reserves continued to rise, mainly because of dollars brought into Britain by GIs getting ready for the invasion of Europe. Leo Crowley, head of the FEA, was unhappy about this and set in train developments that resulted in the Americans finally coming clean with the British in February 1944. 'I have been wondering [wrote Roosevelt to Churchill] whether it would be feasible for you to consider so ordering your financial affairs as to reduce your gold and dollar holdings . . . to the neighborhood of about $1 billion.'[27] This letter was sent despite divided counsel from the State Department and lack of clearance by Morgenthau, who subsequently expressed his disagreement with its content.[28] The British were outraged. Sir John Anderson, Chancellor of the Exchequer, wrote to Churchill:

> If we were to accept the . . . proposal, we should have lost our financial independence, in any case precarious, as soon as lend-lease comes to an end, and would emerge from the war, victorious indeed, but quite

helpless financially with reserves far inferior not only to Russia but even to France and to Holland.[29]

In the days that followed the British remonstrated with the Americans about the President's request, and an apology of sorts was forthcoming, but underlying matters did not go away.[30] By late 1943 the American position on a number of economic issues, as well as their announced plans for the postwar economy, was causing intense concern in London. A spate of papers was prepared for the Cabinet by imperialists such as Robert Hudson, Leo Amery and Max Beaverbrook, criticising American policies. They received support from many in the Labour Party who thought that the economic liberalism espoused by the USA would compromise their chances of achieving both postwar full employment and the creation of the welfare state outlined in the Beveridge Report of 1942. In view of all this, the Cabinet decided that any further talks with the Americans on economic planning should be postponed, with the exception of international monetary talks that were already too far advanced to be stopped without serious problems arising. This decision was not communicated formally to the USA, but the drift of British policy soon became apparent.[31]

Thus by the closing stages of the war there was still something of a stand-off between Britain and the USA with their respective economic aims. The USA had managed to exercise some control over Britain's export trade and over the size of her reserves, but in neither case to the extent it had ideally hoped for. It had a notable success with the Bretton Woods Conference in 1944 and its creation of the IMF, which had more limited liability, smaller resources and controlled exchange rate alterations more rigidly than Britain wanted, and which offered a much shorter transition period to convertibility than Britain thought feasible. It also placed the USA and the dollar in a commanding position in the international monetary system at the expense of sterling.[32] Nevertheless, the USA still had a lengthy list of conditions and policies that it wanted Britain to adhere to, but in 1944 there looked little chance of getting compliance.

The State Department, while it had adopted a sympathetic line on Britain's reserves in the belief that they had to be of an adequate size to enable Britain to resume liberal trade policies after the war, was also deeply uneasy that Britain had not given more unequivocal commitments to the American line on the postwar economy. It also worried about the failure to make progress in talks for economic co-operation in 1944 to which Britain had committed herself in the Mutual Aid Agreement. However, although Britain had evaded the more extreme US demands, its main weakness remained. It needed US help in the difficult transition back to peacetime production and trade, and it was this need that the Americans were to exploit in order to get their way.

At the Second Quebec Conference in September 1944 Roosevelt nearly gave away the bait with which the State Department intended to hook Britain into both reaffirming the conditions of article 7 of the Mutual Aid Agreement and co-operating with the US in the postwar economy. In response to pleas from Churchill, Roosevelt gave commitments to a generous continuation of Lend-Lease supplies to Britain after VE-Day, which would have facilitated reconversion to peacetime production, and furthermore he conceded that conditions governing Lend-Lease should not be such as to hamper the growth of Britain's exports, though of course Lend-Lease items could not be used directly in this. Unfortunately for Britain the Americans blatantly reneged on these commitments during further talks in 1944. After Roosevelt's untimely death in April 1945, Britain's situation became worse economically, because of both the unexpected quick end of the war with the atomic assaults on Japan and the new administration's determination to persuade Britain to its way of thinking on economic matters. Britain's economic plight was dreadful. Reconversion to civilian production was still in its early days, and the export trade was a meagre shadow of its pre-war self.[33]

The abrupt ending of the war and the cut-off of Lend-Lease left Britain economically prostrate. According to assessments made by John Maynard Keynes, British reserves stood at $1.9 billion, and the 1945 balance of payments was $5 billion in the red. The prospective deficit for 1946 was $2.5–3.5 billion. Sterling debts stood at $12–14 billion. Much of Britain's capital equipment needed replacing and there was a massive task ahead in reconverting the economy to peacetime production and in expanding British exports – now one-third of their pre-war volume. Faced with these problems, the new Labour government under Clement Attlee, which had taken office after Churchill's election defeat in July 1945, believed that they needed financial help from the USA and a long transition to fixed exchange rates and freer trade. The Americans determined that things should be otherwise.[34]

William Clayton and Fred Vinson, representing the State and Treasury Departments respectively, took the line that financial help had to be linked with overall British economic policy and the fulfilment of commitments that Britain had made in the Mutual Aid Agreement and at Bretton Woods. The Americans were poised to dictate economic policy to their ally.

In the autumn of 1945 Keynes led a British negotiating team to Washington to seek help. The progress of the talks was excruciatingly painful for the British. Under intense US pressure they shifted from one untenable position to another. At first they asked for a $5 billion gift; then they sought a part gift, part loan arrangement; and then an interest-free loan. In the end Britain was offered and, after crisis meetings of the Cabinet, accepted a loan of $3.75 billion and a further $650 million for Lend-Lease pipeline supplies at 2%. In return for this American largess Britain committed herself to co-operation with the USA in establishing an International Trade Organisation (ITO) which embodied free trade and non-discrimination policies, which brought imperial preference directly under threat. Britain would have to enter the IMF, but also make currently earned sterling freely convertible within twelve months of the loan agreement coming into force, which was much more onerous on Britain than the transitional clauses of the IMF.[35]

The Financial Agreement was signed on 6 December 1945, but it was not ratified by the US Congress for several months. During that time the danger of non-ratification was used to pressurise the British – in particular, to get them to accept the US point of view on postwar civil aviation in the Anglo-American Bermuda Air Services Agreement of 1946.[36] Taking all these things together has resulted in some scholars claiming that the USA dominated the relationship by 1945, that there was thus nothing special in it in the way that most think of a special relationship, and that in a wider context the dominant economic position that the USA had attained by 1945 amounted to hegemony over the free world.[37]

Thus, while the Second World War witnessed unprecedented close co-operation between the USA and Britain, it also saw a massive change in their relative power and serious incursions into the economic sovereignty of the latter. In December 1945 that intrusiveness extended its farthest with the Anglo-American Financial Agreement's provisions and the subsequent pressure on Britain to accept conditions in other negotiations as a price of ratification. There is a certain irony in that neither conditions like those of the US Loan nor wartime intrusions into economic sovereignty would have been or indeed were, accepted by other states. That says something about Anglo-American relations. In a rather perverse way, the intrusions into British economic sovereignty were tolerated because the overall relationship was so close and because both had vested interests in working together to create a better and more liberal postwar economy.

AN INCOMPLETE RESTORATION OF SPECIAL RELATIONS 1946–51

By 1945 the relative decline of Britain and the relative and absolute growth of the USA were self-evident, though one should not overestimate Britain's decline or forget the widespread expectation that it would recover ground in the postwar period: at the end of the 1950s Britain still had the third largest economy in the free world. For Britain and the USA, there seemed less need than ever for defence plans *vis-à-vis* each other, but at the end of the war the significance of that tended to be discounted. The achievements of their economic co-operation, most notably Lend-Lease and Reciprocal Aid, tended to be regarded as past history. For a while, instead of valuing the things that had created and enhanced the special relationship between them, the things that divided them took precedence, and the tending that Craigie had identified as being so important was neglected.

The British felt aggrieved by the conditions of the American loan and resented the way the USA used its economic leverage in other negotiations. At the same time there was a feeling in Attlee's Cabinet that the USA had overplayed its hand and that some conditions could simply not be met. In the meantime, Anglo-American relations deteriorated. Economics underpinned much of this, but there were other problems as well.

As always, war had been a catalyst for social change. In Britain it brought into being a consensus epitomised by the hybrid term Butskellism derived from the names of Rab Butler and Hugh Gaitskell, leading lights respectively of the Conservative and Labour Parties. The consensus was on the desirability of a welfare state along the lines of the Beveridge Report, and full employment. The political values underpinning this, even in the form in which they were held by the Conservatives, placed Britain generally to the left of American politics. As the Cold War settled down into a steady pattern of containment and attrition (albeit punctuated by violent outbreaks), the British tended to pursue economic self-interest through trade with communists, devoted increasing attention to their domestic problems, and were more willing to appease to keep the peace. This British policy line caused persistent friction with the USA, and periodically there were more serious difficulties in relation to Labour policies in government or, more often, over what the USA feared Labour policies might be. Suspicion of the consequences of socialism coloured the way relations developed in the early postwar period.[38]

More specifically, atomic co-operation began to falter at the end of 1945. The Americans professed themselves unable to find a copy of the Hyde Park *aide-mémoire* (it had been conveniently misfiled), and then in 1946 the US MacMahon Act ended further collaboration. This was all quite contrary to the understandings between Churchill and Roosevelt. In 1948 Britain and the USA agreed to a new *modus vivendi* which involved the exchange of non-military information, allocation of uranium supplies, and the ending of the mutual veto over the use of the atom bomb. This was a rather one-sided agreement, especially as little information was forth-coming from the Americans, but the abandonment of the veto was convenient for both as the British were developing their own bomb and had little wish for a US say in its possible future use. The CCS was abandoned at the war's end; there were differences between Secretary of State James Byrnes and Foreign Secretary Ernest Bevin on policy in Europe and toward the Soviets; Harry Truman and Clement Attlee did not get on well; and there was disagreement about the future of Palestine and the creation of the state of Israel, which eventually became the bitterest dispute between the two in the early postwar years.

From this turmoil two important developments impacted decisively on Anglo-American relations. The first was the perception of the growing threat from the Soviet Union. The second was a US shift from the policy of the internationalism embodied in what has become known as the Bretton Woods System (named after the founding-place of the IMF) to a form of economic regionalism. Working within these dynamics and that of their ongoing, if troubled, relationship, the USA realised that policies would have to be modified and more recognition given to British needs in terms of how the British saw those needs. As a result, there developed more harmony in economic and defence co-operation.

But at first the Americans pressed on with their plans for a multilateral trade system with an ITO to oversee things. However, its own negotiating position was undermined by Congressional elections in 1946, which returned a Republican majority sceptical of reform and inclined to protectionism. In the end Truman had to withdraw the ITO from the Congress because he was convinced he could not get it passed. The world had to make do with the more piecemeal approach of the General Agreement on Tariffs and Trade (GATT) to reducing protectionism through complex negotiations based on reciprocal reductions in bilateral agreements, which were then applied to all members through the Most Favoured Nation (MFN) principle. In addition to American domestic opposition to trade reform, other countries, including Britain, tried to modify US policy and lengthen the transition to the dispensation of freer trade.

In the summer of 1947 British determination to maintain economic controls was strengthened by the abortive attempt to make currently earned sterling convertible into other currencies in accordance with the US Loan Agreement. Convertibility could not be sustained because of downward pressure from the market on sterling's value. The Americans acknowledged that and conceded that British discrimination against the USA was permissible if it was necessary for obtaining essential goods.[39] In currency terms, it was recognised that the kind of disequilibria that the IMF was designed to cope with were of a much smaller order of magnitude than those that afflicted the deeply unbalanced world economy of 1947: two years later sterling was still in great difficulty and had to be devalued. The USA, instead of demanding international convertibility, concentrated on regional convertibility in Europe after 1947 and also reluctantly came to the conclusion that it would have to tolerate the sterling area. In fact by 1947 the USA had become more tolerant altogether of regional economic controls and discrimination on the part of its allies. The main priority now was to strengthen Western economies at almost any cost in order to prevent them from becoming weak and vulnerable to communism. The aim of achieving a liberal multilateral international economic order now became a long-term goal to be achieved after a period of economic regionalism which would strengthen Western economies. Once the world economy had recovered the internationalism of Bretton Woods, with fixed exchange rates and full convertibility (accompanied by freer trade), would become possible. Thus the transition period that the British had striven for was achieved. Another of their goals, a close relationship with the USA, was also being rapidly achieved and the underlying cause of both was the Cold War.

The USA was more conciliatory toward the Soviet Union during the final stages of the war and the early postwar period than Britain. Roosevelt's policy of trying to engage their active co-operation in world security, and the expectation, later rendered redundant by the success of the atom bomb, that Soviet help would be needed to defeat the Japanese, were the main reasons behind this. At the end of the war the USA had no intention of staying in Europe for long and the rapid rate of demobilisation shows that she was not seeking confrontation. However, Truman's policy was not consistent. According to some historians there was a sharp reaction against the Rooseveltian line. For example, Truman berated Soviet Foreign Minister Molotov in April 1945 for Soviet action in Poland, and his administration also played cat and mouse with them over postwar US financial help. The other side to US policy is demonstrated by Truman's dispatch of Harry Hopkins, one of Roosevelt's closest advisers and a much respected go-between with the Soviets early in the war, to see Stalin in order to try to sort out problems. Secretary of State Byrnes also tried to deal with the Soviets to establish a *modus vivendi*. Thus until early 1946 the dominant characteristic of US policy appeared to be a search for an accommodation, even though that policy was not consistent and even though there had been something of a shift from the old Rooseveltian line. Certainly the British felt somewhat exposed in Europe. Ernest Bevin, like Byrnes, wanted agreement with the Soviets, but he was not keen on the way Byrnes went about things, and the consequences of failing to reach an accommodation would have more direct consequences for Britain than for the USA. British policy therefore tended to be more cautious and there was more friction between Britain and the Soviets than between the Soviets and the USA.

Historiographical debate continues about the respective roles of Britain and the USA in the origins of the Cold War; why the British and then the US attitude toward the Soviets hardened; and how Britain and the USA interacted in all this. Here we can only touch on some of the pivotal issues involved.[40]

Truman had little experience of foreign affairs before becoming President and so he relied heavily on advisers. The inconsistency evident in US policy toward the Soviets was partly a result of this, but it was gradually eliminated as Soviet actions became more unacceptable, as their rhetoric hardened and as the hard-line anti-communists in the State Department began to exert more influence on Truman. Also, as East–West relations deteriorated, Bevin began to worry that if the Soviets became hostile Britain might have to face them alone, and so he sought to entangle the USA in Europe's defence. That entangling was not easy and the USA was an unwilling accomplice to begin with, but developments by early 1946 changed things.

Wranglings over reparations and the future of Germany, the exclusion of pro-Western elements from the government of Poland and other moves by the Soviets to consolidate their position in central and eastern Europe began to alert US leaders to the potential for trouble with them. These developments also affected public opinion in the USA, which began to swing decisively against the Soviets after feelings of much affection and admiration for what they had done to defeat Hitler (which was more than any other power, including the USA). When the Soviets started to pressurise the so-called Northern Tier states (which ran along the south-western border of the Soviet Union), and especially Iran, the USA took a strong line. In the war, Britain and the USSR had jointly occupied Iran on the understanding that they would withdraw at its end. The British found it easy to keep to this because of their well-established position in Iran: they dominated the oil concessions there. The Soviets were not in such a favourable position and so they tried to expand their influence by encouraging a separatist movement in Azerbaijan and by delaying their military withdrawal. The USA used the pretext of returning the body of the Turkish ambassador from Washington to Istanbul to send the USS *Missouri* on a flag-waving cruise into the Mediterranean and supported Britain in its calls for a Soviet withdrawal from Iran. After the matter was taken up in the UN the Soviets finally complied with Western demands, but US official opinion was now rapidly hardening toward the Soviets.

More or less simultaneously George Kennan wrote his famous long telegram from the US Embassy in Moscow alerting Washington to the dangers of Soviet expansion unless the Soviets were firmly resisted. This arrived in Washington in a context where there were already fears that economic instability in Western Europe might provide opportunity for communist subversion. On 5 March a strident call for Western resolve came from Churchill at Fulton, Missouri in his famous Iron Curtain speech. Things were beginning to swing into the Cold War. The idea of resolve and the need for concerted action to contain communism fed off the knowledge of the shortcomings of the Western response to totalitarian aggression in the 1930s. Appeasement would not be repeated. It only led to humiliation and war. The West was determined it would be neither humiliated nor forced into a war on Soviet terms. Soviet aggressiveness, British encouragement, Kennan's ideas about the need for containment, instability in Western Europe, and a gradual shift of perception of the Soviets within the Truman administration brought the USA to the point where it felt it had to make commitments to Europe.

At first they were of an economic and political sort: the Truman Doctrine, and aid to Greece and Turkey. That was then followed by the Marshall Plan aimed at helping Western Europe as a whole. In 1949 came military aid in the form of the North Atlantic Treaty Organisation (NATO) and the US Mutual Defence Assistance Program (MDAP). On the military side Britain and the USA worked together in a harmony reminiscent of wartime. In 1947 a UK–US Security Agreement was signed which divided up the world into areas of responsibility for signals intelligence between the USA on the one hand and Britain, Canada, Australia and New Zealand on the other. In 1946 General Carl Spaatz, US Air Force Commander, visited Britain and agreed with Air Chief Marshal Lord Tedder that five RAF bases should be prepared to take US B-29 bombers. That paved the way for developments two years later. In 1948, as a direct consequence of the Soviet blockade of Berlin, US bombers were based in Britain. There was no formal agreement governing this until October 1951, long after the bombers had been modified to carry atom bombs. With such ease did Britain become a forward nuclear base for the USA. Little has been done subsequently to alter these loose arrangements.[41]

In developing Cold War strategies, the USA had to postpone its plan for liberal multilateralism and promote the sterling bloc and an integrated European economy, even though both would discriminate against her. The US priority was to rebuild prosperity in order to resist communism, and the quickest way to do that was through regionalism. This new policy, on the whole, suited the British, but there arose a serious disagreement with the USA.

Even after the USA changed direction and realised that it would have to tolerate economic controls, protectionism and discrimination from its Western allies and try to build up regional Western economic blocs, it still found its allies recalcitrant. In the European Recovery Program (ERP), or Marshall Plan as it is commonly known, the USA wanted Britain to lead the movement for European reconstruction. The USA envisaged a regional economic system emerging in Europe that would prosper through intra-European trade and a European system of currency convertibility. To underpin all this, and to provide a political pay-off for the economic discrimination that the USA would have to suffer in the short and medium term, there was to be European integration, which would result in a strong Western political bloc that would be able to help contain communism.

The British refused to integrate and lead Europe from within. They saw its economic chaos as a possible further drain on their already over-stretched resources and in any case the idea was too parochial for them with their Commonwealth and the special relationship. The Labour government decided that it should not commit itself to Europe beyond a point from which it could withdraw with ease.[42] ERP Administrator Paul Hoffman was angered by this and in late 1949 attempted to browbeat the British with threats of suspending Marshall Aid funds unless they involved themselves in integration. It was left to Secretary of State Dean Acheson and his deputy James Webb to point out to Hoffman that Britain was too important to be antagonised in this way and that Truman would not endanger the ERP.[43]

By 1950 it was clear that for one reason or another America's ideal economic world order had been compromised. Imperial preference remained and sterling was only partially convertible. The Bretton Woods System was in limbo, and the GATT was a second-best alternative to the ITO and only had meagre successes until the 1960s. Partly because of domestic politics, partly because of economic realities, and partly because of resistance from Britain, the USA's attempt to create a multilateral liberal international economic order immediately after the war was frustrated. The USA was pushed into tolerating British economic practices and policies which it would have condemned in an ideal world or if it had been the hegemon that some have claimed it was.[44] Above all, the need for British support in the war against communism moderated the pressures that the USA could bring to bear on Britain in the field of economic policy.

In the economic sphere, there had been conflict but eventual accom-modation between Britain and the USA; the situation was similar in the defence arena. Fighting the Cold War and balancing that priority against other interests often caused the two countries to give different emphases to things. Thus, while Britain helped to set up the Co-ordinating Committee

(COCOM) of Western powers to monitor and embargo trade in strategic items with the communists, she also consistently favoured a less restrictive definition of 'strategic' than the Americans. Britain recognised the People's Republic of China (PRC) in 1949, much to the chagrin of the Americans, but they did not have Hong Kong to defend; nor did they have the level of investment in China that Britain had. And the British, after helping the USA into its role as guardian of the West, often exercised a moderating influence: in particular, they took a less aggressive stance on Indo-China than the Americans. In contrast, the British were consistently more aggressive than the USA in the Middle East. Here was still a recognisable sphere of British influence. Well before the celebrated Suez crisis of 1956 there were plans made by the Labour government of Clement Attlee for military intervention in the area. On this occasion it was to have been in Iran, to seize the massive Abadan Oil Refinery, which had been illegally nationalised along with oil concessions belonging to the Anglo-Iranian Oil Company (AIOC). In the early 1950s there was much dispute between the British and the Americans over this, as we shall see in the next chapter. There was also tension between the British colonial and the US anti-colonial tradition, made worse by US fears of Britain alienating newly independent states from the Western camp. In these matters the British were less concerned about the implications for the Cold War and put more weight on their own immediate interests.

Thus it was still quite common for there to be differences between Britain and the USA, even in the defence field, which again brings into question the hegemonic status attributed to the USA by some writers. In fact the USA had to compromise and accommodate her policies in response to differences with Britain on numerous occasions and was not in a position to call the shots unilaterally anywhere, except in the Western hemisphere. She could not pursue a policy independent of Britain in the Middle East and was constrained in her options in Europe and the Far East by the attitudes of Britain and other Allies.

Despite outbreaks of fractious differences a clear pattern had emerged in Anglo-American relations by the early 1950s. Britain had rejected integration with Europe and opted to continue with her international role through co-operation with the USA. At the heart of that co-operation was the war against communism. In the Korean war, the most serious crisis posed by communism in this period, Britain provided troops, albeit a small contingent, to fight alongside those of America. (It should be remembered that at this time Britain also had about 20,000 troops engaged in suppressing communists in Malaya.) Korea caused difficulties in the alliance, particularly over Douglas McArthur's generalship, trade with the PRC, and the cost of UK re-armament. The USA also thought that British policy smacked of appeasement, with its preference for negotiation and fear that the war might spread. Nevertheless, Britain's overall solidarity with the USA was demonstrated, as was the priority they shared of containing communism.

Sadly for Britain, that meant that Labour's original postwar priority of domestic economic regeneration was undermined because of high defence spending at home, overseas in Europe, and in the Middle and Far East. Ironically, in the long run, this proved to be an Achilles' heel for the significance of the relationship in world affairs. Britain overstretched herself, and defence spending contributed to her economic decline, ultimately reducing both her capabilities and her worth to the USA. For its part, the USA abandoned the long-standing policy of no entangling alliances, made her revolutionary commitment to Europe and renewed close co-operation with Britain. Part of the price of that was more tolerance of British economic and colonial policies. However, there were limits to that tolerance. They were not exceeded in the Iran affair, but they were at Suez. Furthermore, the USA did not value the relationship as much as did Britain. Both Dean Acheson and later Eisenhower resisted overtures from Churchill to reinstate the full intimacy of wartime co-operation.[45] One area where there was clearly a contrast with wartime was the lack of collaboration in the field of nuclear weapons. Regarding this, the communist witch-hunt launched by Senator Joe McCarthy at Wheeling, West Virginia in February 1950 combined with British spy scandals to create added difficulties for attempts to renew co-operation, as well as shaking existing intelligence links. Generally, in public at least, the Americans tried to present their relationship with Britain as part of the wider Western alliance rather than something with a bilateral specialness, but in private things were often different. The reality of America's dependence on Britain for help in order to contain communism meant that she was treated as special and different from other US allies in many spheres even if there was not a return to the wartime apogee. The year 1950 provides two good examples of how the Americans valued Britain.

In early 1950 there took place a debate among US ambassadors in Europe about the character of the Anglo-American relationship, and this is what Lewis Douglas US Ambassador to London had to say:

> there is no country on earth whose interests are so wrapped around the world as the UK. Among her crown colonies she is in more vitally strategic areas than any other nation among the community of Western nations. She is the center of a great Commonwealth. The US enjoys the

benefits of being a neighbor to the most important member of this Commonwealth whose relationships with the UK can no more be disguised or eliminated at the moment, or in the future, than can the relationship between the Hawaiian Islands and the US. She is the center of the sterling area. . . . This area is held together not alone by the circulation of an identical currency or other currencies easily convertible into it. It is held together also by an intricate and complicated system of commercial and financial arrangements built up tediously by the British . . . . There is no substitute for the sterling area and none can be erected in any short period of time. But beyond all these considerations the UK is the only power, in addition to ourselves, west of the Iron Curtain capable of wielding substantial military strength. This assembly of facts, though some may disagree with a few of them, make a special relationship between the US and the UK as inescapable as the facts themselves. And no amount of dialectical argument can erase either the facts or the conclusion.[46]

A few months later Truman and his Secretary of State Dean Acheson made comments which illustrated that they too basically subscribed to this view. In December 1950 there was a very difficult conference with Attlee in Washington prompted by indiscreet remarks by Truman at a press conference, which seemed to suggest that atomic weapons might be used in Korea. The Anglo-American talks were very difficult ones and there was little rapport between the two sides on the personal level. Nevertheless, in a National Security Council meeting on 12 December Acheson commented that the conference had shown how important 'a close relationship with the UK is, since we can bring US power into play only with the co-operation of the British. The President said that this was true both in the Atlantic and the Pacific.'[47]

The Americans may have had some qualms about going back to the wartime relationship but, although there were changes and some definite lapses in specific areas of co-operation, the specialness of their relationship with Britain continued into the postwar world during the Truman administration. Accommodations were reached both in the defence and in the economic sphere, and the USA gave help to Britain through its civilian and military aid programmes: over $1.25 billion in the first year of the ERP, and £400 million from the MDAP between 1951 and 1956. Britain was a junior partner in the relationship, but the idea of hegemony is as fatuous as the word is ugly. The USA pressurised Britain on many occasions and sometimes in the pursuit of commercial goals its actions were sullied by a self-interest that damaged Britain's already weakened economy. But she was also generous in the settlement of Lend-Lease and in the ERP and MDAP programmes and she modified her position on discrimination and British economic controls as time went by. Furthermore, as the Cold War developed the USA became dependent on Britain for help in a variety of ways. The fact was that there was an interdependence of needs as well as all the other kinds of ties that still bound Britain and the USA in a special relationship even when there were violent disputes between them over policy in the Middle and Far East. And, as Douglas had put it, those facts could not be spirited away no matter how much dialectical argument was brought to bear on them.

5 Conservatively special 1951–61

I thought that it might do good if we had a
gallop together such as I often had with FDR.
(Churchill to Truman, 22 Aug. 1952)

The joint gallop proposed by Churchill was to tilt against the Iranians in an attempt to end the long-running dispute that had arisen over the AIOC and the nationalisation of its assets in Iran. British oil concessions there and the massive Abadan oil refinery yielded vital hard-currency revenue for the British Exchequer and could not be given up lightly. A joint proposal was put to the Iranians, but when its conditions proved unpalatable to them the US aborted the enterprise. Neither Truman nor his successor would work with Britain as Franklin D. Roosevelt had done in the war. Britain was now clearly a junior partner, and a return to the apogee of co-operation was never achieved.

Fighting the Cold War was different from fighting the Second World War. In the latter, no one needed persuasion to fight. In the Cold War, how to combat the communist threat was not self-evident and conflicting national interests within the Western Alliance impinged upon the priority of combating the enemy. Running an alliance and trying to attract non-committed nations into the Western camp further complicated the politics of Anglo-American relations and, with the USA now the undisputed leader of the West, there was understandable friction with the British as they adjusted to their secondary-power status. Leadership also placed responsibility on the USA to be the most implacable opponent of communism and impartial in dealing with its allies. Both those requirements caused problems. On a number of occasions Britain felt that there was more freedom to manoeuvre than did the USA and sought conciliation with the Soviets or the Chinese: this elicited charges of disloyalty and appeasement from Washington. The British also resented the USA formally treating them on a par with other Allies, especially when it prejudiced the renewal of wartime intimacy. In addition to these circumstances, Americans also had more narrowly based reasons of self-interest for putting distance between themselves and the British. The USA did not want to co-operate with Britain on atomic weaponry until the late 1950s because, notwithstanding the successful British nuclear test in 1952, she had nothing of value to offer the USA in return. The USA did not want an Atlantic community that would draw Britain away from European integration. Nor did they wish to consort with the British in a way that would contaminate them with colonialism in the Middle and Far East.

In assimilating these facts one might be tempted to think that the special quality of the relationship was doubtful and that the revival of co-operation in the Cold War between 1946 and 1951 was less substantial than the previous chapter suggested. However, it should be noted that during the wartime apogee, the USA kept its distance from British imperial policies, negotiated an unequal relationship of nuclear co-operation, and experienced many differences over economic and strategic policies. In the Cold War similar difficulties troubled their relations, but the Americans were sensitive to British needs and policies; recognised her as their staunchest, most stable and powerful ally; often did not object to *de facto* as opposed to *de jure* special relations; and under Eisenhower renewed nuclear co-operation. Britain and the USA continued to share political and cultural values, had a wealth of connections, and most importantly had a large degree of interdependence in the pursuit of their foreign-policy priority of containing communism. Paradoxically, as we shall see later, the strength of their relations was also demonstrated by the speedy consignment to history of the Suez crisis of 1956 and their resumption of the business of containing communism and trying to guide the West along the road to a liberal multilateral economic system.

CHURCHILL AND TRUMAN; CHURCHILL AND EISENHOWER 1951–5

After the first flush of Cold War co-operation disputes were again gnawing at the fabric of Anglo-American relations when Churchill returned to power as Prime Minister after the General Election on 25 October 1951. Anthony Eden accompanied him as Foreign Secretary, and R. A. Butler was Chancellor of the Exchequer. Over the next few years relations improved, but not consistently or linearly so. To try to grasp developments down to the Suez crisis of 1956, I shall adopt two rather different approaches. First, in this section, specific matters will be examined: strategy and the Cold War; Supreme Allied Commander in the Atlantic (SACLANT); a Combined Chiefs of Staff system (CCS); atomic co-operation; the European Defence Community (EDC); and summitry and views on East–West relations. Second, in the next section, broader focus will be provided through looking at regional policies in the Far and Middle East.[1]

At the end of the 1940s, George Kennan's idea of containment was militarised, ironically, by civilians. The USA was confronted with communism that was seen increasingly as a global challenge of both an ideological and a military kind. Atheistic materialism that disregarded individual rights and instituted state control over economic systems was anathema to capitalism and the Western Judaeo-Christian liberal tradition. While the challenge was now world-wide, it had first emerged in Europe, where it had been successfully contained. That experience provided a model that could be applied elsewhere. The imperative to do so became overwhelming in 1949 with the loss of China to communism and with the Soviet explosion of an atom bomb. The problem of how to put global containment into operation had to be addressed.

Kennan was no longer the man to do this and he resigned from chairing the State Department think-tank, the Policy Planning Staff (PPS). He was succeeded by a hardliner, Paul Nitze, who presided over the drafting of NSC-68 (National Security Council Paper 68: the NSC had been set up in 1947 to co-ordinate foreign and domestic policy). The paper assumed that the Soviets would expand militarily if not contained by a military counter-weight: the paper recommended a massive expansion of defence spending to provide that. Truman initialled the document in April 1950. Within weeks the Korean War, 1950–3, seemed to justify NSC-68. The re-armament programme adopted by the USA, and their encouragement of the British one, was not simply to fight the war in Korea; it was part of a strategy to contain communism militarily on a global scale. Britain essentially went along with all this. Military forces were substantially expanded and NATO was to be strengthened by German re-armament. Force levels were agreed at the 1952 Lisbon NATO conference. Militarisation of containment seemed complete. It was, however, soon to change its style.

In January 1952 the British were made privy to the plans of the US Strategic Air Command (SAC) and began to reassess their own priorities in the light of that. The result was the Global Strategy Paper of 1952. One of its aims was to enable the West to win against communism without bankruptcy. Planners suggested that this was possible through limiting expensive conventional forces and emphasising nuclear deterrence. This would be cheaper and the only effective way of both dealing with the Soviet threat and retaining an important say for Britain (which was about to get her own atomic bomb) in Western strategic and defence policy. That same summer Sir John Slessor, the British Chief of Staff, revealed these ideas to his US counterparts. They were not impressed, for the policy was contrary to current emphasis on conventional forces and undermined the rationale of the EDC and the re-armament of Germany. However, American views soon changed.

Dwight D. Eisenhower was elected President of the USA in November 1952 and took office early in 1953 with John Foster Dulles as his Secretary of State. Eisenhower was first and foremost a decent and thoughtful politician; second he was a military man. His choice of the dour, and vehemently anti-communist, Dulles is ample testimony to his anti-communism, but Eisenhower, like the British, was determined that defence spending should not cripple the Western economy. He believed that the West's strongest advantage over communism was its ability to produce goods and services the people wanted. He set in motion Operation Solarium, which investigated strategic options and their costs during the summer of 1953, and from its findings came 'The New Look' – a combination of containment by conventional forces and nuclear deterrence, with the emphasis on the latter. The implications of this for Britain were significant. First, it demonstrated that the two countries were still developing policy in tandem, though not for entirely the same reasons. Second, curbing defence spending led Eisenhower to pursue alliances vigorously in order to spread the defence burden. That increased the value of allies and, by 1957, there was also a will to avoid duplication of effort which had direct consequences for Anglo-American nuclear co-operation.

While there was a drawing-together of US and British global strategies, a specific matter at the beginning of Churchill's premiership caused much acrimony. In February 1951 Churchill had criticised Prime Minister Attlee over allowing SACLANT to be placed in US hands. In fact, SACLANT had not yet been set up by Churchill's return to power in October 1951, and when he and Foreign Secretary Eden met with President Truman in Washington the following January it became the most contentious issue that they discussed.

W. M. Fechteler, Chief of US Naval Operations, explained to Truman that he thought that the matter was largely a domestic political issue for Churchill because of his criticisms of Labour policy. He went on to explain that although the British had made the original suggestion for SACLANT, the US contributed 75% of its naval forces and there was doubt about whether some NATO members would contribute if it were under British command. Truman was determined, in the light of these considerations, that there had to be a unified command with an American at the helm.[2]

Fechteler was wrong. It was not just a political issue for Churchill. It was a matter of pride and national interest. He argued vehemently for a joint Anglo-American command with an appeal structure such as they had used in the war, reaching up eventually to the Prime Minister and the President. Truman would not have this, and discussions became very heated. US Defence Secretary Robert Lovett pointed out that the Soviets had six times as many submarines in the Atlantic as the Nazis had ever had: a proper NATO command was essential and urgent, but Churchill would not give way. At successive meetings he used his persuasive skills: 'British life depended on the sea . . . the British had earned equality with British blood . . . all the British wanted [was] equality, not primacy.'[3] But when he left for a side trip to Canada there was still no agreement.

Lester Pearson, Canadian Secretary of State for External Affairs, informed Acheson that Churchill spent more time on trying to convince the Canadians of the merits of his dual-command proposal than on anything else. The other thing that exercised Churchill was the reinstatement of *Rule Britannia* as the official hymn of the Canadian Navy. He had more success with the latter than the former. After he returned to Washington, it was not until 18 January, his final day in the USA, that he grudgingly conceded ground. The record was still to show that he was not happy with an American commander, but SACLANT should go ahead. Minor amendments to appease the British were incorporated into the agreement: their command was to extend to the 100-fathom mark round the British coast and there would be more command flexibility in the eastern Atlantic.[4] This was a long way from the debate thirty years earlier about Anglo-American naval parity. The episode demonstrated US unwillingness to countenance formal US–UK joint command structures and just how junior Britain was even in NATO, the area of most immediate strategic concern to her. The reasons for this are not hard to find: the USA had the larger naval contribution, had a far stronger economic position, and had the prestige of being the leader of the Western Alliance. On his return to London Eden told the Cabinet that he had returned 'with a renewed conviction of our need to do everything possible to re-establish our economic and financial independence'[5] (a rather prophetic judgement given Eden's experience in 1956). However, one should not read too much into this or ignore ways in which Britain was effective in wielding influence and power. For example, it was more difficult to get Britain to do things as opposed to denying her specific roles such as SACLANT, and the development of Britain's nuclear deterrent gave her a degree of independence and of leverage on the Americans. And, although her independence was later compromised because of reliance on US delivery systems, Britain's nuclear deterrent and its possible use raised problems for the USA and matters of interdependence similar to those for the British caused by the presence of US nuclear bases on British soil.

The rejection of a joint command for SACLANT did not augur well for the re-establishment of a formal Combined Chiefs of Staff, much desired by Britain to give more form to the Anglo-American alliance. The American views on this were consistent through both the Truman and the Eisenhower administrations. Both felt that a CCS would unduly restrict America's freedom of action. That could be most undesirable when US policies diverged from British in certain areas of the world, notably the Middle East. An Anglo-American CCS would also alienate other Allies and add to the tensions already evident within NATO, for example over German re-armament. If Churchill were to raise the matter of a CCS in January 1952, Truman was advised to reject it strongly, but because Britain was such an important ally care should be taken not to 'appear to slight the value of close co-operation with her or to be insensitive to matters of particular importance to them'.[6] The line taken by Eisenhower and Dulles was similar, though more co-operative. In preparation for a meeting between President-elect Eisenhower and Churchill in January 1953, Dulles produced notes dealing with proposals that might come from Churchill:

1. Putting US-UK relations on personalized basis. (There should be many intimate, informal contacts to achieve indispensable harmony. But decisions should be through normal channels.) 2. Combined US-UK chiefs of staff. (*de facto* OK; but *formal* combination would adversely affect other allied relations.)[7]

After Suez in 1956, US policy did not pull away from Britain, indeed, with the renewed threat from the Soviets posed by developments in missile technology in 1957, the USA actually moved into a phase of closer and more overt co-operation.

The most obvious gap in Anglo-American co-operation compared with wartime was in the nuclear field. The 1948 *modus vivendi* did little to alter things, and opposition, particularly from certain sections of the US Congress, prevented substantial progress towards co-operation. Remaining hopes for a renewal were dashed by the Klaus Fuchs spy case in February 1950 and widespread worries about British security which it aroused and which were then compounded by fears unleashed by McCarthyism in the USA. However, notwithstanding all this, one could hardly describe Britain and the USA as being disengaged in the nuclear field. US nuclear bombers were based in the UK, which was an invaluable forward base at this time for the SAC. They also placed Britain in a very dangerous position. Churchill remarked of East Anglia in June 1954, that with its US nuclear bases it was the 'nearest and perhaps only bull's eye of the target' for a Soviet nuclear strike.[8] This situation had a number of implications. It created a certain Anglo-American interdependence which Britain could exploit. It also raised the question of SAC policy – how US nuclear weapons in Britain were to be used. And, finally, it raised the matter of control. Would the Americans use atomic weapons based in Britain without British permission?

The Attlee government had failed to sort out these matters. In Washington in December 1950, Attlee had extracted a concrete commitment from Truman that the atom bomb would not be used without consultation with the British. But, before that commitment could begin to set, Dean Acheson intervened, and after it was pointed out to the President in private that such a restriction was unconstitutional it was deleted from the record. Acheson's argument was strengthened by a horrifying false alarm. It was caused by geese showing up on radar screens and creating the impression that Soviet nuclear bombers were on their way to attack the USA via the short route over the North Pole. Acheson and Under Secretary of Defence Lovett decided the situation was such that there could be no time for consultation with, or the seeking of advice from, allies – even with Attlee in Washington. The imperative of making immediate operational decisions controlled all subsequent commitments to the British. They had to accept a situation governed, in the end, by trust. The only exception to this was the dual-key system, whereby one key in British hands and one in American had both to be used to operate intermediate-range missiles sited in Britain in the late 1950s.

Although Attlee failed to get a formal commitment to consult from Truman, he returned from Washington reassured about the use of the bomb in the Korean context,[9] but once US bombers in Britain were armed with nuclear weapons the question of control and use of the bomb became of even more direct concern to the British. In January 1952 Churchill brought to fruition the publication of a formula to cover the use of US bases in Britain which had been drawn up prior to his arrival in office. It was deliberately vague and, as Acheson later pointed out to the President, nuclear weapons were not specifically mentioned.[10]

The imperative for the USA was that it 'must retain freedom of action regarding a decision to use atomic weapons'. And although both Lovett and Truman assured Churchill that bases in Britain would not be used for atomic war without their 'knowledge and consent', it is clear that Churchill knew what was going on. In an emergency, such as a strike over the North Pole, the Prime Minister said that Britain would not hinder the Americans in the use of their bases in Britain. Of course, if a crisis developed over time the British would expect to be consulted. These were not naïve men. The

British realised as much as the Americans that in an emergency con-
sultations could not be carried out. What was important was to get a
statement for the record that would embody the sense of goodwill and trust
that existed between Britain and the USA, and that is all the joint
communiqué and the various reiterations of it over the years have ever
amounted to.

> Under arrangements made for the common defence, the United States
> has the use of certain bases in the United Kingdom. We reaffirm the
> understanding that the use of the bases in an emergency would be a
> matter of joint decision by His Majesty's Government and the United
> States Government in the light of circumstances prevailing at the time.[11]

Churchill was pleased with this. Furthermore, the Americans also revealed
SAC plans to him in a way that they had never done with his predecessor.
But it was not until Eisenhower came to power that there was any progress
on joint weapons research.

The new President was quickly lobbied by Churchill for more co-
operation. He was reminded of the wartime agreements, and it appears that
Eisenhower was not unmoved by British claims that they had been unfairly
treated. In 1954, on Eisenhower's prompting, Congress revised the
MacMahon act to allow more exchange of information and in June 1956
there was an important agreement with Britain concerning nuclear submarine technology. That was important for an agreement in 1962 that gave
Britain the right to purchase Polaris missiles: if Britain had not had a
nuclear submarine capability to enable her to house Polaris missiles, there
would not have been much point in buying them. Clearly, even before the
1958 landmark agreement, developments were already filling the gap
created by the postwar lapse in collaboration.

Problems for Anglo-American relations in the atomic field arose mainly
because of lack of co-operation: in the conventional field it was the manner
of co-operation that was the problem. The most serious shortcoming
exposed by the Korean War was the military weakness of the Western
Alliance and the consequent fear that the Soviets might exploit that in
Europe. Britain responded magnificently to the challenge with a re-
armament programme costed at £4.7 billion over three years. On this the
British worked closely and generally in harmony with the USA, which
helped with £400 million in defence aid. But even with this effort, military
capability still fell short of the mark. This was partly because of British
commitments in the Middle East and Malaya, partly because a colonial war
in Indo-China absorbed much of France's military capability. More had to
be done and the USA lobbied for German re-armament to solve the manpower

shortage. Just as Germany was indispensable to the economic recovery of the West, so she was indispensable to its defence. But, how could its re-armament be safely accomplished?

In August 1950 Churchill proposed a European army, and two months later the French leader René Pleven produced a plan for a European Defence Community (EDC). At first it seemed that Britain might enter more European integration through defence than she had through the ERP. But neither Attlee nor Churchill was willing to join the EDC. In January 1952 Churchill 'remained unreconstituted to the last':[12] Britain could not take part. What Churchill had had in mind when he had proposed a European army was 'a bunch of faggots bound together, stronger as a bunch than as individual sticks, but each retaining its individual characteristics in the bunch. Pleven's European army . . . is a "bucket of wood pulp"'. On another occasion Churchill invoked a different, but no less disdainful, simile: the EDC was like a 'sludgy amalgam'.[13] The sticking-point for the British was integration and loss of identity. For the French this was the very attraction of the EDC, because it meant no clear identity for the German contingent. But with Britain refusing to take part the French worried about German re-armament even under the Pleven Plan. The Americans, aware of the impact that British non-participation was having on the French, were displeased with the British because they were prejudicing the chances of German re-armament. French procrastination over ratifying the EDC made Dulles angry. He urged France and the British to be more positive and hinted that Congress might not be forthcoming with funds for NATO if things did not improve. In December 1953 he made the ultimate threat of an 'agonising reappraisal' of US defence policy that would involve a turning-away from Europe to the Far East.

In August 1954 the French Assembly rejected the EDC. Ironically, it was Eden who saved the day. He proposed that the Brussels Defence Treaty of 1948 between France, Britain and Benelux should be expanded into the Western European Union (WEU) to include Germany and Italy. Britain would commit herself to keeping four divisions and a tactical airforce in Europe (to reassure France) as long as a majority of the WEU wanted her to. Under this arrangement it would then be possible for Germany to enter NATO and re-arm. The proposal was accepted. Britain had not integrated with Europe, but her commitment there had clearly been expanded and strengthened. The USA was pleased.

By the late 1940s, the British had somewhat shifted from their early combative attitude on containing the Soviets and now consistently, except in the Middle East, found themselves both concerned about US belligerence and trying to moderate US policy. Time after time they worried about the way the possible use of nuclear weapons slipped into US calculations during crises. It was considered in the Berlin blockade; December 1950 in Korea; 1953 during the Korean armistice negotiations after Eisenhower took over; 1954 at the time of Dien Bien Phu; and in both 1953–4 and in 1958 during friction between the two Chinas over offshore islands that lay between Taiwan and the mainland. They fretted about the possible extension of the Korean war, about the support the USA gave to the Chinese nationalists, and over apparent US willingness to seek military solutions to problems. Britain recognised the People's Republic of China (PRC) in 1949 and never saw it as being dominated by the Soviets as the USA tended to. Britain followed a policy of accommodation and trade in order to try to divide the communist camp. In fact, until the Korean War and the McCarthy communist scare US policy also had some inclination to follow a similar route. After hostilities began and McCarthyism took off, that window of opportunity closed. It was left to Britain to try to build bridges, open negotiations, deflate some of the wilder rhetoric about expansionist communism and expose the broad difference between Soviet and Chinese brand names. One tactic they had for trying to improve East–West relations was through reconvening the wartime summits that they had had with the Soviets.

Eisenhower disapproved of this. He never placed much faith in summitry and was unconvinced that any real progress could be made. The death of Stalin in March 1953, however, increased Churchill's buoyant enthusiasm for a four-power meeting between Britain, the USA, the Soviet Union and France. The USA remained wary, especially of likely Soviet tactics at a summit:

> The Soviets wish most of all to upset and break off the free world's NATO–EDC plans. Unity of the free world in Europe is their greatest danger. Therefore the Soviets would like to get us at a four-power conference, while we are divided and not yet settled on EDC. We must resist this move . . . our firm position with the UK must be that we will not agree to a four power meeting date prior to the ratification of EDC.[14]

Churchill never got his postwar summit. It was not until 1955 in Geneva that a summit was convened and it was his successor, Anthony Eden, who attended for Britain. The conference was important in a symbolic sense rather than for any substantial achievement. Eisenhower made a famous proposal for 'open skies' and full monitoring of military capabilities. The Soviets proposed a non-aggression pact between the Warsaw powers and NATO and there was much talk and propaganda posturing about the need for avoiding war, and great concern about the nationalist Chinese 'off-shore islands' and their potential for causing trouble between the USA and the PRC. The most important thing, however, was the spirit of Geneva. In an intangible way it deflated tension in East-West relations and by 1955 the British noted that there was a more conciliatory line developing in Washington. Once again it looked as if British and US policies were converging.

There were other facets to the style and content of British and US foreign and Cold War policies, some of which facilitated co-operation, while others made it difficult. In looking at policies in more detail in the Far and Middle East, an interesting contrast emerges. In the Far East the British often tried to moderate and steer US policy away from its more belligerent inclinations, though one should remember Britain was fighting a hot war in Malaya. In the Middle East things were reversed. Here was one of Britain's remaining spheres of influence and much to US dismay they took a more aggressive line, in pursuit not so much of Cold War as of traditional objectives of national interest.

THE FAR AND MIDDLE EAST

In the Far East Britain had two remaining interests: Malaya (including Singapore), which was important to the sterling area because of its capacity to earn dollars with the export of tin and rubber; and Hong Kong. The former it deemed defendable and so stood and fought for it twice, once against communist insurgents in the early 1950s, and once against Achmed Sukarno's Indonesia a decade later. Hong Kong was not defendable and so accommodation and compromise with the PRC were the chosen route to safeguard British commercial and investment interests. British inclination on all else in the Far East was to negotiate rather than fight, except over the flagrant aggression involved in Korea.

The USA took a different line. It applied containment rigidly to the Far East for fear that just as the Rhineland, Austria, the Sudetenland, and then the rest of Czechoslovakia had toppled like up-ended dominoes in the face of intimidation and subversion from Nazism, so the countries of the Far East would topple under the same kind of pressures from communism. Falling dominoes; appeasement; the need for containment; fear of communism abroad and of being branded soft on communism at home – these were powerful images and they conjured up an imperative for action. After all, containment in Europe had succeeded. Why should it not work in the Far East as well? The USA had not only the general interests of the Western world to consider, but also more specific commitments to safeguard in Japan, the Philippines and Taiwan. Britain was less engaged than the USA, had far less power in the Far East, and did not feel as threatened by the purported global ambitions of communism. One might see a contrast between British pragmatism and US moralistic idealism taking shape here. In any case, the substance of the differences noted above was at the heart of the difficulties they had in co-ordinating policies.

Throughout the Korean War there were serious differences between Britain and the USA. Britain's recognition of the PRC, and trade through Hong Kong with the communists, caused no end of problems with Washington. And Britain was concerned throughout the 1950s by US support of Taiwan and America's desire to foment trouble in the PRC. On returning from the December 1950 trip to Washington, Attlee told the Cabinet that the Americans were 'considering idea of a limited war against China by way of an economic blockade and stirring up trouble in China'.[15] This seemed a dangerous and wayward policy to the British. Also US policy was not always consistent. On the one hand the Americans wanted the British to shadow their lead and yet they negotiated the ANZUS Pact in the autumn of 1951 with Commonwealth members Australia and New Zealand and specifically left Britain out. They reasoned that if she entered, other European states that had interests in the Far East might wish to join as well and the pact would be tainted with colonialism in the minds of would-be allies in the Far East. All these difficulties, however, were kept in check, and no great damage or tragedy arose from them. The problems that became associated with Indo-China were different. They did not directly damage Anglo-American relations in any permanent way, though there were ugly incidents; but American policy in the 1950s led on to the Vietnam war, and that had implications for US policy in general and in some specific ways for relations with Britain.

The fall of China, and the Korean War, accelerated the changes of attitude that the USA was then currently undergoing. First, those events pushed the USA into a vigorous containment policy in the Far East. It added to the global perspective on the communist threat and caused the USA to revise its view of the importance of south-east Asia. After according it little significance in the postwar period, in December 1949 a Defence Department study stated: 'The loss of an area so large and populous would tip the balance of power against the United States.'[16] Second, the USA became more tolerant of the policies of the European colonial powers, particularly France and Britain. The USA still remained opposed to colonialism, but not as much so as against communism. With regard to France, the USA found itself in something of a quandary. It approved even less of French colonial policies than of British, but it could hardly give France aid to help redress the balance of power *vis-à-vis* the Soviets in Europe and oppose French policy in Indo-China. Once China fell and Korea began, the USA supported the French war against the Vietnamese revolutionaries led by Ho Chi Minh, but at the same time wanted independence for Indo-China. The French ended up fighting a war to defeat communism in order to give up their empire in the Far East: not surprisingly, they were not terribly enthusiastic about that.

As the war in Korea ground to a halt the situation in Vietnam deteriorated badly. In one of the great strategic blunders of the twentieth century the French miscalculated the Vietminh's ability to move heavy artillery across rough terrain and found themselves, at their great military base in Dien Bien Phu, sitting at the bottom of a valley surrounded by Vietminh forces constantly dropping shells on them. By this time, 1954, the USA was providing a large proportion of the finances for the French effort, and Dulles was determined to prevent the Indo-China domino from toppling. He wanted to give military help to the French, but Congressional leaders, while not ruling this out, stipulated that intervention had to be on an allied basis, which meant bringing the British on board. Eisenhower agreed. Dulles also wanted to form a South East Asia Treaty Organisation (SEATO) to harden the containment line and strengthen the West's hand.

Churchill and Eden would have nought to do with the proposal for military intervention. Churchill thought that to agree to Dulles's suggestion would have the effect of 'misleading Congress into approving a military operation, which would in itself be ineffective, and might well bring the world to the verge of a major war'.[17] Furthermore, Britain also refused to prejudice a negotiated settlement of the Vietnam problem by trying to set up a SEATO before the talks had had a chance to succeed. Dien Bien Phu duly fell to General Giap, the Vietminh commander, and at the Geneva Conference, convened to end Korean hostilities, Vietnam was also on the agenda. The French, with strong support from the British, negotiated the Geneva Accords, which divided Vietnam between the communists and non-communists along the 17th parallel, provided for free elections in 1956, prohibited military alliances and foreign bases for either side and gave neutral status to Laos and Cambodia.

Dulles was furious. This was not containment and it was a long way from rolling back communism. Relations between him and Eden never fully recovered from this. The USA refused to sign the Accords but agreed not to disturb things. In fact, over the following years it did disturb them, by installing Ngo Dinh Diem as leader of the South in Saigon, by providing military advisers and money, and by opposing elections which, if held, would have unified Vietnam under Ho Chi Minh. The British had managed to put off the day of active military involvement in Vietnam by the USA, but that was all. By the end of the 1950s there were growing problems with unrest in Laos and a less than adequate performance by the South Vietnamese regime.

British ability to affect US policy in the Far East was limited to persuasion, which rarely worked, and the power to say no when the USA wanted to use ground troops on an allied basis. Britain was impotent to affect US dealings with the nationalist Chinese, because the power they used was either naval or threats of nuclear retribution. Britain also had to stand on the sidelines when ANZUS was formed. But the British in turn proved fairly immune to pressure to change their own policies. They would not enter Vietnam or set up SEATO prior to Geneva and despite many demands they did little to bring their trade policies with the PRC in line with what the USA wanted.

The situation in the Middle East was different. Here Britain was the leading military power, and although the USA had both a growing economic and political say in the region, not only was it unable to dictate policy, but it found itself following the British lead most of the time. That was until the British overreached themselves, and rediscovered the fact that for any significant military operation they had to have, at the very least, US benevolent neutrality. Eden should have consulted Austen Chamberlain's views on such things, expressed in the CID in 1928, before he authorised the Suez campaign in 1956.

Britain and the USA collided repeatedly in the Middle East. Truman's behaviour during the crisis over Britain's Palestine Mandate and the emergence of Israel had infuriated the British, who tried to be as even-handed as they could. Truman was not helpful. He was inconsistent and eventually came down in favour of an independent state of Israel, partly on the basis of election calculations to do with the US Jewish vote. In 1950 there was something of a *rapprochement* with the Tripartite Declaration by France, Britain and the USA, aimed at securing peace between the Arabs and the Israelis and the avoidance of an arms race that might bring the Soviets into the picture. Another attempt at constructive co-operation, namely a Middle East Defence Organisation to include Britain, France, the USA, Turkey and Egypt, was abandoned by the USA after Egyptian opposition. Instead the Americans continued to look to the British to take the lead in the area's defence and promoted a Northern Tier alliance of Iran, Turkey and Pakistan to contain the Soviets on their south-western border. That strategy was flawed: there was a breach in the tier, Afghanistan, and the mainstay of any such pact would have to be Britain, but the Americans recognised that she did not have the power to play that role.

The Americans knew what they wanted: stability with an orderly transition to Western-style democracy in the region, prosperity and the containment of communism, but they relied on Britain to carry much of this policy.[18] The flaws and problems of the US position are well illustrated in the following observations. The Americans had Arab enemies in the region because of their support of Israel; they promoted a defence strategy that depended upon Britain, which was too weak to effect it; they urged Britain to continue to defend the area, but distanced themselves from her because of her colonial legacy; and they increased their economic and political influence in the area, though that could never be decisive without the back-up of military power, which they were not prepared to develop before 1956. At the heart of the problem of Anglo-American relations was that the USA saw things in terms of containment and Cold War; the British had other interests to nurture – oil, and strategic and commercial communications through the Suez Canal. These different priorities caused trouble and accentuated problems over colonialism and anti-colonialism. Bearing these factors in mind it becomes easy to demonstrate why relations in the Middle East were, by the USA's own reckoning, the most difficult of all that she had with Britain.[19]

The AIOC crisis spanned both the Truman and the Eisenhower presidencies. The Abadan oil refinery and Iranian oil were seen as crucial components of Britain's economic livelihood. The British felt that the illegal seizure of the AIOC assets by the nationalist government of Mohammed Mossadeq could not be tolerated because of the actual economic loss to Britain, but also because of the potential impact it might have elsewhere for British assets in the Middle East if Mossadeq were seen to get away with it. Some ministers, most notably Herbert Morrison, after succeeding Ernest Bevin as Foreign Secretary, felt that military action should be taken and plans were drawn up. In the end they were abandoned largely because of diplomatic pressure from the USA. The Labour government did not make the mistake Eden's Conservative one was to make in 1956 over Suez. But perhaps the most interesting thing is that a Labour government actually seriously countenanced such a course of action in the first place. After abandoning the military option, the British concentrated on squeezing the Iranians economically and seeking international legal redress.

Truman and Acheson were dismayed by the high-handed British approach. They had sympathy for Iranian desires for a fairer share of their oil wealth and feared that British policy would destabilise Iran. The staple diet the Americans fed the Middle East was aid and investment in the hope that prosperity would bring stability and stave off any inclination to communism. They saw British policy running directly against this over the AIOC dispute and they feared that unrest in Iran could be taken as a pretext by the Soviets for intervention when the West was desperately over-stretched militarily because of the Korean war.

These different perspectives and interests caused much difficulty between Britain and the USA. However, as time went by the Americans began to realise that their options in the Middle East were severely limited because they lacked military power there. In the face of Britain's resolute pursuit of her interests the USA could not impose a solution, but only attempt to mediate.

By 1952 the USA had developed doubts about both the wisdom of mediation and supporting Mossadeq. In August, Churchill called for an Anglo-American gallop together and the two countries considered how they might jointly approach the Iranians, but difficulties still remained. Acheson commented at one point: 'the only resemblance I could see between the *aide-mémoire* we had given the British Government and Mr. Eden's reply was that they were both written on paper and with a type-writer'.[20] In the end this attempt to concert action failed.

Things changed with Eisenhower. By now the Korean War had settled down and the Americans no longer saw Mossadeq as the man to bring stability to Iran. At the same time they did not wish to act with overt force in the Middle East. A US memorandum of November 1953 stated: 'The US is not attempting to replace the British in the Middle East or to vie with her on matters of prestige. We would in fact be little interested in the situation there but for the perilous state of affairs arising from East-West tensions.'[21] For the time being at least, the interest was not sufficient to justify the major step of taking over the role of Western defence in the Middle East. Instead the Central Intelligence Agency (CIA) co-operated with British intelligence. A CIA team led by Kermit Roosevelt was set up to execute an audacious coup that his grandfather Theodore would undoubtedly have approved of. Mossadeq was removed and the Shah reinstalled. The oil concessions were carved up between Britain and the USA. In the end the USA had had to follow Britain's lead, but it benefited by gaining further economic interests in the Middle East, and it learnt for the first time about what appeared to be the easy gains to be had from covert activity. Further cases followed in Guatemala, Cuba, Chile and elsewhere with varying degrees of success and failure.

Notwithstanding the growing realisation of shortcomings in US policy toward the Middle East, the USA still stood back from a major military commitment, though it supported the creation of the Baghdad Pact of 1955 (later renamed the Central Treaty Organisation after Iraq's withdrawal). The Americans were uneasy about Britain's relations with Egypt and the fraught negotiations that eventually resulted in agreement in 1954 for

British withdrawal from its enormous base in the Suez Canal zone. There were also difficulties brewing in Cyprus between the Greeks and Turks, which caused the Americans concern for fear that NATO members Greece and Turkey might be drawn into conflict. But it was Egypt and the Suez crisis that changed US policy and had important consequences for Anglo-American relations.

SUEZ AND ITS CONSEQUENCES 1956–61

On 26 July 1956 the Egyptian nationalist leader Abdul Nasser nationalised the Suez Canal with the declared intention of using its tolls to finance the building of the Aswan Dam on the Nile. The West had previously withdrawn offers of financial help for the project because of Nasser's links with the Eastern bloc and domestic US pressures. Britain and France, who were the joint owners of the canal, decided that Nasser could not be allowed to get away with his illegal action. The reasoning and circumstances were similar to those in the AIOC crisis, except Suez was symbolically more important, Nasser was a more formidable challenge to the West than Mossadeq had ever been, and Eden failed to assess both the consequences of military action and US reaction accurately.

Britain and France decided to use force if Nasser would not give way in negotiations. In the end they colluded with Israel to provide a pretext for an Anglo-French invasion to safeguard the Canal from Israeli–Egyptian fighting. It was a pretty transparent pretext. Furthermore, the success of military action depended upon the USA. With added clarity from hindsight, Chancellor of the Exchequer Harold Macmillan later wrote:

if the Americans would give reasonable support to sterling and help us in an emergency by paying for dollar oil, we and the European countries should be able to maintain our position even in the worst conditions. Of course, if the Americans were to sell sterling – officially or unofficially – and act not even as neutrals but in a hostile manner, we stood no chance.[22]

As in the 1920s and in 1940, Britain without US economic backing would be constrained to the utmost in the type of policy it could conduct. There had been a sense of that in the AIOC crisis, but it was not strong enough to prevent the Suez fiasco. Instead, Eden became angry with US policy, particularly when Dulles declared that there would be no shooting of a way through the Canal, undermining the threat of force from France and Britain. From then on Eden, disillusioned with the Americans (how many times had the British had to put up with what they considered over-reliance by the

USA on the threat of force?), increasingly misread the situation and embarked upon secret military plans.

Initially, Eisenhower, Dulles and US Congressional leaders seemed to condone the idea of force, but as the crisis dragged on to the autumn attitudes changed. When the shooting started several things determined Eisenhower's response. He was angry that he had not been consulted and that the invasion took place on the eve of the US Presidential election. He feared that this type of gunboat diplomacy would tarnish the US reputation in the Third World unless he came out against it. The crisis coincided with the Soviet invasion of Hungary to suppress liberalisation of the regime there and Suez would reduce the propaganda opportunity Soviet actions presented to the West. And finally Eisenhower was standing as a peace candidate in the aftermath of the Geneva Summit. All these things led Eisenhower to the conviction that Britain and France had to be stopped and forced to withdraw and he bent all his efforts to achieve those goals. Most crucially of all, the Americans did the very thing that Macmillan was frightened of: they sold sterling and blocked British efforts to get help from the IMF. The sterling crisis occasioned by Suez and exacerbated by the Americans gave Macmillan no option but to recommend acceptance of Eisenhower's demand that they halt the military operation. Britain had to withdraw ignominiously under unrelenting pressure from the USA after the ceasefire. The sense of betrayal and anger in Britain was intense. The British felt that the USA and the UN did not act even-handedly in requiring Britain to withdraw while tolerating dilatory action by Nasser over clearing the canal, which had been blocked during the fighting. Just how bad relations were was shown in a meeting between Rab Butler (expected by many to succeed Eden) and US Ambassador Winthrop Aldrich in late November. Butler said if the UN did not 'act with firmness to bring about immediate clearance of the canal Great Britain would withdraw from the UN and the situation might even reach the point where the US would be asked to give up its bases in Great Britain'.[23]

Things never went that far. Once Britain withdrew its troops US policy became helpful. Oil, a $500 million credit from the US Export–Import Bank, and IMF assistance soon flowed to help Britain to recover its economic stability. But Eden was done for and resigned within months because of a collapse in his health, and Harold Macmillan became Prime Minister in January 1957. These events constituted the biggest storm in Anglo-American relations since the nineteenth century, but within little over four months a remarkable reconciliation was under way.

Macmillan was well equipped to reforge friendly relations with the USA: he was half American and had a long-standing friendship with

Eisenhower that went as far back as their time together in North Africa during the Second World War. The President for his part went along with views expressed by Churchill to him at the height of the crisis: 'to let events in the Middle East become a gulf between us would be an act of folly, on which our whole civilisation may founder' and from which the Soviets alone would benefit.[24] Eisenhower invited Macmillan to talks and they arranged to meet in Bermuda in early March. Meanwhile, there were two important developments: a UK defence review and the Eisenhower Doctrine.

The review by the Defence Secretary, Duncan Sandys, proposed a 40% reduction of the British Army of the Rhine (BAOR), the ending of conscription, and more reliance on nuclear defences, but little change in Britain's commitments east of Suez.[25] Eisenhower and Dulles were deeply worried by the prospects for European defence in the light of proposed British cut-backs and France's wavering commitment to NATO in the aftermath of Suez.

One solution to Europe's problem would have been a larger US commitment, but America was beginning to worry about costs and balance of payments and overstretch. Those feelings were particularly acute because after Suez Eisenhower felt the need to make defence commitments to the Middle East to try to stabilise things. On 7 March 1957 Congress approved the Eisenhower Doctrine, offering military and economic aid to countries in the area that requested it. The USA thus moved to eliminate the problem of having a policy without the means to implement it. From now on the USA became increasingly active in the Middle East; this culminated in Desert Storm in 1991. In 1957 it joined the military committee of the Baghdad Pact and in July 1958 Britain and the USA co-ordinated operations to stabilise things in the Middle East after an anti-Western coup in Iraq. US marines landed on the beaches of the Lebanon, and British paratroopers went into Jordan. Memories of Suez were beginning to fade.

Prior to the meeting with Macmillan at Bermuda, Eisenhower had time to ponder on the West's disarray and the shortcomings of its defences, which were exacerbated by proposed British cut-backs, escalating costs, and US overstretch – made even tauter by the Eisenhower Doctrine. A briefing paper for the conference demonstrated just how valuable Britain was to the USA:

> The US needs the alliance for much the same reason as does Britain. We rely on British help . . . material and psychological, to implement our policies towards the Commonwealth, Eastern Europe, South Asia, and some areas of the Far East. We recognize the two acting in concert, with the aid of the Commonwealth, form a more persuasive combination than

the US acting alone. In addition we rely heavily on Britain in the military field. Their contribution, next to our own . . . forms the largest national component in NATO and UK territory aford essential bases for US forces in the British Isles, Caribbean and other areas.[26]

Before the conference, the USA acted in a most conciliatory way. During Suez the Soviets had threatened nuclear intervention. Now, in order to deter such blackmail, the USA proposed stationing intermediate-range ballistic missiles (IRBMs) in Britain. At Bermuda the proposal was firmed up, steps were taken to broaden Anglo-American nuclear co-operation, and the Americans went out of their way to be tactful and friendly. Eisenhower later declared the conference 'by far the most successful I have attended since the close of World War 2'.[27]

Bermuda laid the groundwork for both the renewal of the special relationship and the response to the crisis that hit the West in October 1957 with the Soviet launch of Sputnik: the Soviets now had an inter-continental ballistic missile capability. Before the end of the month Macmillan and Eisenhower met again and decided on even closer nuclear co-operation. Soon the MacMahon Act was repealed and after yet another meeting in July 1958 the Agreement for Co-operation in the Uses of Atomic Energy for Mutual Defence Purposes was concluded. It created a preferential relationship under which a wealth of technical information and hardware was exchanged.[28] Britain was by far the main beneficiary but the US got some benefit as well, and the West gained in general by avoiding duplication of effort. The first climax of the new nuclear special relationship came in 1960. Macmillan and Eisenhower agreed that Britain could buy the air-launched Skybolt missile from the USA to take the place of Britain's Blue Streak Rocket, which was obsolete before it was completed because of the time it took to fuel in preparation for firing. There was also a gentleman's agreement that gave Britain an option on Polaris missiles. There were separate *quid pro quo* arrangements on the British side which granted the USA a Polaris submarine base at Holy Loch and an early-warning spy station at Fylingdales in Yorkshire.

By the start of the new decade Britain and the USA had repaired their fences. A new dimension to their relations had been created through nuclear co-operation and the development of a new phase of US bases in Britain. But not all was forgotten or forgiven. Some became convinced that Britain's destiny lay in Europe, not in an Atlantic community. Some economic developments in the 1950s supported that view, but for the time being the main trend still emphasised Britain's internationalism.

INTO THE 1960s

Economically, the 1950s was a time of preparation for the 1960s: a transition period to the normality that US and British wartime planners had defined in terms of stable, convertible currencies and progressive liberalisation of trade, overseen and facilitated by the IMF and GATT.[29] In 1958 sterling was made fully convertible and in 1960, in response to an American initiative, the Dillon Round of GATT trade talks tried to reduce protection.

Neither Britain's transition to convertibility nor its economic relationship with the USA was easy. In one specific area, that of embargo policy toward communist states, they were consistently difficult. Britain repeatedly called for relaxation of controls and the abolition of the China differential: during the Korean war controls on trade with China became more severe than those applicable to the Soviet bloc and even after 1954 the differential was maintained. Britain wanted to expand trade and in June 1957 she unilaterally abandoned the China differential. The rest of COCOM, except the USA, followed suit. In 1958 there was liberalisation across the board, but again the USA was unhappy and resented Britain's role as instigator of new policy. Relations between the two continued to be difficult and volatile over COCOM policy into the 1960s and beyond.[30]

The main economic issues between them, however, were freer trade and convertibility. On the latter there was a steady relaxation of controls and little disagreement on the end goal. Indeed, early in the Churchill administration, Chancellor of the Exchequer, Rab Butler proposed 'Operation Robot', which would have returned sterling to convertibility at an early stage, but the Cabinet thought that it was too risky and could involve severe domestic deflation. On matters of trade the situation with the USA was more difficult.

After the abandonment of the ITO, and US acceptance of discrimination by Europe and Britain, American trade policy had reverted to a cautious conservatism. In 1953 there was a major Anglo-American economic conference in Washington, at which Butler argued the case for 'trade not aid', but, while Eisenhower was sympathetic, there was opposition within his Cabinet and in Congress to trade liberalisation. In January 1954, the Randall Commission, headed by Clarence Randall, Chairman of the Commission on Foreign Economic Policy, recommended modest liberalisation, but even that was difficult to implement. It was only through collaboration with Democrats that extension of the RTAA, authorising trade reductions, was pushed through Congress. But Eisenhower also used executive powers to ease non-tariff barriers to trade and, no matter how much the British moaned, the fact was that in 1956 the USA replaced Australia as Britain's biggest single export market, though there was still a big trade deficit.[31]

Economically, Britain looked primarily to the Commonwealth and the USA. Furthermore, with Bretton Woods coming into operation and need for management through the IMF and GATT, Britain believed that it still had a pivotal role to play in the international economy. However, at the same time it could no longer ignore economic developments in Europe. As an area this was extremely important for British exports, and Macmillan became increasingly worried about the prospect of a common tariff being adopted by the six members (France, Germany, Italy and Benelux) of the European Economic Community (EEC), formed by the Treaty of Rome in 1957. Macmillan had helped to create a competitor organisation, the European Free Trade Association (EFTA – Britain, Austria, Denmark, Norway, Portugal, Sweden, and Switzerland) – but there were doubts that this could compensate for the effects of EEC protection. In July 1960 he started to move toward the possibility of applying for EEC membership by appointing the passionately pro-European Edward Heath as Lord Privy Seal in charge of European affairs.

The 1960s thus posed both great opportunities and challenges for Anglo-American relations. Suez had been overcome and nuclear co-operation had been fully renewed. The nuclear agreement of 1958 was a postwar milestone which put Britain in a position that no other ally of the USA enjoyed. Economic co-operation and friction continued, but new possibilities for collaboration opened up in the 1960s as Bretton Woods came fully on line and momentum gathered for trade liberalisation. Cultural and educational exchanges flourished. More tourists crossed the Atlantic in both directions than ever before. Intelligence and conventional military co-operation intensified with more US bases and intelligence installations being developed, not only in Britain, but later on Ascension Island in the Atlantic, on Diego Garcia in the Indian Ocean, and elsewhere. Personal relations between Macmillan and Eisenhower were good, and renewed tension because of the Soviet nuclear challenge and then the collapse of the Paris Summit in 1960 (because of the shooting-down by the Soviets of a US high-altitude U-2 spy plane on the eve of the conference and Eisenhower's subsequent refusal to apologise for such missions) pushed Britain and the USA closer together.

In short, there seemed great promise for Anglo-American relations, but there were some variables that were to cause disappointment. These were to do with Britain's economic troubles; America's growing preoccupation with Vietnam; the parochialisation and Europeanisation of British politics; and the collapse of the Bretton Woods system. In 1960 one variable that was thought would damage the special relationship, the presidential victory of John F. Kennedy, turned out instead to be a constructive factor for its continuance. Even so, with Kennedy in the White House, the reign of the conservatives on both sides of the Atlantic was broken: four years later the Labour Party's General Election win under Harold Wilson made the break complete. A more liberal, more progressive and less fastidious dispensation was being ushered in.

6 Years of transition 1961–79

Treated now as just another country, now as
an ally in a special and unique category.

(Harold Macmillan)

It was not just the British who were to lament the interchanging of ordinary and special treatment: Richard Nixon experienced similar sentiments to those of Macmillan because of Edward Heath in the early 1970s. These variations in the relationship were partly symptomatic of broader role changes that Britain and the USA underwent at this time. These changes included their respective roles in the Cold War and in the international economy; British entry into the EEC; and changing patterns of immigration into the USA, which further emphasised the drawing of US attention to the Far East because of the Vietnam War and the growth of the Japanese economy. In their turn these developments impacted on the special relationship, which faltered and lost direction for much of the 1970s. The faltering seemed all the more dramatic after the promise of the early 1960s.[1]

In November 1960 Macmillan wrote to Eisenhower that he would continue to work for good Anglo-American relations with his successor, but with President Kennedy he could not 'of course ever have anything to replace the sort of relations that we have had'.[2] Macmillan was wrong. He was the 'Western leader whom he [Kennedy] saw first, liked best and saw most often'.[3] Disagreement over how to deal with instability in Laos troubled their first meeting, but that did not prevent the growth of their friendship. In June 1961 Macmillan reassured and sympathised with Kennedy after his difficult meeting with Soviet leader Krushchev in Vienna in a way that consolidated their affection and respect for each other. In 1961 alone the two leaders met four times.

Another significant actor on the personal level was David Ormsby-Gore, the British Ambassador in Washington, who was a long-standing friend of

John Kennedy and had privileged access to him. Ormsby-Gore was a catalyst in the chemistry of good Anglo-American relations in the early 1960s. That was important because the opportunities for co-operation in the defence and economic spheres also held challenges that caused difficulties.

ECONOMIC POLICIES

Economic policies at home and abroad troubled Britain and the USA in the early 1960s. Britain had an uncompetitive economy, large overseas debts and obligations, and the task of maintaining confidence in sterling as a convertible international reserve in the face of balance of payments problems. The USA suffered similar if less serious ills. From 1957 to 1963 she lost $7.4 billion from her gold reserves. This was a small fraction of her total, but in the long term continuing losses affected the stability of the Bretton Woods system and undermined US foreign policy.

Pressures on sterling and the dollar were interconnected as they were the mainstays of the international monetary system. If they weakened, so did Bretton Woods. This problem also had connections with defence policy. Recurring economic problems caused Britain to threaten and later to implement cut-backs in overseas defence spending: that in turn meant more burdens for the USA to shoulder and more overseas defence spending, which weakened the dollar further and threatened the international monetary system. In short, the fortunes of sterling, the US dollar, the Bretton Woods system, and Western defence were all interconnected and they all affected the special relationship. One way that the British felt that they might break out of their economic troubles was to enter the EEC, but this was also not without problems and had important implications for Anglo-American relations.

By the early 1960s Macmillan concluded that the Commonwealth held little prospect as a major foreign-policy platform for Britain, especially with the withdrawal of South Africa in 1961 and the fragility of the political ties within the Commonwealth that its leaving exposed. There were also those who harboured doubts about the wisdom of dependence on the USA, remembered Suez and looked to Europe for a route to more strength and independence. However, ties with both the USA and the Commonwealth were strong. Indeed, Macmillan continued to look first and foremost to the USA as an ally. These things complicated Britain's application to the EEC and provided President de Gaulle of France with evidence of Britain's equivocation about becoming truly European.

At their meeting in Washington in April 1961, Kennedy told Macmillan that he favoured British entry into the EEC. The Americans had always sought a strong, integrated Europe, but as the EEC prospered, the USA became less tolerant of its discriminatory and protectionist policies, especially of those arising from the Common Agricultural Policy (CAP). This was a major issue for the USA and they hoped that British entry would not only strengthen the EEC politically but also make it more outward-looking and less protectionist. The USA ideally wanted a pro-Western European bloc, including Britain, that would embrace a free-trade area extending over the whole North Atlantic community.[4] So, while the USA wanted Britain in the EEC, it also strove to reassure the British that her move into Europe would strengthen rather than weaken Anglo-American links. But that view and the parading of their close friendship had a negative impact on Britain's European venture.

While the Americans adopted a low profile on UK–EEC relations so as not to incite opponents of British entry, they were active behind the scenes. Shortly after Britain made her formal application in the summer of 1961, Under Secretary of State George Ball smugly informed Kennedy that they had successfully opposed Britain's policy of trying to take the whole of EFTA into the EEC. So far as the USA was concerned this had two benefits: it simplified things and made Britain's chances of getting in better; it also prevented the possibility of the neutral members of EFTA, Sweden and Switzerland, entering the EEC and diluting its character as a strong pro-Western bloc.[5] Notwithstanding this success, Ball was still anxious because he thought that Macmillan was trying to slide sideways into Europe and that formidable problems remained: there was still the matter of preferential access for Commonwealth agricultural imports, which was opposed by the EEC because of the CAP, and by the USA as a further spread of discrimination that would damage US agricultural exports. But, perhaps most important of all, was the symbolism of Britain's close link with the USA, which placed her Europeanness in question, not least in the mind of General de Gaulle. He was suspicious of Anglo-Saxon collusion, especially in promoting free trade, which could strike at the heart of French economic nationalism in the shape of the CAP. Furthermore, he feared that Britain would challenge his leadership of Europe and be an American Trojan Horse that would influence European policy on the basis of Atlantic rather than European interests.

As Britain and the EEC continued to haggle over the terms for entry, the question of her commitment to becoming truly European increased in importance and was doubted more by her would-be partners. Then in December 1962 ex-Secretary of State Dean Acheson, who favoured British entry, made a now famous comment about Britain losing an empire and failing to find a new world role. It had widespread repercussions and caused an outcry in Britain. The White House soon instructed Secretary of State Dean Rusk to reassure Britain that she still had a special relationship with the USA, but rather perversely one result of that was increased French suspicion that Britain would continue to look to her Atlantic rather than her European interests.[6] Just a few days later developments in Anglo-American nuclear-defence co-operation provided further substance for de Gaulle's suspicions and he decided to veto British entry into the EEC. The rebuff was much resented in Britain, but de Gaulle was quite right: Britain was not truly European and had no intention of becoming so in the early 1960s. The veto also dashed US hopes for their plan for a politically stronger, more stable Europe which, with British encouragement, might have been receptive to an Atlantic free-trade area of benefit to America's ailing exports. The special relationship had undone both America's grand design for an expanded EEC more to its own liking and Macmillan's plan for entry into Europe. Equally important for the future, Britain had still not found a strategy to solve her economic troubles.

NUCLEAR DEFENCE

The renewal of Anglo-American nuclear-weapons co-operation was not without its problems. This was definitely the case in 1962, when a crisis arose over Britain's purchase of the Skybolt missile in an atmosphere already soured by Acheson's remarks about Britain's diminished status. The Skybolt affair became so serious that it was likened to Suez. If Kennedy and Macmillan had not been such close friends it could have caused long-term damage.

The Kennedy administration, under the tutelage of Defence Secretary Robert McNamara, developed ideas different to the Eisenhower administration's about nuclear strategy. McNamara telegraphed his views to the British and the French (who were busy developing their independent nuclear *force de frappe*) in a speech at Ann Arbor, Michigan, on 16 June 1962. The USA wanted to bring all the West's nuclear forces under central control (i.e. US command, while allowing Britain and France to save face by creating a kind of multinational nuclear force) for the publicly stated reasons of economy and rational targeting. Unspoken reasons were the fear of Germany demanding nuclear equality with her allies, and realisation that US and European interests were not identical – problems that might arise from this were soon highlighted by the Cuban missile crisis.

The discovery in October 1962 of Soviet nuclear missiles in Cuba posed the USA with a political challenge, if not so much a strategic one given its nuclear superiority over the Soviets, that it had to meet head on. Anything other than a resolute response could have triggered serious domestic political problems, and the USA might have been seen as an appeaser by the Soviets, which could have led to a train of events like those of the 1930s with a similar ending, except on a nuclear scale. However, as McGeorge Bundy was quick to point out at the first meeting of EXCOM (the executive committee of the NSC), the European perspective on the crisis would be different because Europe's interests were not immediately challenged and therefore it would not be wise to involve America's NATO partners in the process of deciding how to respond.[7] This raised the possibility of one side of the Atlantic Alliance involving the other in a full-scale nuclear exchange for the sake of interests the other side did not regard as vital. One logical inference to be drawn from this was that both needed to have the capability to use nuclear weapons independently to safeguard interests that they unilaterally regarded as vital. But what McNamara was trying to do was to deny the luxury of that logic for the Europeans. He wanted to remove their independent nuclear capability to avoid the possibility of their starting a nuclear war that the USA disapproved of but might nevertheless be drawn into as a member of the Western camp. In the Cuban missile crisis the Europeans had to risk a similar fate as the USA unilaterally decided policy and eventually forced a Soviet climb-down and the withdrawal of the missiles.

It was shortly after this that the Skybolt missile crisis arose. The effectiveness of Britain's nuclear deterrent depended upon Skybolt, and the British regarded the continuation of their independent nuclear deterrent as vital. It was also important that the USA should be seen as a good friend of Britain because of the way that Macmillan had presented his friendship with the USA to the British people as special. Unfortunately, the Skybolt affair placed Britain's deterrent, the special relationship and the life of Macmillan's government all in jeopardy.

By the end of 1962 there were budgetary and technical problems with Skybolt, and McNamara wanted to end the project. Unfortunately this decision leaked to the British before they were formally informed, which did not help things. Also, part of the problem was that British Defence Secretary Peter Thorneycroft and McNamara had what might charitably be called a personality clash. But there was also a failure on the US side to appreciate the sensitivity of the issue. This was partly excused by Kennedy's aide Theodore Sorensen, who later wrote: 'After Cuba, it seemed a small problem. All problems did.'[8] However, it was not just a presentational problem. McNamara saw Skybolt's demise as an excuse for restricting, or indeed ending, Britain's independent deterrent and for persuading her to pool its weapons in a multilateral Western nuclear force under US command.

In Britain the threatened cancellation of Skybolt had serious implications, especially as there was already a troubled domestic political situation caused by economic difficulties, problems with the application to the EEC, a panic Cabinet re-shuffle, and the celebrated Vassal spy case. Under these conditions further setbacks, especially at the hands of Britain's supposedly closest ally, could be fatal for Macmillan's government. If Skybolt were axed then that would mark the end of Britain as a credible nuclear power unless she could persuade the USA to give her Polaris missiles instead. Because of the 1956 agreement, Britain had the submarine technology to house the missiles, and Eisenhower had made a gentleman's agreement to give Britain an option on Polaris, so its acquisition became Macmillan's main objective at his forthcoming meeting with Kennedy at Nassau, scheduled for late December 1962.

The State Department shared McNamara's reasons for not wanting to prolong British nuclear capability, but they were also concerned about the effect that an Anglo-American nuclear deal might have on France, and in turn on Britain's application to the EEC. Much hinged on this because if Britain did not get in then the likelihood of an Atlantic free-trade area receded rapidly. In short, the cards were stacked heavily against Macmillan winning Polaris from the Americans. Why, then, did Kennedy go against his senior advisers and agree to sell Polaris to Britain? First of all, it was already clear that Britain stood little chance of getting into the EEC, and Macmillan took pains to reassure Kennedy that an Anglo-American nuclear deal would not upset the French. At least that is the view he reported that de Gaulle had expressed at their recent meeting at Rambouillet. Second, there was the matter of the survival of Macmillan's government. A State Department briefing paper made it plain that the USA did not want a Labour government to come to power because it would be equivocal about membership of the EEC and it could drift towards a Scandinavian type of neutralism that would undermine the defences of the West.[9] Such developments could also threaten the Holy Loch base and the Fylingdales early-warning station.

These kinds of fears were skilfully played on by Ormsby-Gore and by Macmillan, who pointed out to Kennedy at Nassau that he might precipitate the fall of his, Macmillan's, government if he did not sell Polaris to Britain. Kennedy was moved by the arguments that were made and he did not wish to be instrumental in the downfall of his friend. He was also unhappy with the way the Skybolt saga had unfolded and was mindful of understandings reached between his predecessor and Macmillan. He later commented to Sorensen that 'it might well be concluded that . . . we had an obligation to provide an alternative'.[10] A deal on the sale of Polaris missiles to Britain was thus struck.

The wording of the agreement was equivocal: Britain undertook to commit her nuclear missiles to a multilateral force, but could still use them unilaterally in a supreme national crisis. One might facetiously enquire: in what other situation would a responsible state be likely to want to use nuclear weapons? The Polaris deal perpetuated a nuclear special relationship between Britain and the USA. But over the following years it was clear that its importance to Britain was vastly greater than to the USA. One of Britain's aims since the 1940s and the inception of her independent nuclear programme was to keep a presence in the superpower conference hall. In 1963 that tactic still worked and she played a major role in the Partial Nuclear Test Ban Treaty, but it was the last time that Britain participated at the nuclear summit table. The arsenals of the USSR and the USA now so far outstripped Britain's that in the overall strategic balance her forces became insignificant.

Nevertheless, the special nuclear relationship with the USA continued and still does so at the present (1994). The supply of missiles and the considerable amount of back-up that the USA gives Britain to keep them serviced creates a problem similar to the one posed by the possible use of US nuclear bases in Britain. The situation is not exactly alike, but there are parallels. A unilateral strike by Britain against the Soviet Union with missiles supplied and serviced by the USA would clearly have raised problems in US–Soviet relations, just as a unilateral strike by the USA against the Soviets from bases in Britain would have caused problems in Anglo-Soviet relations. This was the kind of contingency McNamara had sought to obviate, but now, with US missiles supplied to Britain, it became even more of a danger for the USA. The clause in the Nassau Agreement that the missiles could only be used independently by Britain in a crisis of supreme national importance was similar to US undertakings concerning the use of US nuclear bases in Britain in an emergency. Both arrangements came down to reliance on mutual trust. Thus Nassau was important, not just because of the actual nuclear-weapons system involved, but also because it was evidence of the continuing closeness of Anglo-American relations.

Attempts to create a multilateral nuclear force continued for some time. When Labour Prime Minister Harold Wilson visited Washington in December 1964, President Johnson tried to persuade him of its desirability by saying that the 'object was to keep the Germans with us and keep their hand off the trigger'.[11] Wilson, despite the Labour Party's perennial doubts about the wisdom of British nuclear weapons, remained unconvinced. The multilateral force never came into being and over the years Polaris was up-dated and eventually replaced with a new US missile system.

The Skybolt episode is fascinating for what it reveals about Anglo-

American relations and their complexity. It was an unholy row and yet at the end of the day Britain got what it wanted despite much official opposition in Washington. The outcome was largely because of Kennedy's friendship with Macmillan and the legacy inherited from Eisenhower. The trust required for the kind of nuclear relationship that they were perpetuating demonstrated that special the relationship remained, but it was changing. The fact that the USA miscalculated the importance of Skybolt to Britain was indicative of how Britain's defence role had declined in US eyes. There was also evident a certain arrogance of power that the British would have been well advised to take on board in future policy calculations. US arrogance of power was to grow in the next few years, and the attention the USA paid to the UK diminished as it became riveted in the Far East by the Vietnam war.

STERLING, DEFENCE AND BRETTON WOODS 1964–70

Relations with the USA during the Labour government of Harold Wilson were far from being as bad as many had expected. In some ways they were better than the later part of Macmillan's premiership and the brief period of his successor, Alec Douglas Home. Denis Healey was preferred to Thorneycroft as Defence Secretary, and Chancellor of the Exchequer James Callaghan had very good relations with US Treasury Secretary Henry Fowler. Many in the Wilson government were strongly pro-American, but relations were soured by Britain's recurring economic problems and by the war in Vietnam. Henry Brandon, one of the astutest commentators on affairs in Washington, remarked that 'Americans never failed to support sterling in a crisis but relations were not good'.[12] Reading Harold Wilson's memoirs one might find that judgement surprising. However, one should not be misled (as possibly Wilson was) by Johnson's extravagant compliments: on one occasion he compared Wilson with Churchill. Such praises were part of the political coinage in which Johnson had learnt to conduct his affairs in the US Senate. Beneath the surface, although he had respect for Wilson's political skills, there was resentment that Britain did not participate militarily in Vietnam, and irritation over Wilson's attempts at mediation. There were no strong feelings of friendship for the Prime Minister. On 26 February 1965, when Johnson was under threat of a visitation from Wilson, Johnson's close aide Jack Valenti informed him: 'Dean Rusk says there is no escape from seeing the Prime Minister Wilson when he is here in April.'[13]

When Wilson formed the Labour government in October 1964 he inherited an £800 million balance of payments deficit which threatened sterling, Britain's defence programme and ultimately Bretton Woods. The crisis demanded action, and the government responded by imposing a 15% import surcharge, by raising the bank rate 2% and by acquiring, with US help, a $3 billion loan from Western banks. A brief breathing-space was thus created in what was in effect a long-term sterling crisis.

The other immediate concern that had impact on Anglo-American relations at the outset of the Wilson administration was Healey's review of defence policy. A picture began to emerge from a conference at Chequers 20–22 November and from talks that Wilson had with the Americans in Washington 7–8 December. Much of the outcome was dictated by Wilson's determination both to maintain Britain as a major power and to sustain close links with the USA. Not too surprisingly then, contrary to election pledges, Polaris remained – the government argued that the programme was already too far advanced to cancel. Much to US satisfaction, Britain also reaffirmed both her commitment to the BAOR, despite its cost, and to a presence east of Suez. The latter took on more importance in the mid-1960s because of the war in Vietnam. The Americans tried to get Wilson to send a token military force there and were bitterly disappointed when they failed. Some have suggested that they then pressed Britain into a formal arrangement to continue at least their role east of Suez in return for US economic support for sterling. Although it was understood that Americans were willing to help Britain partly because of its military efforts on behalf of the West, claims about a formal agreement linking help for sterling and the continuation of Britain's defence role east of Suez have not been substantiated. James Callaghan, in fact, has specifically denied any knowledge of such an agreement. There is no hard evidence to contradict him, and circumstantial reasoning also places in doubt the suggestion that there was a formal link.[14]

The underlying determinant of so much of British policy was her economic performance, and that gave serious concern to the USA. Johnson realised that speculation against sterling also threatened the dollar and Bretton Woods. In the summer of 1965 he directed Fowler to set up a study group which should give

> urgent and thorough consideration to the special situation of the United Kingdom, which is of major foreign policy concern. Specifically, it should consider what steps the United States could take to arrange for a relief of pressure on sterling, so as to give the United Kingdom the four-or-five year breathing space it needs to get its economy into shape, and thereby sharply reduce the danger of sterling devaluation or exchange controls or British military disengagement East of Suez or on the Rhine.[15]

In April 1965 Wilson made important trips to Paris and Washington: high on the agenda for both were economic and particularly monetary matters. In Paris things went remarkably well, heralding something of a thaw in Anglo-French affairs during which Britain first explored possibilities and then in May 1967 re-applied for EEC membership. However, at the meeting in 1965 there was an ominous note of discord over monetary policy. The French thought that the EEC would be damaged if Britain entered with a weak currency which still had a major reserve role. They also resented the prominence of the dollar and sterling in the IMF and wanted them replaced with gold.[16]

In Washington Wilson and Fowler reaffirmed their commitment to the existing Bretton Woods system and rejected the French idea of an increased role for gold. They both regarded the value of the dollar and sterling as sacrosanct and Fowler promised to help Britain get more support from the IMF for sterling. The meeting added emphasis to an already existing pattern. The Americans, particularly Fowler and William McChesney Martin, Chairman of the Federal Reserve Board, regarded the possibility of a sterling devaluation with almost as much horror as did the British. Over the following eighteen months the USA responded helpfully on every occasion that sterling wobbled. When Britain asked for $1,400 million under the auspices of the IMF's General Agreement to Borrow on 29 April, the US supported her; when Britain needed more funds in September 1965, Fowler helped to arrange a $1 billion aid package from the main Western banks. By July 1966 the US bilaterally had put over $1.7 billion at Britain's disposal; and in September 1966 its SWAP facility (i.e. a temporary swap of currencies at a fixed exchange rate) was increased to $1.35 billion as a result of an American initiative. From outside there appeared to be no wavering of US support for sterling, but there were changes. In June 1965 when Callaghan went to Washington, he was disappointed by US reluctance to commit the dollar to assist sterling in the future. The Americans had identified some restraints and conditions, of which Callaghan was by no means fully aware, which affected their commitment to support sterling.

During the summer of 1965 Fowler concluded that the US should not give the UK further unilateral aid: first, because of its limited effectiveness; second, because of damage involved for America's own balance of payments, which was $1.3 billion in the red that year. The collective view of Fowler, Ball and McNamara was that 'we will not foot the bill without substantial help from others'.[17] Fowler still adamantly believed that it was contrary to US interests to let sterling be devalued, but defence considerations gave others in the Johnson Administration a different perspective. National Security Adviser McGeorge Bundy, in a memorandum for the President in July 1965, after noting Fowler's view, went on to say:

My own interests, and those of Bob McNamara and Dean Rusk are wider. We are concerned with the fact that the British are constantly trying to make narrow bargains on money while they cut back on their wider political and military responsibilities. We want to make very sure that the British get it into their heads that it makes no sense for us to rescue the Pound in a situation in which there is no British flag in Vietnam, and a threatened British thin-out in both east of Suez and in Germany.

What I should like to say [to the British] . . . myself, is that a British Brigade in Vietnam would be worth a billion dollars at the moment of truth for sterling. But I don't want to say it unless you want it said.[18]

Johnson never put things to the British as bluntly as this, but US opinion of Britain was not improved by Healey's defence review, which had begun in 1964 and appeared as a White Paper in February 1966 (a further instalment came in 1967). In it he recognised how defence expenditure exposed Britain's financial Achilles' heel and he thus proposed cut-backs and a ceiling on defence spending of £2 billion at 1964 prices.[19]

The Americans, despite worries about their own balance-of-payments problems and defence spending and their misgivings about the direction in which British defence policy was heading, responded generously in order to try to bridge the gulf between British resources and defence commitments. They committed themselves to buying $325 million worth of British arms and promised to help Britain sell more in the Middle East. Washington set up a credit facility to help with payments (postponed until 1968) for US aircraft. And in the summer of 1965 a 5% R&D payment on Polaris was waived in return for communication and refuelling facilities on Diego Garcia in the Indian Ocean.

These measures were helpful, but insufficient significantly to alleviate British economic problems. With the picture still gloomy, pressure mounted within the Labour Party to adjust Britain's defence posture further both east of Suez and regarding her support of US policy in Vietnam. On 20 June Wilson, who was committed to a continuing presence east of Suez, successfully argued his position before a meeting of the Parliamentary Labour Party, declaring that it could be a recipe for disaster to leave the PRC and the USA eyeball to eyeball in the Far East. The USA could take some comfort from that, but suspicion that Britain might withdraw persisted. Matters were not helped at the end of June when Wilson felt obliged to dissociate his government publicly from the US bombing of North Vietnam, and in July worse was to follow.

The British economy had already been hit by a damaging seamen's strike, and this was now followed by a run on the pound. With help from abroad, and particularly from the USA, sterling's parity was saved, but in the course of the crisis Wilson again turned down a request from Johnson to send British troops to Vietnam. Then on 20 July Wilson announced an austerity package in a bid to strengthen sterling, but it contained some provisions that agitated the Americans. In particular a threat (largely bluff) to make major cuts in the BAOR looked likely to sour things at a meeting between Wilson and Johnson scheduled for July in Washington. The meeting, however, went better than expected: there was even talk of coupling the dollar and sterling. But, beneath the surface, US unease continued to grow. Even Wilson's claim that he was prepared to sacrifice 10% of his public-opinion ratings in order to correct Britain's economic malady through a deflationary package did not impress Fowler, who was worried about the discrimination involved in Britain's policy and her selling of dollars, which adversely affected the US economy.[20]

During the first half of 1967, however, the deflationary measures adopted the previous summer began to have beneficial effects. The balance of payments moved into surplus, the bank rate was reduced in May to 5.5%, its lowest for two years, and confidence in the pound increased. Nevertheless, there was still apprehension in the USA about the weakness of the UK economy and its likely consequences. A solution to Britain's economic problems remained elusive. Her attempt to get into the EEC was running into trouble again with de Gaulle. In November he finally dashed British hopes for the second time because of his dislike of the special relationship, especially as evidenced by co-operation to uphold Bretton Woods and the pre-eminence of the dollar and sterling. A successful application to the EEC might have strengthened the British economy and helped her to carry defence and international monetary responsibilities. Instead, Britain had to struggle on haphazardly with wage restraints and government cut-backs and threats to her defence commitments. All this had a gradual but cumulative effect in Washington on the quality of the relationship Americans perceived of themselves as having with Britain. In May 1966 a composite report from members of the US Embassy in London largely agreed with the statement that the Anglo-American alignment had been the 'most important single fact of international life in the postwar world'. But just over twelve months later Ambassador David Bruce, commenting on Britain's application to join the EEC and looking to the future, wrote: 'The so-called Anglo-American special relationship is now little more than sentimental terminology, although the underground waters of it will flow with a deep current.'[21] Bruce was not entirely right. There was more left of the special relationship than he thought and it was to have more consequence than he

imagined. Among other things he had overlooked was that shared sentiment often determines shared interests and helps set policies, and that was
to be the case several years later; but there was also a kernel of truth in what
Bruce observed. Things were changing and it was difficult to see how the
special relationship would operate in radically different circumstances.

When Wilson met Johnson for talks in Washington in June 1967 there
was renewed speculation that Britain was intending to withdraw from east
of Suez. To Wilson's surprise, the President made no reference to that.
Instead discussions focused on Arab-Israeli tensions and the danger of war
in the Middle East. Preoccupied with the war in Vietnam, Johnson hoped
that Wilson might successfully mediate in the Middle East. His hopes were
vain. The Israelis crushed the Arabs in the June Six-Day War. Its effect on
the British balance of payments was very damaging. The closure of the
Suez Canal cost Britain about £20 million a month and it also had to buy
more expensive Western-hemisphere instead of Middle Eastern oil. These
things along with another dock strike and a less-than-helpful attitude on the
part of the French government caused speculation and a drastic weakening
of the strength of the pound.

A crucial question in the new crisis was: how would the Americans
respond? Those in Washington who had hoped that financial help for
Britain would stave off the need for her to cut back on her overseas
defences were dismayed by the July instalment of Healey's defence review,
which stated: 'our military strength outside of Europe will have little value
if it is achieved at the expense of economic strength at home . . . . We plan
to withdraw altogether from our bases in Singapore and Malaysia in the
middle of the 1970s.'[22] Britain's east-of-Suez defence policy was finally
buried by the devaluation of sterling in November, but the writing was
clearly on the wall before then.

With the US defence and security people disaffected with British policy,
it was left to the Treasury and the Federal Reserve Board to champion the
defence of sterling. Mindful of the growing vulnerability of the US
economy and following the 1965 decision not to give unilateral assistance
to Britain, Under Secretary at the US Treasury, F. L. Demming, set about
trying to muster international support for sterling.

By 10 November things were reaching a final crisis. Callaghan, in
pessimistic mood, told Fowler that he feared that if Britain did not act soon
devaluation itself might not work. He went on to make sure that Fowler had
not overlooked the consequences for the dollar if Britain had to devalue,
and others, in particular the French, followed suit.

Of course I realise that in the end this will depend on the General [de

Gaulle], but it seems to me that the French have stepped up their campaign against sterling with their eye on their main target of bringing down the dollar, and they will do whatever they think will achieve this.[23]

On 13 November the results of multilateral efforts to save sterling were conveyed to the British, but conditions were draconian:

> In our view [Wilson later wrote], this must lead to the most searching intrusions not only into our privacy, but even into our economic independence, not least from the French. And all this would be against the background of unacceptably high unemployment, and the play that would be made in Parliament about sacrificing the unemployed to the bankers.[24]

The decision to devalue on 18 November from $2.8 to $2.4 to the pound was taken on the 15th and conveyed to the full Cabinet on the 16th. During that time, the US Treasury, now thoroughly alarmed at the prospect of devaluation, proposed a last-minute rescue plan, but according to Wilson it was not backed by a cheque book. More interestingly, according to Callaghan, it contained unacceptable conditions regarding British support for the USA in south-east Asia. This looked very much like an attempt to reverse British policy on withdrawal from east of Suez. Britain would have nothing to do with this, and the pound was duly devalued.[25] This marked the end of an era and accelerated developments which were to shape the next.

Both US and British policies were in disarray at the close of the 1960s. Britain had failed to get into Europe, the Commonwealth continued to decline in what little use it had for Britain, and the special relationship was looking less special than it had at any time since the late 1920s. The postwar framework within which the special relationship had gained such prominence was changing. Britain's defence role was becoming increasingly confined to Europe. After devaluation Britain began its withdrawal from east of Suez. The Conservatives slowed things down marginally on their return to power; even so, the USA was soon bemoaning not just the state of affairs in the Far East but also the power vacuum in the Persian Gulf – responsibility for which they laid at the door of the British. Nuclear co-operation continued, but Britain's contribution was marginal except for the bases that she could provide for the USA: her actual weapons capability was insignificant in the international strategic equation. In the economic sphere the basic consensus on the shape of the West's international economy began to break down as the Bretton Woods system itself broke. After sterling devaluation, pressures on the dollar increased. Despite some imaginative innovations by the USA to safeguard the system through a two-tier gold system (operating with an official and a market gold price), and attempts to co-ordinate policies to achieve exchange-rate stability, by 1971 the new Republican President, Richard Nixon, decided that there had to be a New Economic Policy. The USA devalued the dollar, introduced a new phase of protectionism and floated the dollar in 1973. Bretton Woods was finished.

Thus much of the economic and defence framework, within which fruitful Anglo-American co-operation had taken place in the twenty-five years since the end of the Second World War, disappeared. The USA also turned more to the Far East and away from Europe (and thus Britain as well), because of the war in Vietnam, the growing economic importance of Japan, and increasing irritation with her European allies. The USA resented European criticisms of her leadership, and their unwillingness either to make constructive policy proposals or to shoulder a fair share of the cost of their own defence. Not surprisingly, US Senator Mike Mansfield's regular proposals for US troop withdrawals from Europe curried favour in several quarters in the USA and, even though they were unsuccessful they worried those in Europe, especially in Britain, who wanted to maintain strong trans-Atlantic ties. Britain's declining economy and her ever-contracting defence role made changes and a devaluing of the importance of the special relationship inevitable, but it did not follow just because its importance was devalued that its quality would necessarily be also. If there was a willingness to adjust the policies and manner of Anglo-American co-operation to fit the new circumstances, then there was no reason why the special relationship should not continue, albeit at a less exalted level in the overall affairs of the world. Richard Nixon, the new American President, was an Anglophile and, despite Vietnam and preoccupation with the Far East, looked to perpetuate the trans-Atlantic friendship. In January 1969, shortly after coming to power, he wrote to Prime Minister Wilson:

> For many decades one of the great sources of strength in the cause of freedom has been the close relationship between Prime Ministers of the United Kingdom and Presidents of the United States. This is as it should be, for it but reflects the depth of feeling and kinship existing between our two nations.
>
> I intend, in the years ahead, to see that this tradition is upheld and nourished.[26]

Perhaps if Wilson had remained in power a personal element in the relationship might have done something to help the upholding and nourishing that Nixon spoke of, but that was not to be. In 1970 Edward Heath took over as Prime Minister after a surprise Conservative victory in the General Election.

Now, combined with the disappearance of the structure within which the special relationship had flourished in the postwar period, there were to be personality problems at the top of the political ladder between Britain and the USA. Heath would not regard Anglo-American relations as special in the way his predecessors had done or, indeed, in the way that Nixon desired. He also turned decisively to Europe, which added a new structural perspective to the systemic landscape in which Anglo-American relations operated.

ON LOSING ONE'S WAY 1970–4

The Anglo-American relationship in the 1960s and 1970s underwent change not only because of its own internal dynamics, but also because of a broader-based transition that afflicted the Western world as a whole as it moved away from the postwar Keynesian consensus toward a more market-orientated economic and social experience.

Rapid growth in the 1960s, and high government spending for domestic reform and overseas defence, especially in Vietnam, along with a balance of payments deficit, led to strains in the US and then in the international economy, culminating in the abandonment of Bretton Woods. Among other reasons for this was the fact that the Kennedy and Johnson administrations ignored Keynesian strictures about reining in expenditure at times of high levels of economic activity. Inflation built up and was exacerbated by the rise in energy prices because of the 1967 and 1973 Middle East conflicts and the OPEC (Organisation of Petroleum Exporting Countries) cartel. These problems combined with inflexibilities in Western economies to produce stagflation (low or falling production and high inflation) which proved immune to Keynesian remedies. The net result was that the world faced an insecure and volatile economic future. The postwar framework was crumbling and with it the postwar consensus.

The crumbling took quite a while, but from it there emerged an alternative put forward by neo-conservatives, who were anything but conservative in economic policy. They called for radical change involving supply-side economics, monetarism and deregulation. It amounted to more than an economic doctrine. It was also a backlash against the sexually promiscuous 1960s in Britain, the counterculture in the USA, Johnson's Great Society reform programme, and Wilson's and later Callaghan's versions of democratic socialism. High taxation, high levels of regulation and of government intervention in the economy, and expensive welfare policies – all Keynesian shibboleths which had been seen by many as the measure of a civilised society in the postwar period – were gradually cast aside or cut back. This development was accompanied by the decline of the atmosphere of tolerance. The ideologues of the right asserted the inextricable link between a free economy and a free people, but they were not noticeably as libertarian in their attitudes towards cultural, educational, moral and social matters as they were on economic questions. The ushering-in of the new economic dispensation, which was largely defined by people like Milton Friedman and others of the so-called Chicago School, was not easy or quick, but it gathered momentum from the end of the 1960s and came into its own twenty years later. By 1980 the initiative in Britain and the USA was held by the New Right. The losing of the way appeared to have ended: the way ahead branched to the right.

In addition to these great changes there were momentous happenings in other aspects of national and international affairs. Britain joined the EEC. The USA opened relations with the PRC and went on to formal recognition during President Jimmy Carter's term of office. The Vietnam war reached its tragic climax in 1973 but then continued to trouble America for several years after that, as also did the debilitating Watergate affair. Japan and West Germany emerged as economic giants. In the Middle East terrorism took its toll, and Moslem fundamentalism began to make its mark. Concerns grew about the environment and sustainable economic development. The Soviets enjoyed *détente* with the USA in the early 1970s, but then fell back into their old ways at the end of the decade. It was against this background of upheaval and change that the special relationship lost its way in the early 1970s, but it rallied somewhat in the latter part of the decade and began to adjust to new circumstances.

The years 1970–4 were rather barren for Anglo-American relations. The Heath government slowed down the east of Suez withdrawal and pledged itself to maintain some military presence in the Far East in co-operation with Australia and New Zealand, which gave Americans some satisfaction, until they realised that the changes to Labour policy were largely cosmetic. Nuclear co-operation was maintained, though with no significant new developments. The overriding characteristic of the period was that the two countries were distracted away from each other by policy commitments elsewhere, and personal rapport did not materialise to ameliorate the consequences of that. The USA desperately sought to end involvement in Vietnam and, after the 1972 re-election of Nixon, became engulfed in the Watergate scandal. It involved illegal activities and their cover-up by the President and some of his senior aides, and raised questions about the imperious use of executive power and constitutional integrity. In Britain, economic difficulties occupied much government time, and the main foreign policy issue was Heath's determination to take Britain into Europe.

Hopes that the things the two leaders had in common might compensate for lack of engagement in policy matters were disappointed. Both were conservatives of the moderate school, had returned from defeat at the polls to hold the highest political office in their respective countries, and were self-made men, but they were also awkward in personal relations and despite Nixon's hopes and desires for close links with Heath, the latter's determination to get into Europe, and his preference for Europe over the USA, persuaded him to keep Nixon at arm's length.

Heath's vision of the future did not include an Anglo-American special relationship. It was now an American President's turn to lament treatment – now as an ally in a special and unique category, now as just another country. Heath looked to an Atlantic partnership of equals between the USA and the EC. This view logically entailed that Britain should be treated as just another European power. This was a view that had held currency on and off in Washington since the time of the Marshall Plan, but Nixon and his National Security Adviser, Henry Kissinger, a follower of the European tradition of diplomacy, did not favour downgrading the special relationship.

> My own personal view [he told Nixon] . . . is that we do not suffer in the world from such an excess of friends that we should discourage those who feel that they have a special friendship for us. I would think that the answer to the special relationship of Britain would be to raise other countries to the same status, rather than to discourage Britain into a less warm relationship with the United States.[27]

The logic of all relationships being special is that none is, nevertheless, Nixon and Kissinger hoped to enjoy close relations with the Heath government. By contrast Heath, determined to be a good European, kept his distance – both metaphorically and geographically. His first official meeting with Nixon was in December 1970, some six months after coming to office, which was an unusually long time compared with normal practice. When they did meet it 'was a new experience for American leaders: a British Prime Minister who based his policy towards the United States not on sentimental attachments but on a cool calculation of interest'.[28] On the question of the EEC, Heath, during a brief informal meeting with Nixon at Chequers in the autumn of 1970, rejected the idea of discreet US assistance for Britain's third application, and in Washington in December he made it clear that:

> he could not risk making any concessions to us [i.e. Nixon and Kissinger] in advance; he wished neither to negotiate Common Market issues bilaterally with us nor appear as – or, for that matter, to be – America's Trojan Horse in Europe.[29]

This made sense as the Americans wanted Britain's application to succeed: they did not want a re-run of the previous failures. However, things were now different, especially as de Gaulle had left office and there was clearly no equivocation in Heath's commitment to Europe. There was thus more scope for some Anglo-American co-operation on Europe, but Heath would have nothing to do with that. His attitude gradually distanced Britain from the USA. There was also disarray in his personal relations with Nixon. In interviews that Henry Brandon had with Nixon and Kissinger in 1972, Nixon claimed that he had invited Heath to his home in San Clemente, but later the White House denied this and Heath claimed that the invitation had never been tendered. Kissinger tried to gloss over the matter by saying that this had taken place the year before and Nixon had perhaps forgotten things. Whatever the case, Heath did not visit San Clemente. And Nixon confessed: 'I don't know him well.'[30]

By 1973 US relations with Western Europe in general were poor. In July 1969 Nixon had announced the 'Nixon Doctrine' on the island of Guam in the Pacific. As he later reported to Congress, its theme was, that while the USA would help allies, it would not 'conceive *all* the plans, design *all* the programs, execute *all* the decisions and undertake *all* the defense of the free nations of the world'.[31] The idea was to have partnership and a sharing of the burden, but things were not turning out that way, so Nixon and Kissinger tried to improve relations with, and get more co-operation from, Europe by declaring 1973 'The Year of Europe'. Again things did not go quite as planned. The Europeans thought the idea patronising and reacted coolly to the American overture. In fact there was a real gulf between Europe and the USA, and its seriousness was amply exposed by the Arab–Israeli Yom Kippur war. When the war erupted in 1973 Europe failed to co-operate with the USA. The most serious difference arose over help for the Israelis. At one point they were in dire straits, and the USA airlifted supplies to help them out. They requested the use of airbases in European NATO countries but, except by Portugal, were denied. Heath refused access to British bases on Cyprus which were ideally situated strategically for American needs. Some in Britain rather malevolently saw this as belated revenge for Suez. Kissinger and Nixon were enraged by their European allies, and Britain in particular. Anglo-American relations were in a very serious state during Nixon's final months and the early period of his successor, Gerald Ford. Many of the problems were of a temporary nature, but they were symptomatic of the loss of direction in Anglo-American relations. On the other hand, British Europeanists saw this period as characterised not by a loss of way but by the finding of a new one. They had successfully taken Britain into the EEC in 1973. Heath had achieved his main objective, but it posed more difficulties for the special relationship, and, despite all the changes it had undergone between 1967 and 1974, there was still no denying its importance to Britain and to a lesser extent to the USA.

PICKING UP THE PIECES 1974–9

In addition to problems over policies, and difficult relations between British and US political leaders, there had also been a serious lapse in general communications between the two countries during the Heath period. After Labour's victory in the 1974 General Election, Prime Minister Harold Wilson's Foreign Secretary, James Callaghan, took immediate steps to remedy this: he instructed the Foreign Office to improve relations with the USA.[32] After all the doubts about socialism which periodically arose in US administrations, it is rather amusing that fences were mended by Labour leaders in 1974. Just how successful they were is illustrated in a US briefing paper prepared for Harold Wilson's visit to Washington in January 1975. 'With the advent of the Wilson Administration relations between our two governments have been particularly warm and cordial. This is in large part to do with Wilson's determination to ease the strain and tension which developed between us during the latter months of the term of his predecessor.'[33]

Wilson and Callaghan, who succeeded to the premiership in 1976 after Wilson's resignation, had friendly relations with their US counterparts. Callaghan developed a particularly warm and intimate friendship with Gerald Ford despite their different political convictions. During the period 1974–9 the two countries had good relations regarding dealings with the Soviets, trying to solve the problem of the illegal Smith regime in Rhodesia after its unilateral declaration of independence and its attempt to maintain white minority rule, and in helping Portugal's transition to democracy. In the latter, Secretary of State Kissinger was supportive of Callaghan, who took the policy lead. The Turkish invasion of Cyprus caused considerable friction as Kissinger tended to see things from a NATO perspective and worried about the danger of two of its members, Greece and Turkey, going to war over their respective expatriate groups in Cyprus, whereas Callaghan was more concerned that a member of the Commonwealth had been invaded.[34] But the most telling episodes in these years were in the economic sphere.

Despite improved relations with Britain, there was an episode in October 1975 that revealed the uncomplimentary way Americans increasingly regarded her. In April 1975, Alan Greenspan, Chairman of the Council of Economic Advisers, passed an article to President Ford from the *Economist* which painted a frightening picture of UK government overspending and poor economic performance. His comment was that this was a model of what the USA must not do, and Ford seems to have taken the comments to heart. In October that same year, addressing the annual conference of US Mayors, Ford was reported by the *New York Times* as having said that a 'horrible example of a government that spends itself sick was Britain's with its Labor [sic] Government and its welfare state'. UK Ambassador Ramsbotham was quick to protest and seek assurance that Ford had said no such thing. Matters were considered so sensitive that National Security Adviser Brent Scowcroft undertook to reply. He lamely told Ramsbotham that they had no script of the President's speech so could not confirm or deny the report, but he assured him that the President's feelings towards Britain had not changed.[35]

Another illustration of the way Britain's relations with the USA were changing can be made with reference to a matter of more substance: the sterling crisis of 1976 and the infamous letter of intent that the British government had to send to the IMF. In the summer of 1976 sterling was once again in trouble. Ideally, Callaghan wanted a long-term rescue operation for sterling – an idea that he had toyed with for some time – that would provide enough funds to cope with speculation arising from the sale of overseas-held sterling. The only way to achieve this was with US help. At the beginning of June, crisis point was reached, but it looked as if the USA was going to mount a salvage operation. The Americans helped to arrange with central banks and the Bank of International Settlements a standby credit of $5.3 billion, of which the USA put up $2 billion. However, on 5 June Edwin Yeo, Under Secretary for Monetary Affairs in the US Treasury, explained to Callaghan and his Chancellor of the Exchequer, Denis Healey, that there was a time limit of six months on the credit, after which it would have to be repaid in full. Normally there were no such strings attached, but neither William Simon, the flamboyant right-wing US Treasury Secretary, nor Arthur Burns of the Federal Reserve Bank had much faith in the economic policies of the Labour government. They had no intention of cushioning the British economy so that it could avoid taking the harsh road Simon and Burns felt that the market dictated.[36]

The standby arrangement provided only the briefest of respites. Soon the only avenue left for Britain was the IMF, which, it was widely known, would require that strict conditions be met in return for help. Speaking of the deflationary measures that Britain had to adopt in order to receive IMF aid, Callaghan some years later rather sadly noted that William Simon was not nearly as helpful as Henry Fowler had been a decade earlier.[37] The fact was that there was now little inducement for the Americans to be helpful. Britain no longer had troops east of Suez and there was no Bretton Woods system to defend.

The USA refused to take any further steps to help until the conditions of the IMF assistance had been finalised. In return for help Healey had to send a letter of intent to the IMF committing Britain's public-sector borrowing right to £8.7 billion for 1977/8, and £8.6 billion for 1978/9. In effect, this dictated the amount of deflation the government had to impose. Callaghan claims that the end result was little different from what he and Healey had independently worked out as necessary before the IMF discussions took place, but others disagree about that. There is also debate as to just how limiting of economic growth the package was, but there is little debate about how symbolically damaging it was to Britain's prestige and to the standing of the Labour Party in Britain. Its economic policy was in difficulties prior to the sterling crisis: in particular, the 'Social Contract', under which the unions agreed to wage restraint in return for high welfare spending was already in jeopardy, but the IMF crisis put the final nail in the coffin of that casualty of the country's ongoing poor economic performance.[38]

An overall assessment of the state of affairs between Britain and the USA during the Labour administrations of Wilson and Callaghan is not easy, and the unavailability of documentary sources does not help matters. Wilson and Callaghan both strove to improve relations and return to a special relationship. Policy became distinctly less pro-European and there was discernible equivocation about membership of the EEC made manifest because of splits within the Labour Party and because of the referendum Wilson called in 1975 to determine whether or not Britain should remain within the Community. As Europe declined in importance, the USA took on its old mantle of being Britain's special ally. Relations between Callaghan, Ford and Carter were good, and while that did not affect matters in Britain's favour in the 1976 IMF crisis, on other occasions the importance of friendship for Britain did have effect: this can be seen in both the economic and the atomic spheres.

In 1976–7 there was a series of extremely difficult negotiations to try and replace the 1946 Bermuda Air Service Agreement, which governed the operation of commercial scheduled air services between Britain and the USA. The British, as provided for under the 1946 agreement, denounced it with the required twelve months' notice on the grounds that the USA was gaining unfair benefit. It was replaced in the end by the Bermuda 2 Agreement, which was arguably the most restrictive bilateral the USA ever agreed to with an important civil-aviation partner. This fact is all the more remarkable as the USA was in the throws of deregulating its domestic market and launching a drive for more liberal air-service agreements world-wide. Part of the reason why the British were so successful in getting what they wanted was that Carter liaised with the US negotiators and ensured that an agreement was reached that would not embarrass Callaghan politically. Also the head of the US delegation, Alan Boyd, said some years later that if he had not been an Anglophile there would have been no Bermuda 2.[39]

In the nuclear field the Heath and the subsequent Labour administrations continued to work closely with the Americans. The British undertook a secret £1 billion programme called Chevaline to improve the warheads on their Polaris missiles and in 1974 started a new phase of test explosions at the US underground site in Nevada. However, by 1979 Callaghan was having doubts about the wisdom of putting new wine into old bottles: the warheads might be new but Polaris submarines were now ageing. In January, at the Guadeloupe Summit, he asked Carter if the USA would be prepared to sell Britain the new Trident system on similar terms to Polaris, and Carter responded that in principle he would have no objection to that and was sure an arrangement suited to the British pocket could be worked out. The nuclear special relationship was about to get a new lease of life.[40]

So the currents of the Anglo-American special relationship continued to run deep and have impact. Callaghan got on well with Carter. They spoke informally to each other on the telephone about various matters of concern fairly frequently and Callaghan helped mediate between the German leader Helmut Schmidt and Carter when their relations deteriorated badly. The two leaders co-operated in economic summits that grappled with the international economy, growth and the environment. Carter's National Security adviser, Brzezinski, confirms in his memoirs how Callaghan endeared himself to Carter and that they had close relations. Nevertheless, Callaghan and Wilson had not been able to create an ostensible special relationship of the kind that had prevailed, with only brief interruptions, from the Second World War until the early 1970s. Britain's main preoccupation now was her domestic affairs: poor economic performance, industrial unrest and, after the 1978–9 'winter of discontent', when the dead lay unburied and rubbish uncollected, there arose the question of Britain's governability. Her standing in the world sank, not just in the eyes of America but just about everywhere. Britain no longer played an important defence or economic role in the world, was troubled domestically, had little prestige and lacked leadership. In this situation irritants in Anglo-American affairs such as indiscreet remarks by President Ford and, more notably, the troubles in Northern Ireland took on a significance that would have been dwarfed in earlier decades by the importance of Anglo-American co-operation. Now the case was different, and periodically there were outbursts on both sides of the Atlantic about British policy and US reaction to it. For her part the USA was also having to come to terms with a less exalted status in the world. Carter was not a successful President. In foreign affairs America was still nursing its wounds after Vietnam and was deeply troubled by the shockwaves of Watergate and by domestic problems arising from rising energy prices, poverty, crime and the challenge from the more competitive economies of Japan and Germany. America was having to adjust to new circumstances just as Britain had to and for a while the special relationship was a casualty of these changes.

However, in 1979 and 1980 three things happened that were to bring the two countries closer. First of all world tensions increased and the Cold War heated up. The Shah, America's main ally in the Middle East, fell from power, and Iran became a major problem for the USA. The taking of hostages from the Embassy in Teheran by Moslem fundamentalists was a final humiliation for Carter. America appeared impotent to act and in this new world such a country could well do with staunch allies. At the same time the Soviets invaded Afghanistan, and East–West tensions were fully renewed. The US Senate lost what little inclination it had to pass the much-debated SALT 2 (Strategic Arms Limitation Talks 2) agreement, and a new arms race gathered pace. Second, Margaret Thatcher came to power at the head of a Conservative government in Britain and swiftly moved to establish good relations with Carter and the USA. In December 1979 she had a most successful trip to Washington, and she soon clinched a deal on the sale of Trident that ensured that Callaghan's hopes for continuing the nuclear special relationship would be realised. The final act in the preparation for the renewal of the special relationship came in November 1980, when Republican Ronald Reagan won the Presidency. At the time of Margaret Thatcher's victory the previous year Reagan had said: 'I couldn't be happier than I am over England's new Prime Minister.'[41] One suspects that Margaret Thatcher's sentiments were the same about America's new President in November 1980.

At the start of the 1980s there was a renewal of the Cold War. There were right-wing ideologues in power in both Downing Street and the White House and they felt that they had to respond to the Soviet challenge, strengthen the defences of the West and do some reasserting with regard to the status and fortunes of their respective countries. Somewhat to the surprise of many, they were also to reinvigorate the special relationship and reassert its importance. It had never died away entirely as we have seen, but it was now to have a period of remarkable salience after the erosion of its significance in world and Anglo-American affairs in the late 1960s and the 1970s. It not only became more special but, more remarkably, it counted for more in the affairs of the world, at least for a short period.

7 Of interests and sentiment 1980–95, and beyond

Interests can generate warm sentiments.
Sentiments often lead to strong interests.

In the relationship between Thatcher and Reagan there has been a tendency to see a predominance of sentiment and an absence of policy substance, because of both the asymmetry in power between Britain and the USA and the shrinkage of shared national interests. There is some truth in this, but it has been overdone.[1]

Relations between the USA and Britain have declined in importance over the years, particularly during the transition period of the 1960s and 1970s, when much of the postwar structure within which their co-operation flourished changed or disappeared. The Bretton Woods system collapsed. The drive to a more liberal world economy slowed down. The USA looked more to its own domestic affairs and to the Pacific region. Britain entered Europe and contracted her defence role. Simultaneously, she continued to decline as a world power, and that had an effect that has been generally overlooked. It has often been emphasised that Britain's decline reduced her importance as an ally to the USA, but it also reduced the importance of the USA to Britain. At the end of the 1960s the US National Security Council (NSC) perceptively noted: 'The special relationship the UK has with us is less important to them now because the British have less interest in maintaining a world role. . . . Close bilateral relations with the British, however, will certainly continue.'[2] In a rather unexpected way, Britain's decline in power and the shedding of her international responsibilities gave her more freedom of action in some respects, including in her relations with the USA. All these developments reduced the importance of Anglo-American relations in one way or another. The questions to be addressed regarding the last two decades of the century are: have such changes removed substantial common interests to an extent that the scope for bilateral co-operation is diminished to insignificance, and does the reduction in importance and scope of the relationship necessarily involve the death of its special characteristic?

In answering those questions, it would be a mistake to juxtapose interests and sentiment in such a way that they are regarded as separate and distinct. What comes to be seen as an interest is often moulded by common sentiment, and the existence of friendly sentiments often creates common interests. An important reason why the special relationship has flourished in the twentieth century has been the mutually supportive strength of shared interests and sentiments – sentiments covering a wide range of feelings from friendship to political and moral convictions. In such a climate, ties that bind can take on a life of their own. Writing two decades ago at a time when Anglo-American relations were not good, and from a personal viewpoint that was sceptical about the overall quality of the special relationship ('It meant something quite different to the British for whom it represented a central element of their foreign policy, and for the Americans, for whom it was much less important'),[3] Joseph Frankel wrote:

> The most effective and important layer was the official one, the habit of the military, intelligence, and civilian personnel, not exclusively of the highest rank, of engaging in a constant interchange of information and views on all issues of common interest, with the normal barriers of secrecy, both about security and technology, being, on the whole, fairly drastically reduced.[4]

This comment seems to capture something more special than it was perhaps intended to convey. It encapsulates a type of culture of co-operation based upon a long experience of shared interests and friendly sentiments that have produced what could be termed as good, or ideal, practice between allies. Among other consequences some writers have noted that a tendency has developed for British and American policy-makers to see world problems in similar ways and within similar frameworks of analysis. Good habits of co-operation and the absence of barriers to co-operation must play important roles in any relationship to warrant the accolade of 'special'. This does not rule out the possibility of clashing interests and communications breaking down, as in the Suez and Skybolt affairs, or differences intruding upon normally good relations to disrupt things in less spectacular ways. But, if the general pattern of easy co-operation remains possible and normally in place, and is evident, especially in times of crisis, then there are good grounds for the use of the term 'special relationship'.

REAGAN AND THATCHER 1981-9

Four things have repeatedly worked together to create good habits of Anglo-American co-operation: friendship at the highest political level; a desire to promote a liberal capitalist economic system; shared political values concerning the worth of the individual, free elections and civil rights protected by law (even if at specific times the political learning curve had not progressed beyond votes for adult males only or for adult whites only); and a common perception of an external threat.

When Reagan came to power in 1981 all these four features were soon in evidence: friendship between the President and Mrs Thatcher – there were a record fifteen Anglo-American summits during Reagan's two terms as president; the dominance of a muscular form of capitalism in both countries; clarion calls from Downing Street and the White House to rally round the value of individual freedom and for release from government controls; and a renewal of the Cold War.

Relations with the Soviets began to deteriorate in the mid-1970s as they deployed a new generation of nuclear weapons in Europe: the SS-20 missile. President Carter's initial response was to propose deploying a neutron bomb that would kill people but leave buildings intact. European dislike of this idea resulted in a reconsideration and the decision to deploy Pershing 2 and Cruise missiles instead. In 1979 NATO decided on a two-track policy, or carrot-and-stick approach: the threat of deploying new US missiles unless the Soviets withdrew the SS-20s (the so-called zero option, i.e. no new system deployed on either side), and later, after US deployment had to go ahead, negotiations with the Soviets to try to get mutual reductions in nuclear-arms levels, but things did not go as smoothly as might have been hoped.

The invasion of Afghanistan by the Soviets in 1979 forced the West to make a strong response. The US defence budget rose dramatically and in January 1980, in his State of the Union Address, the President issued the Carter Doctrine as America's way of dealing with the instability caused by events in Iran and the Soviet invasion of Afghanistan: 'An attempt by an outside force to gain control of the Persian Gulf region [would] be repelled by any means necessary, including military force.'[5] With a hard line adopted by both sides, a severe deterioration in East–West relations was inevitable, and talks about nuclear arms reduction looked like having little chance of immediate success. At the same time, the prospect of more nuclear weapons being deployed in Europe by the USA prompted a renewal of fears of nuclear annihilation among west Europeans and a revival of the Campaign for Nuclear Disarmament. In 1980-1 there were large and widespread demonstrations against the deployment of Pershing 2 and Cruise missiles.

It was in this context that Reagan and Thatcher considered the security of their respective countries and the need for both a renewal of the defences of the West and a concerted effort to deal with the new bout of Soviet aggressiveness. Thatcher was convinced of the need for a strong response to be taken towards the Soviets and believed that only the USA had the resources and the will to do that effectively. Reagan was determined to reassert US leadership and counter the threat from the Soviets and was keen to have staunch allied support: the kind Mrs Thatcher was willing to give. Visible co-operation soon flowed.

There were four factors that determined Mrs Thatcher's attitude towards the USA in the sphere of defence. The first was her inclination to be well disposed towards the USA, strengthened by her personal friendship with Reagan and a wish for close co-operation. The second was her reassertion of Britain's importance in world affairs. The third was her conviction that only the USA could maintain the West's security. And the fourth was a fear that vestiges of isolationism, and exasperation with both Western Europe's criticisms of US leadership and refusal to shoulder its fair share (in America's judgement) of the costs of the defence of the West, would result in a US withdrawal from Europe. The net result of all this was a very friendly disposition towards the USA and its prosecution of the Cold War, but not at the expense of what were perceived to be British interests. Thus, while there was British support for US policies in general, there was nothing automatic about it and differences did arise. This has led some to assert that there was more rhetoric than substance to Anglo-American co-operation in the 1980s, but the kinds of differences experienced in the Reagan–Thatcher years were remarkably similar to those that afflicted the relationship during periods more readily recognised as having been special in substance as well as appearance. Differences over strategic export controls, economic embargoes, negotiations with the Soviets, the possible use of weapons systems, friction over economic policies, all sound remarkably familiar to anyone who has studied Anglo-American relations in the 1940s and 1950s.

Mrs Thatcher, in stark contrast to her Conservative predecessor Heath, lost no time in visiting the new President of the USA. In February 1981 she travelled to Washington and began the intimate and mutually supportive relationship with President Reagan which was to be a significant factor in Anglo-American and world affairs for the next eight years. Defence and the unstable world situation were prominent on the agenda, and Mrs Thatcher gave strong support and pledged a British contribution to the US proposal for a rapid deployment force, designed to cope with sudden and aggressive moves by the Soviets or their sponsored agents. Although Britain's contribution would be small, Thatcher's move was an important gesture of 'symbolic support and involvement in out-of-(NATO)-area operations' for the USA: an act of solidarity with a close ally.[6]

Several months later Reagan acted in an equally supportive way towards Britain on the matter of nuclear missiles. The USA had developed an updated and more potent version of Trident, and the President made it available for the British to buy if they so wished. Thatcher seized on the opportunity and in an exchange of letters in March 1982 the conditions on which the Trident 2 (D-5) missile system would be supplied to Britain were set out. Both Reagan and Defence Secretary Caspar Weinberger expressed their belief in the importance of maintaining Britain's independent deterrent, and British Defence Secretary John Nott expressed his government's pleasure with the agreement and with the evidence that it provided of the continuing, close relationship between the USA and Britain. It was quite a remarkable deal. For a mere $116 million contribution toward the R&D costs, an undertaking to man Rapier air-defence systems round US bases in the UK, and a vague commitment to 'employ additional savings represented by the remainder of the United States waiver to reinforce its efforts to upgrade its conventional forces', the British got a deterrent that would last well into the next millennium at an off-the-shelf price.[7]

Nuclear co-operation was complemented by the continuation of intelligence, special forces, conventional defence and Cold War diplomatic collaboration. Revelations in the 1980s about 'policing assistance' and help from British special forces for the US war in Vietnam were indications of the political risks British governments had been prepared to shoulder for the sake of their American friends in the past. Under Thatcher, actions, known to the public, were taken even when the government was aware that they would be unpopular. Intelligence co-operation continued and the discovery that the US system was no more immune to penetration than Britain's brought about a somewhat more tolerant attitude in Washington to British intelligence. The importance of Britain to the USA was demonstrated by a former Director of the US National Security Agency when he described the Menwith Hill Station as 'the most important station for our national security in the world'.[8] And faith in Britain's reliability, after grave doubts about its stability and probity in the 1970s, was reaffirmed with the decision to relocate US European war headquarters from Germany to High Wycombe. Mrs Thatcher was supportive of the USA in its deployment of Cruise missiles, the first of which arrived at Greenham Common in 1983 amidst an outcry by disarmers, who then proceeded to set up a women's protest peace camp outside the base. Greenham Common was just one of over 130 bases and facilities that the USA had in Britain. The British supported the US policy of aid to rebel forces in Afghanistan and also followed the US lead in protesting about martial law being imposed in Poland in December 1981 in an attempt to crush the Solidarity reform movement. And all this was accompanied by rhetoric which paraded close ties between Britain and the USA and condemned the Soviet communists.

While there was little daylight between the British and US governments' general positions regarding the Soviets (there were, however, some differences which will be discussed later), the crisis that arose between Britain and Argentina over the latter's invasion of the Falkland Islands in 1982 posed more of a problem.

Britain and Argentina had been in dispute over which of them had sovereign rights to the remote and sparsely populated Falkland Islands for many years. Prior to the outbreak of war, tension over the islands had eased during a period of negotiation about their future. There was hope for an arrangement that would safeguard the life-style of the British people on the islands, while eventually giving sovereignty to Argentina. Two factors disrupted this optimistic scenario. The first was the unpredictable nature of the military dictatorship of General Galtieri. The second was a miscalculation by the British of the effect of withdrawing *HMS Endurance* from the South Atlantic: Galtieri read this as evidence that the British would not be prepared to take military action in the face of a *fait accompli* military occupation of the islands by Argentina. Galtieri was wrong. The Thatcher government could not let the attack on British territory go unanswered. They asserted that it was a matter of principle and, amidst an outbreak of patriotism that surprised most of the world and seemed an anomalous anachronism to many, set about sending a task-force to the South Atlantic to retake the islands by force if necessary. The logistics of conducting a campaign over the enormous distance involved were extremely difficult and seriously jeopardised the chances of success. Britain needed all the help that she could get from the USA to wage her military campaign.

Whether or not to give help posed problems within the Reagan administration. Reagan's policy in the Western hemisphere had abandoned Carter's attempt to press unsavoury right-wing dictatorships into better human-rights conduct by manipulating US aid. Reagan reverted to a more traditional policy of blanket support for any anti-communist regime: notable among them was Galtieri's Argentina. Justification of this policy was forthcoming from Jeane Kirkpatrick, the US Ambassador to the UN. She argued that right-wing regimes were corrigible, preferable to communist dictatorships, and valuable to the USA in the fight against the spread of the ultimate evil – communism. Argentina was thus supported by her and others in Washington. If the USA was to help Britain, that would alienate an important Western hemisphere ally and possibly offend other Latin American allies as well. It was this kind of consideration that caused Reagan to hesitate in giving all-out and public support to Britain. So, at first, the US reaction was to try to mediate between the two sides through the shuttle diplomacy of Secretary of State Alexander Haig.

Haig's attempts at reconciliation were not always appreciated in London. The Secretary of State's 'haigravation' of language did not endear him to upper-class *aficionados* of English in the FO: on one occasion he criticised Congressmen who were making economies and cutting back US capabilities overseas for 'castrating our eyes and ears around the globe', which, at one's most charitable, one could describe as the use of a mixed metaphor. While, for his part, Haig was less than happy with Foreign Secretary Lord Carrington, and was reported to have called him a 'duplitious bastard' on one occasion. Caspar Weinberger, Haig's strongly pro-British colleague at the US Defence Department, later recorded rather contemptuously in his memoirs that Haig, in one of his 'more convoluted sentences' said: 'The United States has not acceded to requests that would go beyond the scope of customary patterns of cooperation based on bilateral agreements.' Weinberger went on to comment: 'That verbal mess was correctly translated by the British to mean that Secretary Haig was trying to keep the United States neutral in a war between an aggressor and America's closest friend, whose territory had just been invaded.'[9]

This is rather an uncharitable slant on what Haig tried to do. He had to maintain a public front of impartiality if he was to have any chance of success in his search for a peaceful solution to the crisis. But, in the end, Haig's work was in vain. Even before that became obvious, the USA was giving discreet help to the British. Weinberger had been very receptive to British requests for help right from the start and ensured that any calls for assistance would be answered promptly and effectively. That belies the suggestions made by some that the question as to whether the USA would help Britain hung in the balance. Further evidence against such a claim is given by Weinberger: 'He [Reagan] was willing to allow Haig's attempts at negotiations, but I never had any doubt that the President's heart was with Britain.'[10] Once the shooting began at the end of April, Reagan condemned the Argentinians as aggressors and pledged open support for Britain.

The support was very important, if not vital, to the British military campaign. Sidewinder air-to-air missiles, aviation fuel, equipment and supplies all flowed freely from the US Defence and Navy Departments. The

US facilities on Ascension Island were made available to the British as a staging-post on their long trek to the South Atlantic and, perhaps most important of all matters of substance from the Americans, they supplied intelligence about Argentine military plans and movements. It took six weeks, over 250 British lives and a brilliantly executed campaign to recapture the islands. The prestige of Mrs Thatcher and of Britain in general rose internationally, and nowhere more so than in the USA, where the overwhelming majority of people rejoiced at the British victory.

The USA, after appearing hesitant because of the likes of Kirkpatrick, and because of the peace-keeping efforts of Haig, had strongly supported Britain, not just in the end but also surreptitiously from the beginning. The US government had both the moral sensitivity to distinguish between the merits of British democracy and Argentinian military dictatorship, and the rational capability to perceive the strength of interests it still had in maintaining good relations with what Weinberger openly referred to as the closest friend of the USA: a sentiment Reagan instantiated personally in his relationship with Mrs Thatcher. But perhaps an even more telling aspect to the whole Falklands affair, so far as Anglo-American relations are concerned, was not the substance but the way in which aid was given by the USA to Britain.

Weinberger's immediate response to make aid speedily available to the British was taken without having to set up any new arrangements or make any new agreements with the British. All that was needed was to speed up the Pentagon's bureaucratic procedures. US Navy Secretary at the time of the Falklands crisis, John Lehman, in an interview with David Dimbleby, explained much of what happened in terms that exemplified the judgement of Joseph Frankel several years earlier about the importance of the co-operation of British and American officials:

> One has to understand the relationship of the United States Navy to the Royal Navy – there's no other relationship, I think, like it in the world between two military services. . . .
>
> There was no need to establish a new relationship . . . it was really just turning up the volume . . . almost a case of not being told to stop rather than crossing a threshold to start.[11]

Working together in NATO, and the UKUSA framework of intelligence co-operation, intermixing of British and American officialdom, and the legacy of long Anglo-American friendship, as well as strongly pro-British sentiments among key figures such as the President and the Defence Secretary, resulted in what Lehman described as almost automatic support for Britain in the Falklands war.

Good and supportive relations between the two countries in the Falklands War and in the Cold War, and the Reagan–Thatcher friendship, were somewhat counterbalanced by economic friction, the US invasion of Grenada and differences about tactics in the Cold War.

Notwithstanding their similar economic ideologies, Thatcher and Reagan pursued rather different policies. High US interest rates caused volatility in the international monetary field and damaged the British economy. There were also significant differences about trade with the Soviets and Eastern Europe. Despite her reputation as the Iron Lady and as a fierce opponent of communism, Thatcher pursued a traditional British policy, independently of the USA, of trading with 'the enemy'. The Macmillan government had done exactly the same in the early 1960s in refusing to ban the export of steel pipes to the Eastern bloc.

There was also the EC and its traditionally more protectionist policies, especially in agriculture, which had impact on British trade relations with the USA and created some areas of friction, even though Mrs Thatcher preferred relations with the USA to ties with Europe. Part of the problem here was that her succession of Foreign Ministers, Peter Carrington, Francis Pym, Sir Geoffrey Howe and Douglas Hurd, were all notably more pro-European and less sanguine about relations with the USA than the Prime Minister. There were also increasingly institutionalised pulls towards Europe, which in the long term could erode the easy and familiar interaction of British and American officialdom; but as late as 1986 there was little evidence of that, as we shall see when looking at the US raid on Libya. Britain's close relations with the USA cut right across attempts at foreign-policy co-ordination in the EC during the Libyan crisis.[12]

More dramatic and embarrassing than economic problems was the US invasion of Grenada. Throughout his term of office, Reagan and his defence people were deeply troubled by the threat of a further spread of communism, sponsored by Cuba and the Soviets, in Central America and the Caribbean. The Reagan Doctrine, issued in his State of the Union Address in 1985, captures the tone of American concerns and determination:

> We must stand by all our democratic allies [democratic here had a very elastic definition]. And we must not break faith with them who are risking their lives – on every continent, from Afghanistan to Nicaragua – to defy Soviet-supported aggression and secure rights which have been ours from birth.[13]

One such danger spot was the small British Commonwealth island of Grenada. During 1983, instability on the island seemed to be deteriorating into chaos. The Americans, already fearful because of Cuban aid to the island and close ties between Castro and the leftist Prime Minister Maurice Bishop, decided, when Bishop was overthrown in October in a bloody coup by a more radical leader, that they had to act to protect the substantial number of American students on the island. Unfortunately they disregarded the fact that Grenada was a member of the Commonwealth and did not consult with Britain beforehand.

This was a slight to Britain's newly refound dignity that Mrs Thatcher could not let pass unremarked. Francis Pym, Foreign Secretary 1982 to June 1983, commented: 'the usual close co-operation between London and Washington failed completely on this occasion'.[14] Mrs Thatcher criticised the USA, and Pym's successor, Sir Geoffrey Howe, was equally disturbed by what was widely perceived in Britain as cavalier American behaviour. But the Americans did not see it like that. They saw Britain as a pernickety and ungrateful ally: where was the *quid pro quo* for support in the Falklands War? Newspaper reports in the USA were highly critical of the way Thatcher and her colleagues had reacted. The whole episode went deeper than just a breach of diplomatic etiquette, it demonstrated the willingness of the USA to back up its anti-communist rhetoric with actions, whereas Britain, even under Mrs Thatcher, was more pragmatic in the way she chose to deal with the communist menace.

In the broad span of affairs Grenada, while embarrassing and awkward, was only a passing irritant. Differences about how to deal with the Soviets and the implications of the US Strategic Defence Initiative (SDI) were more substantive and important matters. Thatcher was all in favour of taking a strong stand against the Soviets (was she not ever so on all things!) and, at considerable political cost, welcomed the new generation of US missiles into Britain. At the time there was a revival of anti-nuclear feeling, renewed debate about the effectiveness of British controls over the use of US bases, and suggestions that the two-key system, used for US missiles in Britain in the 1960s, be expanded. But Mrs Thatcher was resolute in her determination to see new American nuclear missiles deployed; however, she was also keen to begin negotiations with the Soviets and was disappointed when nothing happened.

The main problem was that Weinberger and his hard-line assistant Richard Perle did not want to talk with the Soviets. The British worked with George Shultz, the Secretary of State and a warm friend of Britain's, to try to break the impasse. When things finally began to move in 1983, however, other difficulties arose so far as Thatcher was concerned. In March of that year, without any warning, President Reagan announced the SDI, which was a futuristic plan to use space-age technology to make the USA immune to nuclear attack. Mrs Thatcher in her memoirs recounted: 'I did not share

President Reagan's view that it was a means of ridding the world entirely of nuclear weapons.'[15] In fact, Thatcher had several worries about the SDI, most important of which was the fear that it could lead to a decoupling of the USA from European security and destroy the nuclear deterrence upon which she believed the security of Western Europe depended. In 1984 there were proposals from Senator Sam Nunn in the US Congress to reduce US forces in Europe by 25%, unless the Europeans increased their own defence efforts. That added to the worries about the possibility of US cut-backs and eventual withdrawal, even though the Nunn amendment failed.

On 22 December 1984 Mrs Thatcher went to Camp David in Maryland to talk with the President. It was the first time that she had talked with him about the SDI. She was disturbed by what Reagan had to say and began to work on a statement that would limit his freedom of action. In conversation with US National Security Adviser Robert MacFarlane, she drafted out a number of points, one of which stated that the USA, because of its treaty commitments, would negotiate with its allies before deploying the fruits of SDI research. Afterwards, Shultz was rather concerned that Mrs Thatcher had had too much say in what was essentially a US policy matter, but in fact the statement did little to limit US actions.[16]

By 1985 the British were still worried and Foreign Secretary Howe, in a speech at the Royal United Services Institute in March, openly criticised the concept of SDI. Nevertheless, in December Britain signed up to participate in the hope of getting lucrative research contracts for British industry. Little came of that, but US strategic and negotiating policy with the Soviets continued to cause London concern. Between 1985 and 1987 there were dramatic breakthroughs by Reagan and the Soviet leader Gorbachev, who was desperately seeking reform of the Soviet system and labouring under ever-increasing economic problems, which demanded some easing of the Soviet defence burden. The negotiations for Intermediate Nuclear Force (INF) reductions reached agreement in principle in Geneva in 1985, but ran into trouble at Reykjavik in 1986 because of Gorbachev's attempt to link the agreement to SDI; and then in early 1987 actual agreement was reached when Gorbachev dropped his attempt at linkage. In Washington in December 1987 an agreement was signed. While all this was going on, Mrs Thatcher was uneasy and repeatedly cautioned the President about the possible dangers of his policies. After Reykjavik she flew to Washington for urgent talks and urged Reagan to reaffirm both US commitments to the defence of Western Europe and the need to modernise remaining nuclear-weapon systems. Only after receiving them did she agree to support the INF treaty. If Reagan had not had such respect and affection for her it is doubtful that her hectoring and overt interference would have been tolerated. When

George Bush came to power in 1989, Mrs Thatcher had to adopt a more low-key approach, allow the President to have more of a say in their conversations and, as she later put it, have 'no hesitation in eating a little humble pie' in order to secure British interests.[17]

There were various other matters that hit the headlines from time to time in Anglo-American relations. One such instance involved difficulties arising out of their civil-aviation relations, an area traditionally afflicted with political controversy. Freddie Laker, after going bankrupt in 1982, brought antitrust lawsuits in the USA against British Airways, and several other European and US companies, alleging predatory pricing and a conspiracy to put his airline out of business. Furthermore, the US Justice Department also took up the matter and began an investigation. This did not please the British government, which was looking to privatise British Airways, and that plan was jeopardised by the possibility of punitive damages being awarded to Laker by US courts. Damages would be three times the value of whatever losses he had suffered as a result of any collusion with others by British Airways to put him out of business. Things were coming to a head in 1984, but it was an election year for Reagan and so Mrs Thatcher kept her peace. But after his safe re-election the sparks flew with a vengeance. US officials were astonished by what they saw as the inappropriate amount of pressure the Prime Minister exerted on the President. They were equally astonished when he gave in and ordered that the Justice Department case be discontinued. He later intervened again in order to help resolve the civil case brought by Laker, and an out-of-court settlement was made. British Airways could now safely be sold off to the private sector.[18] There was little doubt after incidents like this just how influential Mrs Thatcher could be in Washington and how close she was to the President. She had endeared herself to him in a number of ways, but perhaps nowhere more so than in relation to the problem of terrorism in the Middle East and the support she rendered the US air strike on Libya.

Anglo-American relations concerning the Middle East had been fraught with difficulties throughout the postwar period. Even as late as 1973 there had been the incident in the Yom Kippur War when Heath had refused to allow US planes to refuel at British bases to facilitate the supply of material for the Israelis. Since then, North Sea oil had started to flow ashore and Britain was now able to take a line more independent of considerations about the importance of Middle Eastern oil for its economy. However, the rest of Western Europe was still highly dependent on that source for its oil and thus cautious about action that might offend the Arab world. In the 1980s Britain, on the one hand, had achieved a position whereby it could exercise a freer hand in its policy decisions on the Middle East because of

North Sea oil. On the other hand, as the EC tried to co-ordinate its foreign policy, and as that tended to be conciliatory towards the Arab world, the British had a new potential restraint upon their policy options.

European Political Co-operation (EPC), an attempt to co-ordinate the foreign policy of the member states, was given formal standing in 1970 and proceeded through regular ministerial meetings, but with little of substance to show for its work. However, in 1980 the EC issued the Venice Declaration, which called for the participation of the Palestinians in the Middle East peace process. That caused some difficulties between the British and the Americans because of the latter's close relations with the Israelis, though, generally, Britain's line was often closer to that of the USA than to its partners in Europe.It was supportive of US actions in the Lebanon that tried to facilitate Israel's withdrawal after its invasion to clear out terrorist groups. The USA provided the bulk of troops in an international contingent to try to stabilise things, but the British made a small contribution as well. Britain also took a similar hard line to the USA on terrorists in general. The slaughter of US marines in Beirut by a suicide attack in 1983, and bomb outrages at Rome and Vienna airports in December 1985, and on a TWA jet and at a discothèque in Berlin in April 1986, caused a hardening of attitudes towards Libya, which was largely held responsible by the USA for sponsoring these massacres of innocents. Britain's attitudes were supportive, much more so than those of her European partners, despite attempts by the EPC to establish a common policy. Mrs Thatcher's lack of sympathy for things European hardly needed much demonstration, but there had been an incident at the end of 1985 involving the future of Britain's helicopter manufacturer Westland that left no one in doubt. The company was in difficulty and needed a partner. Mrs Thatcher and most of her colleagues looked to the USA in the form of the Sikorski Corporation to answer that need, but Defence Secretary Michael Heseltine had other ideas and turned the whole affair into an EC versus USA controversy. Heseltine argued for a European consortium to salvage Westland's fortunes, but Thatcher would have nothing to do with that. In the end, Heseltine resigned and the Sikorski deal went ahead, but not before many had drawn the lesson that in the Thatcher government the USA still held predominance over the EC in many spheres of co-operation, not least of which were foreign relations themselves and defence policy. That became even clearer in the planning and execution of the US punitive raid on Libya in April 1986.

With Americans falling victim to terrorist attacks, domestic political pressure mounted within the USA for an effective response, giving support to the convictions of the President and some of his senior advisers that a punitive lesson should be meted out. The difficulty was where such action should be taken. In April 1986 the answer became clear. There appeared to be conclusive evidence that the Libyan leader Qadaffi was behind much of the terrorist activity in Europe and the Middle East. Reagan decided to act: US forces would strike at targets in Libya itself. Once that decision was made, the next problem was the difficulty of logistics. Rather like Britain in the Falklands war, the USA was confronted with the need to cover a long distance before its forces could deliver their strike.

The USA approached its European allies for help, but all, with the exception of Britain, refused. President François Mitterand of France advised that the strike should be a hard one, but refused to allow US aircraft to use French air space during their mission. The plan was for F-111 fighter bombers to fly from their bases in Britain to inflict the main blow on Libya. Weinberger later commented: 'The long flight of the F-111s, from Britain, made many hours longer by Mitterand's refusal to let us use French air space, required four refuelings, all at night, with radio silence.'[19] After the raid had been carried out Weinberger refrained from criticising the French, but he believed the facts spoke for themselves and: 'The contrast to Mrs Thatcher's agreement to let the bombers go from England could not have been more marked.'[20] These facts showed Britain had adopted a clearly different line from at least one of its major EC partners, but there was more to it than that.

Not one of America's allies, apart from Britain, had actively supported the US strike. Furthermore, six minutes before the F-111s took off from Britain, EC foreign ministers at the Hague issued an appeal for restraint on all sides: British Foreign Secretary Sir Geoffrey Howe was party to that, even though Britain was then colluding with the USA to mount the air strike. There was little evidence of European political co-operation in this and, indeed, Britain's partners felt that Howe had misled them and that once again Britain's friendship with the USA was preferred to solidarity with her EC partners.[21]

Although British links with the USA have cut across EPC on several occasions, it must not be overlooked that the pull from Europe has had an impact on British policy. Whenever Mrs Thatcher believed that EPC could be constructive in strengthening the economy or security of Western Europe she seized the opportunity to push British policy within that framework. Results have been modest in most areas except economics and trade. Trade negotiations are now conducted by representatives of the EC, not by national delegations. Even in monetary matters, Britain was first supportive of, and then eventually joined, the European Monetary System. But, more than the other member states, Britain has retained a degree of worrying ambiguity about its policy on Europe. In the 1990s, controversy over the merits of a single currency, and the September 1992 sterling crisis, which forced Britain out of the European currency system, raised worries about Britain's role in Europe and caused concern about its pattern of international relations in general.

Looking back on the Thatcher–Reagan years, it is still difficult to assess their impact on Anglo-American relations. Those who thought that the 1970s had witnessed the demise of special relations between the two were clearly proved to be in error. Nuclear, intelligence and conventional military co-operation, continuing ethnic and cultural ties and the sharing of political values that led the two countries into partnership against the great authoritarian and totalitarian threats of the twentieth century, would have guaranteed the continuation of special relations in some form, even without Reagan and Thatcher. With Reagan and Thatcher in charge in the USA and Britain, their warm personal relationship helped things and was made manifest in mutual support against renewed activism by the Soviets, in removing the Argentinians from the Falklands and in combating terrorism. There were differences and difficulties over specific problems and often over tactics, but on the major dangers confronting the world the British and the USA continued to see things remarkably similarly. Structural and economic forces were not as supportive of Anglo-American relations as they had been in the past: Britain felt the attraction of Europe, even under Mrs Thatcher, and the USA became more and more orientated towards the Pacific, but such pulls were nothing like fatal for their good relations. In the broad context of things they are not even necessarily incompatible with close Anglo-American relations. At the same time, it is also now clear that, while Reagan and Thatcher imparted renewed strength to the pattern of a special relationship, the configuration changed after their departures, first with President Bush's succession and then, after Thatcher was forced out of office, with the arrival of John Major as Prime Minister. Interestingly, one of the main reasons for Thatcher's loss of office was to do with her lack of constructive attitudes towards the EC. Would a government more committed to Europe find, like Heath, that in pursuit of a more Europeanist policy there would necessarily be a devaluation of the importance of the ties with the USA?

CHANGES AND RE-ADJUSTMENTS 1990–5

Before Mrs Thatcher was dethroned by her own party, she had nearly two years of working with President Bush. They were years of accelerating change in East–West relations. Gorbachev made further arms-control concessions in 1988 and over the following three years there was more concern about the danger of instability within the Soviet Union than about its direct potential threat to the West. In August 1991, the abortive coup against the forces of reform in the Soviet Union marked its disintegration as a united power. The demise of the main external threat to the West removed one of the main factors that had encouraged Anglo-American co-operation in the postwar world. As the Cold War went into its death throes, Germany reunited, the EC continued to grow in influence, and further integration was high on the agenda. Much seemed to be pulling Britain away from the USA, and President Bush and some of his advisers welcomed that. They looked for a more cohesive EC with Britain acting out a constructive role within it. The Bush–Thatcher relationship was initially a more low-key affair than the Prime Minister had experienced with Reagan, and Secretary of State James Baker was not as friendly as Shultz had been.

In December 1989 Baker spoke in Berlin of the need to strengthen US–EC relations. The main response to that came from Germany through Hans Dietrich Genscher, but at the end of the day it did not amount to a great deal. In November the following year a declaration on US–EC relations was signed, pledging collaboration on crime and terrorism, the environment and the non-proliferation of biological weapons. The fact was that Bush's attempt to get close to the EC by wooing its main power was not bringing the results that had been hoped for. Problems with German reunification and the limitations of German foreign policy were making close collaboration difficult, as were problems arising out of the Uruguay GATT trade talks, which soured relations generally between the USA and the EC. But the most obvious drawback to US–EC collaboration was exposed by the Gulf War. The EC failed to develop a coherent and unified policy. And, as had so often been the case in crises in the past, it was the British who reacted in closest harmony with the USA, saw the problem in a similar way and acknowledged that force would probably have to be used.

On 2 August 1990 Saddam Hussein invaded Kuwait. That same day Mrs Thatcher received a telephone call from the President, who was at his home in Kennebunkport, Maine. They discussed the crisis, and Mrs Thatcher argued for a strong response: it was 'no time to go wobbly' she told the President. Bush wavered at times but never wobbled. By the time war was joined, Mrs Thatcher had been replaced by John Major, but British policy remained unchanged and supportive of the USA. Britain provided the largest European component of the military force that took on the Iraqi army and was the most outspoken and staunchest supporter of the US-led mission to liberate Kuwait. Bush was soon praising the British effort and the special relationship his country enjoyed with them. After the Gulf War relations between Major and Bush were warm and cordial, but never anything more than that, and after Bill Clinton beat Bush in 1992 a man even cooler to the idea of close ties with Britain was at the helm in the USA. During his first two years of office there was hardly a single incident or event that one could point to as indicative of close relations. Indeed, the years were peppered by minor, but no less worrying, disputes and arguments to do with GATT trade talks, problems over the Anglo-American air-service agreement, and the visit of Gerry Adams, the Sinn Fein leader, to the USA in 1994 after the lifting of a twenty-year ban. Once the visit was over there was a public attempt to smooth Britain's ruffled feathers. Protestations were forthcoming from Clinton about the importance of good and close Anglo-American relations, and a number of friendly 'photo. opportunities' were arranged during the visit of John Major to Washington. But, for the most part, neither of the present administrations in Britain and the USA has done much to continue the kind of relationship Mrs Thatcher and Reagan had in the 1980s. Both are more preoccupied with domestic economic and political problems, have shown little skill in foreign affairs, and seem content with a lower-key and less overt relationship. When they have expressed views on the major issues of the day, such as the condition of the former Yugoslavia, there has been little rapport.

Anglo-American relations have gone through worse doldrums than this in the past without any permanent damage being done. At the present, it is difficult to say what effect the dip in relations will have. It could be just a passing phase, or it could be symptomatic of a continuing contraction of the scope, and a decline in the importance, of Anglo-American relations and, more importantly, of their quality as well: only time will tell.

CONCLUDING OBSERVATIONS

In writing about Britain and the USA in the twentieth century, one is confronted with a vastly complex and rich relationship. That very characteristic has led writers to seek some shorthand means, or, in the jargon of my generation of international-relations scholars, a hermeneutic device to explain the fundamental character of the relationship. Some of these have taken the form of analytical theories, others have involved metaphors of varying degrees of complexity. Before concluding this account, some brief comment on these approaches to the problem of explaining Anglo-American relations will be made.

During his long career, Harold Macmillan had much to do with Americans, and he used the conventional picture of the way ancient Greece related to Rome as a metaphor to suggest how Britain might relate to the USA in the latter part of the twentieth century. Whether or not he believed that this was a useful image for explaining Anglo-American relations is difficult to say. More likely than not, it was only a witticism to indicate a rather unwarranted sense of political and cultural superiority over the Americans, but it has had considerable appeal and has been used from time to time by writers on Anglo-American affairs. In what is admittedly a pastiche of impressions and anecdotes, Christopher Hitchens nevertheless makes an effective attack upon the picture conjured up by Macmillan. He points out that Britain has had more in common with Rome than with the cultural excellence of Greece: Britain in the mid-twentieth century was more like an old Rome to America's new Rome.[22] While this seems more appropriate, it is still vague. Macmillan's notion of educating and leading the Americans by British experience, worldly wisdom and cultural example was little more than arrogant wishful thinking. America's culture has had more impact than Britain's throughout the century, and British foreign policy has not been of such excellence that it stands out as a role model. The USA has ploughed its own distinctive furrow in the twentieth century, little affected by British advice, and its foreign policy has coincided with British policy when interests and sentiments coincided, not because of the wily British leading her by the nose along a diplomatic or any other kind of learning curve. That judgement seems to be borne out in two obvious areas where Britain might be seen as an obvious contender for the role of 'teacher' or 'leader': in the development of foreign intelligence operations in the 1940s, and during the early period of the Cold War. In neither case could the British be said to have held the initiative for long. Whatever tutelage there was, the Americans soon matured beyond it.

Another image that has been invoked is of America in Britain's place: *Pax Americana* replacing *Pax Britannica*. Only the prestige and eminence of Donald Watt give this idea sufficient currency to be of note.[23] In fact the image does not actually seem to play a major role in Watt's work on Anglo-American relations, except in that it allows him to pass some comparative judgements and make critical comment on the rise of the USA to the status of world power at the expense of Britain's accelerated decline, which is generally seen as a bad thing, particularly in relation to the forced pace of empire dissolution. But the USA is not in Britain's place in anything other than a misleading or very general sense. The USA has never had a large formal empire (or to my mind an informal one). It is a truly world superpower in a way that Britain never was. Britain in her heyday was *par excellence* a great trader, the first industrial nation and the leading naval power; the USA is a great trading nation and the leading naval power, but it is also the dominant military power in a world of many other industrial powers. Its period of world leadership has also coincided with a different form of world conflict – ideological, and Cold War. One could go on, but it is unnecessary. The image of the USA in Britain's place can only be used in the loosest kind of metaphorical way: it is no substitute for detailed explanation, and Watt, I am sure, never intended it to be: other writers, however, can be less astute.

Two other ways of dealing with the relationship are more persuasive: the idea of the USA as a hegemon, and variants on the theory, or theories, of economic imperialism. In their more sophisticated forms these two are often related. Theories of economic imperialism became popular in the early twentieth century because of radical liberal writers such as J. A. Hobson and socialist writers like Lenin.[24] Their ideas were elaborated upon in the postwar period by a wave of New Left historians in the USA, with William Appleman Williams as their mentor.[25] There is not space to rehearse their arguments here, and the plural is deliberately used, for there is more than one view expressed by them. However, at the heart of their arguments is the following. The affairs of men are dictated by the economic structure of production under which they live. In the USA this is advanced corporate capitalism, which seeks exports, investment and markets wherever they might be in order to command sources of raw materials, expand production and markets and maximise profits. With the inbuilt dynamic of maximising profits, the system leads to cartelisation and monopoly, in order to control both the costs of production and the price system. The result is international capitalism. It exploits workers (low wages mean higher profits) and ultimately foreign governments. International corporations will undermine the aspirations of states whenever they wish to take actions contrary to the interests of the corporations and their elite managers and directors. In this system, a notion of false consciousness is deployed to explain away the face-value or appearance of political life. The reality behind the appearance is that the political is only a means to an end controlled by corporate capitalism. In this scenario of advanced capitalism, the leading country logically always tends towards hegemony, and the reality of economic power exercised through capitalism is imperialistic by its very nature. The dynamics of capitalism determine relations within and between states. The relationship of Britain to the USA is always determined by the economic equation, not by anything else.

Many of these ideas have a certain attraction and persuasiveness. Economic matters are important and in the present account much has been made of them in Anglo-American relations. Austen Chamberlain in 1928 and Churchill in 1940 both recognised the constraints on British policy exercised by Britain's economic circumstances and the possibilities that would open or close depending on whether or not help was forthcoming from the USA. In 1956 Eden failed to think lucidly about economic constraints and led Britain into a disaster. This kind of historical material is grist to the mill of the economic determinists and of those who are not so deterministic but who nevertheless invoke forms of hegemony or economic imperialism theory. Things that are more difficult to explain are: the peaceful transition from Britain's leadership of the capitalist world to America's; why corporate America gave socialist Britain economic assistance after the war, which helped it to develop a welfare state; why Britain refused America's demands to abandon imperial preference and sterling controls for so long; why she refused to become part of Europe in the 1940s; and why she took such harsh measures in the AIOC crisis, in the Suez crisis, and in the Falklands War, contrary to what the USA would have preferred. The points made here are by no means an adequate challenge to the work of those who employ hegemony theory, and theories of economic imperialism. What they require is a fuller theoretical exegesis and critique, for really they are theoretical arguments and not historically or empirically based. All that is intended here is to alert the reader to some of the possibilities and limitations of these approaches, albeit in a very crude way.[26]

Finally, there are two common approaches, though often appearing in different mutations, which might loosely be referred to as the sentiment and realist approaches: the former emphasises common Anglo-American sentiments, and the latter interests. Both these approaches are useful, providing two things are borne in mind. First, as I have argued elsewhere, it is a mistake to juxtapose interests and sentiments as separate and distinct: the two are inextricably linked. It is extremely rare to be able to isolate a sentiment in such a way that it is totally at odds with an identified interest, and vice versa. Second, both sentiments and interests exist in multiple and varied forms and are not carved in stone. They change over time, and competing interests and sentiments always co-exist. In Britain, the Conservative and Labour Parties have been traditionally pro-American, but there has also been a long tradition and an unholy alliance of imperialists, the Conservative right wing and the Labour Party left wing that has disliked the USA and tried to steer Britain away from too close an alliance with her. Similarly, in the USA certain ethnic minorities, isolationists, American populists and progressives, with a strong strain of anti-imperialism, have all opposed close ties with Britain. Nevertheless, there is a certain persuasiveness in the suggestion, most notably made by H. C. Allen, that there has been a natural development of close Anglo-American relations because of the shared sentiments of their cultural and linguistic inheritance, their blood, and their commercial and historical ties. But in the end it sounds like a form of determinism reminiscent of, even if different from, theories of economic imperialism. Was Anglo-American friendship in the twentieth century really that inevitable?

Other historians clearly think not, or at least seek to explain the relationship in a different way by emphasising British and American common interests. One particular form of this argument finds expression in terms of the two countries reacting in harmony to commonly perceived external threats: the Kaiser's Germany; Hitler, Mussolini and Tojo; communism; and possibly also Saddam Hussein. Again, there is much to recommend this approach, but it has its flaws. Britain and the USA failed to react in a concerted way in the 1930s to the threat of totalitarianism until it was almost too late. When they did respond they had somewhat different reasons for doing so and developed plans and ideas for the future that were not always compatible. Similarly, regarding the Cold War, to say that Britain and the USA responded to a commonly perceived threat only identifies the contours of the way they acted. It fails to explain the different tactics, for example regarding economic warfare, or to account for the different approaches to dealing with the PRC and problems in south-east Asia. And it is in those kinds of differences that much of the substance of Anglo-American relations is to be found. Perhaps most fundamentally important, while historians have invoked the existence of common threads in British and US foreign policy, they have sometimes failed to ask the question why they conceived of things as being in their common interest and why they saw certain states as being a common threat. To answer those questions one must return to sentiments: political, legal and cultural values, friendship, historical experience and economic beliefs.

My own approach I leave to the reader to discern from what I have written, and in particular from what I wrote about method at the outset.

What of the future?

Thatcher and Reagan demonstrated that, at least until the beginning of the last decade of the century, the scope of Anglo-American mutual concerns had not diminished to insignificance and that the quality of the relationship was still special. The quality of the relationship does not have to be devalued just because it operates at a less exalted level in world affairs: the USA has had a special relationship with Israel for many years, and no one raises an eyebrow at that claim, despite the facts that it has less military power than Britain, has a smaller economy, fewer people and less say generally in the world.

Britain has declined to a mid-range power and is more inward and Europe-orientated than at any other time in its recent history. In the process, one of the asymmetrical aspects of the Anglo-American relationship has diminished: Britain no longer needs the USA as much as it used to when it had international military and monetary responsibilities. One could argue that Britain's decline has given it more, not less, freedom of action. For its part, the USA has also suffered relative decline, but unlike Britain it has not shed its international economic and military responsibilities. Some may have been abandoned, but a formidable amount remains. In this respect, US freedom of action has somewhat diminished over the years, and one could argue that the need for a supportive ally has therefore increased. Whether or not Britain should remain the supportive special friend, or whether, indeed, its entanglement in the European Union will allow it the freedom of action to pursue that independently of its fellow member states, cannot be predicted with any guarantee of accuracy.

However, although Britain is now tied politically to Europe, strong ties still bind it to the USA. There is a popular Atlantic cultural community, facilitated by a common language, by easy access to films and books and by buoyant tourist, commercial and educational intercourse. Britain is still the single most popular destination for US tourists outside the Western hemisphere. Public opinion polls have shown fluctuating views about mutual perceptions. In the early 1980s, after a decade that was notable for troubled and cool Anglo-American relations, US opinion still consistently viewed Britain as being friendly and 'together with Canada seen by a majority of Americans as "a close ally". A significant majority (66–80%) assert[ed] that the United States has a vital interest in both countries.'[27] In Britain in the 1980s public opinion was volatile, often expressing concern at Reagan's strong rhetoric, his deployment of nuclear missiles in Britain, and his strong anti-communist stance in general. At the same time, when unilateral nuclear disarmament became an issue in the 1987 General Election, the Labour Party's antinuclear policy showed as consistently unpopular, and it should not be forgotten that the nearest thing Britain had politically to Reagan – Margaret Thatcher – was repeatedly returned to office by the electorate.

In addition to all this, intelligence, nuclear and conventional defence co-operation continue. There are habits of co-operation acquired over a long period of time and during all the great crises of the twentieth century. The historical legacy is a powerful one. The pattern of Anglo-American co-operation has been challenged at many times and in many ways over the years, but perhaps no more so than now. Notwithstanding its resilience, it has still not fully adjusted to the challenges posed by British and US decline, the demise of the Cold War, the reorientation of the USA toward the Pacific, the impact on the US world view of new patterns of immigration from Latin America and Asia, and the consequences of Britain's membership of the European Union. The last may be the biggest challenge of all, but as David Owen wrote at the end of the 1970s: 'I see no incompatibility whatever in maintaining a strong commitment to the Atlantic Alliance with Community Membership.'[28] It should not prove to be beyond the wit and wisdom of humanity to achieve that, providing sound interests and good sentiments continue to thrive in a mutually supportive manner within the Anglo-American relationship. For, in crisis after crisis – the Falklands; Libya and terrorism; countering Soviet nuclear power in the 1980s; and the Gulf war – Britain and the USA have approached things similarly and in a partnership that is suggestive of there being further life in the special relationship. To liken it to a song: the lyrics may have changed, but the tune remains the same – even though it has been transposed over time from a major to a minor key.

Notes

1 THE LION AND THE EAGLE: OF TWISTED TAILS AND PLUCKED FEATHERS

1 The reader must persevere well into the first chapter to find out the circumstances of the prisoners of war.
2 For contrasting views on Anglo-American relations, see H. C. Allen, *Great Britain and the United States: A History of Anglo-American Relations 1783–1952* (Odhams Press, London, 1954); D. C. Watt, *Succeeding John Bull: America in Britain's Place 1900–1977* (Cambridge University Press, Cambridge, 1984); Max Beloff, 'Is There an Anglo-American Political Tradition?', *History*, 36 (1951), 73–91; C. J. Bartlett, *The Special Relationship: A Political History of Anglo-American Relations Since 1945* (Longman, London, 1992); H. G. Nicholas, *The United States and Britain* (University of Chicago Press, Chicago, 1975). For further reading, see D. A. Lincove and G. R. Treadway, *The Anglo-American Relationship: An Annotated Bibliography of Scholarship, 1945–1985* (Greenwood Press, Westport, 1988). For some guidance on the pros and cons of the special relationship, see H. C. Allen's review of Watt's *Succeeding John Bull* in *Journal of American Studies*, 19 (1985).
3 Public Record Office London (all Cabinet and FO papers cited are from the PRO unless otherwise indicated), CAB 24/128, CP 344, memo by Craigie, 13 Nov. 1928.
4 H. V. Hodson, 'The Anatomy of Anglo-American Relations', an inaugural lecture, 27 Apr. 1962, published by the Ditchley Foundation.
5 Interview with the Rt Hon. James (now Lord) Callaghan, 26 Feb. 1987, conducted by the author.
6 For quantification, and comment on the respective changes in British and American power, see Paul Kennedy, *The Rise and Fall of the Great Powers: Economic Change and Military Conflict from 1500 to 2000* (Fontana Press, London, 1989); for the economic relationship, see Alan P. Dobson, *The Politics of the Anglo-American Economic Special Relationship* (Harvester Wheatsheaf, Brighton, and St Martins, New York, 1988); on the wartime economic relationship, see R. N. Gardner, *Sterling Dollar Diplomacy in Current Perspective* (Columbia University Press, New York, 1980), and R. B. Woods, *A Changing of the Guard: Anglo-American Relations 1941–46* (University of North Carolina Press, Chapel Hill, 1990).

7   Washington's farewell address: text in Henry Steele Commager, *Living Ideas in America* (Harper, New York, 1951), 143–7.
8   Monroe Doctrine 1823, ibid., 656–60.
9   Department of State publication prepared by Carlton Savage, *Policy of the United States toward Maritime Commerce in War, vol. 1, 1776–1914* (US Government Printing Office, Washington, 1934).
10 Roosevelt Corollary 1904: see Robert D. Schulzinger, *American Diplomacy in the Twentieth Century* (Oxford University Press, New York, 1984), 29–31.
11 P. J Cain and A. G. Hopkins, *British Imperialism: Crisis and Reconstruction 1914–1990* (Longman, London, 1993); Paul Kennedy, *The Realities Behind Diplomacy: Background Influences on British External Policy 1865–1980* (Fontana, London, 1981).
12 Foreign Relations of the United States (published from time to time by the US Department of State, hereafter FRUS), 1902, 463–98: correspondence between Hay and Choate (especially 16 Oct. 1900 and 29 Oct. 1902; latter includes letter from Lansdowne).
13 Harold and Margaret Sprout, *The Rise of American Naval Power 1776–1918* (Princeton University Press, Princeton, 1914), chs 13–15.
14 *Hansard*, 26 June 1923, vol. 165, col. 2142.
15 P. Gibbs (ed.), *Bridging the Atlantic: Anglo-American Friendship as a Way to World Peace* (Hutchinson, London, 1944).
16 C. Bell, *The Debatable Alliance* (Oxford University Press, London, 1964), 11–12.

2 ASSERTION AND RESPONSE 1900–19

1   For the broad brush strokes of international relations in this period I have relied on: Kennedy, *Rise and Fall* and *Behind Diplomacy*; Cain and Hopkins, *British Imperialism*; Walter Lafeber, *The American Age: United States Foreign Policy at Home and Abroad Since 1750* (W.W. Norton, New York, 1989); Schulzinger, *American Diplomacy*; the Sprouts, *Naval Power*; for Anglo-American relations, Allen, *Great Britain and the United States*; Lionel M. Gelber, *The Rise of the Anglo-American Friendship* (Oxford University Press, London, 1938); R. B. Mowatt, *The Diplomatic Relations of Great Britain and the United States* (Edward Arnold, London, 1925); Nicholas, *The United States and Britain*; D. Dimbleby and D. Reynolds, *An Ocean Apart* (Hodder & Stoughton, London, 1988).
2   FRUS, 1895, part 1, 552–62 (Secretary of State Olney to London).
3   Sprouts, *Naval Power*, 230.
4   Quoted from Gelber, *Friendship*, 92–3.
5   Quoted from Mowatt, *Diplomatic Relations*; 284; source W. R. Thayer, *The Life and Letters of John Hay*, vol. 2, 221.
6   Quoted from Mowatt, *Diplomatic Relations*, 331.
7   Quoted from Lloyd C. Gardner, *Safe for Democracy: The Anglo-American Response to Revolution 1913–23* (Oxford University Press, New York, 1984), 54.
8   Charles Seymour, *The Intimate Papers of Colonel House*, vol. 1 (Ernest Benn, London, 1926), 210 (diary 21 Jan. 1914).
9   Sprouts, *Naval Power*, 253.

10 PRO, CAB 11/118, memo. by Colonial Defence Committee, 7 Apr. 1909, CO No. 1018/09.
11 Cain and Hopkins, *British Imperialism*, 58.
12 Schulzinger, *American Diplomacy*, ch. 3.
13 Carl Parrini, *Heir to Empire: United States Economic Diplomacy 1916–23* (Pittsburgh University Press, Pittsburgh, 1969), chs 1 and 2.
14 F. A. Mckenzie, *The American Invaders* (Grant Richards, London, 1902); James McMillan and Bernard Harris, *The American Take-over of Britain* (Hart Publishing, New York, 1968). For investment figures, see the *Independent*, 20 Jan. 1989, 'Change and Exchange Across the Atlantic'; source US Commerce Department.
15 Savage, *Maritime Commerce*, 454–60 (opinion of the US Supreme Court in the case of the *Bermuda*, Dec. 1865, delivered by Chief Justice Chase).
16 Viscount Grey of Fallodon, *Twenty Five Years 1892–1916* (Hodder & Stoughton, London, 1947), 103.
17 Quoted from Allen, *Britain and the United States*, 681.
18 Quoted from Mowatt, *Diplomatic Relations*, 336 (Page to Wilson, 11 May 1914).
19 Cain and Hopkins, *British Imperialism*, 59.
20 Quoted from Watt, *Succeeding John Bull*, 32.
21 Seymour, House, 461–2, (Lane to House, 5 May 1915).
22 Cain and Hopkins, *British Imperialism*, 60; for a full account of the financial and supply relationship between Britain and the USA, see Kathleen Burk, *Britain, America and the Sinews of War, 1914–1918* (Allen & Unwin, Boston, 1985).
23 Michael Simpson, 'Admiral William S. Sims, U.S. Navy and Admiral Sir Lewis Bayly, Royal Navy: An Unlikely Friendship and Anglo-American Co-operation 1917–1919', *US Naval War College Review*, 41: 2 (1988), 66–80.
24 Commager, *Living Ideas*, 683–87.
25 J. M. Keynes, *The Economic Consequences of the Peace* (Macmillan, London, 1920), 26, 29, 37, 39, 40.

3 STABILITY AND CHANGE 1919–39

1 Keynes, *Economic Consequences*, 2.
2 F. Venn, 'A Futile Paper Chase: Anglo-American Relations and Middle East Oil 1918–34', *Diplomacy and Statecraft*, 1 (1990), 165–84; Michael J. Hogan, *Informal Entente: The Private Structure of Co-operation in Anglo-American Economic Diplomacy 1918–28* (University of Missouri Press, Columbia, 1977).
3 Kennedy, *Rise and Fall*, 366–7.
4 For the overview I have drawn liberally on: Kennedy, *Rise and Fall* and *Behind Diplomacy*; Lafeber, *American Age*; Cain and Hopkins, *British Imperialism*, Schulzinger, *American Diplomacy*; F. Costigliola, *Awkward Dominion: American Political, Economic, and Cultural Relations with Europe, 1919–33* (Cornell University Press, Ithaca, 1984); Parrini, *Heir to Empire*; Nicholas, *The United States and Britain*; Allen, *Britain and the United States*; Dimbleby and Reynolds, *An Ocean Apart*; D. Reynolds, *The Creation of the Anglo-American Alliance 1937–41* (Europa, London, 1981); Watt, *Succeeding John Bull*.

5 CAB 24/100, CP 842, 11 Mar. 1920 (Houston to Chamberlain via Lindsay, dispatched 5 Mar. 1920).
6 CAB 24/116, CP 2214, 30 Nov. 1920, and CP 2214A, 3 Dec. 1920. Geddes reported that House advised procrastination as the USA would deliver a generous settlement in the end: both Geddes and Chamberlain concluded that House had misjudged the situation.
7 Ibid.
8 CAB 24/123 (memo by Secretary of State for Foreign Affairs, Lord Curzon, 9 May 1921). 'Unwarrantable interference' was a US proposal of relief for Ireland. It was rejected; on 8 July there was a truce with the Sinn Fein and in December 1922 the Irish Free State was proclaimed. For a while, the Irish question ceased to be an irritant in Anglo-American affairs.
9 FRUS, 1920, vol. 2, 608–81, (Acting Secretary of State Polk to Ambassador Davis, 10 May 1920).
10 CAB 24/123, CP 2957 (memo, 'Anglo-Japanese Alliance', by Lee of Fareham, 21 May 1921).
11 For more detail on the Washington Naval Conference, see Kennedy, *Behind Diplomacy*, 359–63; Lafeber, *American Age*, 319–23.
12 CAB 24/ 138, CP 4112 ('Draft Dispatch to Allied Debtor Governments' by Balfour, 17 July 1922).
13 Quoted from K. Middlemas and J. Barnes, *Baldwin: A Biography* (Weidenfeld & Nicolson, London, 1969); see also H. Montgomery Hyde, *Baldwin: The Unexpected Prime Minister* (Hart-Davis, MacGibbon, London, 1973), 125–35.
14 Costigliola, *Awkward Dominion*, 20.
15 CAB 24/198, CP 344 (note by acting Secretary of State for Foreign Affairs, Lord Cushenden, circulating memo to Cabinet by R. L. Craigie on 'The State of US–UK Relations', 14 Nov. 1928).
16 Ibid.
17 CAB 24/171, CP 48 (memo by Secretary of State for Foreign Affairs, Austen Chamberlain, 'United States and the Geneva Protocol', 27 Jan. 1925).
18 J. Wheeler-Bennett, *The Disarmament Deadlock* (Routledge, London, 1934). Dick Richardson and Carolyn Kitching, 'Britain and the World Disarmament Conference', in Peter Catterall with C. J. Morris (ed.), *Britain and the Threat to Stability in Europe, 1918–45* (Leicester University Press, London, 1993), think the conference was doomed from the start. See also Alan P. Dobson, *Peaceful Air Warfare: the USA, Britain and the Politics of International Aviation* (Clarendon Press, Oxford, 1991), ch. 3.
19 Costigliola, *Awkward Dominion*, 131. I have drawn from this for the US side of economic diplomacy; from Cain and Hopkins, *British Empire*, for the British, and from Kennedy, *Rise and Fall*, for both.
20 CAB 24/174, CP 364 (memo by Austen Chamberlain on meeting with US Ambassador Houghton, 22 July 1925).
21 FRUS, 1925, vol. 2, 263–5 (Kellogg to Houghton, 1 Dec. 1925) and ibid., 1926, vol. 2 (Vansittart for Chamberlain to Sterling, US charge in London, 6 Apr. 1926). For the rubber dispute, see Joseph Brandes, *Herbert Hoover and Economic Diplomacy* (Pittsburgh University Press, Pittsburgh, 1962), chs 5 and 6.
22 CAB 24/188, CP 258 (Austen Chamberlain memo, 'Belligerent Rights at Sea and the Relations Between the United States and Great Britain', 26 Oct. 1927).

23 Martin Gilbert, *Winston S. Churchill, vol. 5: Companion, part 1* (Heinemann, London, 1979), 1033.
24 CAB 24/198, CP 344, 14 Nov. 1928.
25 CAB 24/199, CP 367 (memo by L. S. Amery, Dominions Secretary, 'Anglo-American Relations', 26 Nov. 1928).
26 CAB 24/199, CP 358 (memo by W. S. Churchill, Chancellor of the Exchequer, 'Anglo-American Relations,' 19 Nov. 1928).
27 Ibid.
28 Quoted from Lafeber, *American Age*, 325.
29 CAB 28/198, CP 344, 14 Nov. 1928.
30 CAB 24/199, CP 368 ('Three Questions of Imperial Defence Related to Anglo-American Relations', note by Secretary to CID M. P. A. Hankey, circulated on the authority of the Prime Minister to the Cabinet: CID on Naval Policy, 236 Meeting, 5 July 1928, Austen Chamberlain).
31 CAB 24/201, CP 26, 7 Feb. 1929(Howard to Chamberlain, 25 Jan. 1929).
32 CAB 23/60, C7/29, 15 Feb. 1929; CAB 24/202, CP 71, 8 Mar. 1929 (2nd Report of subcommittee of CID on Belligerent Rights).
33 CAB 24/207, CP 312 (memo, 'Conversations Between the PM and President Hoover at Washington (October 4 to 10, 1929)', undated).
34 FRUS, 1933, vol. 3, 17–19 (Bingham to Secretary of State, 11 Oct. 1933). Britain helped throughout Prohibition: a convention was signed in 1924, and executive action in 1926 clamped down on smuggling via Canada and British territories in the West Indies.
35 I. M. Drummond, *Imperial Economic Policy 1917–39* (George Allen & Unwin, London, 1974).
36 David Bergamini, *Japan's Imperial Conspiracy* (Heinemann, London, 1971).
37 FO 371/17603 (Vansittart to Lindsay, 24 Sept); 1934, this is taken from Venn's article 'A Futile Paper-Chase'.
38 FRUS, 1936, vol. 1, 629–35 (Hull meetings with Lindsay, 22 Jan. and 5 Feb. 1936).
39 In 1938 a dispute over islands in the Pacific was also resolved, albeit temporarily: See M. R. Megaw, 'The Scramble for the Pacific: Anglo-American Rivalry in the 1930s', *Historical Studies*, 17 (1977), 458–73.

4 IN WAR AND COLD WAR 1939–51

1 Interview with Callaghan, Feb. 1987, conducted by the author.
2 Alan P. Dobson, *US Wartime Aid To Britain* (Croom Helm, London, 1986)
3 Warren F. Kimball, *Churchill and Roosevelt: The Complete Correspondence*, 3 vols (Collins, London, 1984), I, 9.
4 Bradley F. Smith, 'Admiral Godfrey's Mission to America June/July 1941', *Intelligence and National Security*, 1(iii) (1986), 441–50 (source, CAB, 122/1021, 7 July 1941).
5 J. T. Richelson and D. Ball, *The Ties That Bind* (Allen & Unwin, Hemel Hempstead, 1985). See also F. Hinsley *et al.*, *British Intelligence in the Second World War*, 4 vols (Cambridge University Press, Cambridge, 1979–88); Bradley Smith, 'America and Wartime Changes in Intelligence', in Warren F. Kimball (ed.), *America Unbound: World War 2 and the Making of a Superpower* (St Martin's Press, New York, 1992).

6   John Bayliss, *Anglo-American Defence Relations 1939–84* (Macmillan, London, 1984); Margaret Gowing, *Britain and Atomic Energy 1939–45* (Macmillan, London, 1964); A. Pierre, *Nuclear Politics: The British Experience with an Independent Strategic Force, 1939–1970* (Oxford University Press, London, 1972).

7   Kimball, Complete Correspondence, 9; M. A. Stoler, *The Politics of the Second Front: American Military Planning and Diplomacy in Coalition Warfare, 1941–1943* (Greenwood Press, Westport, 1977); Lafeber, *American Age*; Bayliss, *Defence Relations*; W. R. Louis, *Imperialism at Bay: The United States and the Decolonisation of the British Empire 1941–45* (Oxford University Press, Oxford, 1978).

8   Kimball, *Complete Correspondence*, Introduction; Alex Danchev, *Very Special Relationship: Field Marshal Sir John Dill and the Anglo-American Alliance 1941–44* (Brassey's, London, 1986).

9   Henry B. Ryan, *The Vision of Anglo-America: The US–UK Alliance and the Emerging Cold War 1943–1946* (Cambridge University Press, Cambridge, 1987), section 2.

10   Dobson, *Peaceful Air Warfare*, chs 5 and 6.

11   Dobson, *Economic Special Relationship*, ch. 2.

12   Ibid.; Robert A. Divine, *Roosevelt and World War 2* (Penguin Books, Harmondsworth, 1970); R. Dallek, *Franklin D. Roosevelt and American Foreign Policy* (Oxford University Press, New York, 1979); Warren F. Kimball, '"The Family Circle", and "Naked Reverse Right"', in his *The Juggler: Franklin Roosevelt as Wartime Statesman* (Princeton University Press, Princeton, 1991).

13   US National Archives (hereafter NA), RG 169, box 163, folder – British Capital Goods, Knollenberg to Crowley, 15 Oct. 1943).

14   Alan P. Dobson, 'A Mess of Pottage for Your Economic Birthright: The 1941–42 Wheat Negotiations and Anglo-American Economic Diplomacy', *Historical Journal*, 28 (1985), 739–50; Dobson, Peaceful Air Warfare, chs 5 and 6.

15   Dobson, *Mess of Pottage*.

16   For much of this section I have drawn from my own and the following publications: Gardner, *Sterling Dollar Diplomacy*; G. Kolko, *The Politics of War* (Weidenfeld & Nicolson, London, 1969); Fred Block, *The Origins of International Economic Disorder* (University of California University Press, Berkeley, 1977); Woods, *Changing of the Guard*; G. John Ikenberry, 'A World Economy Restored: Expert Consensus and the Anglo-American Post-War Settlement', *International Organization*, 46 (1992), 289–323.

17   Kimball, *Complete Correspondence*, I, 49–51.

18   R. G. D. Allen, 'Mutual Aid Between the United States and the British Empire', *Journal of the Royal Statistical Society*, 109 (1946); Dobson, *US Wartime Aid*.

19   CAB 66, WP(41)202 and 203; H. V. Morton, *Atlantic Meeting* (Methuen, London, 1943); T. A. Wilson, *The First Summit: Roosevelt and Churchill at Placentia Bay* (Houghton Mifflin, Boston, 1969); Dobson, *Economic Special Relationship*, ch. 2.

20   Ibid.; see also CAB 66, WP(42)21, 5 Jan. 1942; and CAB 65, WM(14)42, 2 Feb. 1942.

21   Kimball, *Complete Correspondence*, I, 357–8 and 360–1.

22 NA, State Department, 841.24/720 (hereafter only decimal number references are given), (Ambassador Winant to Secretary of State, 3 Sept. 1941); Cmnd 6311 'The Export White Paper', 10 Sept. 1941); for more detail, see Alan P. Dobson, 'The Export White Paper of 1941', *Economic History Review*, 39 (1986), 59–76.

23 FO 371/40883 (memo by Dalton, 'Supersession of the Export White Paper', 28 June 1944).

24 Dobson, 'Export White Paper'.

25 F. D. Roosevelt Library (hereafter FDR Lib.), Morgenthau Diary, vol. 592, 292 (Stettinius to Morgenthau 3 Dec. 1942), where he quotes Cox's memo to him of 23 Nov. 1942; ibid., pp. 110 and 150–78, 17 and 18 Dec. respectively; NA RG 169, box 163 (minutes of Dollar Position committee, 29 Dec. 1942); ibid., box 721 (BEW Board Meeting, 29 Dec. 1942).

26 FDR Lib., Morgenthau Diary, vol. 607, 99 (White to Morgenthau, 8 Feb. 1943).

27 FDR Lib., PSF, box 49, folder GB 1944–45 (Roosevelt to Churchill, 22 Feb. 1944).

28 NA, State Department 841.24/2197A (draft letter and memo by Acheson, 21 Feb. 1944); FDR Lib., Morgenthau Diary, vol. 709, 109, 13 Mar. 1944.

29 FO 371/40881 (Anderson to Churchill, 24 Feb. 1944).

30 Kimball, *Complete Correspondence*, III, 35–6 and 65–6.

31 CAB 66, WP(43)566 (Hudson memo, 14 Dec. 1943) and WP(43)576 (Amery memo, 20 Dec. 1943); Kenneth Young, *Churchill and Beaverbrook: A Study in Friendship and Politics* (Eyre & Spottiswoode, London, 1966), 261; Lionel Robbins, *Autobiography of an Economist* (Macmillan, London, 1978), 203.

32 A. Van Dormael, *Bretton Woods: Birth of a Monetary System* (Macmillan, London, 1978); Block, *International Economic Disorder*; Dobson, *Economic Special Relationship*.

33 Dobson, *Economic Special Relationship*, 65–74.

34 FO 371/45699 (Keynes, 'Overseas Assets and Liabilities of the UK', 12 Sept. 1945).

35 CAB 128/4, CM(45)59, 5 Dec. 1945; Cmnd 6708 ('Financial Agreement Between the Government of the United States and the United Kingdom', 6 Dec. 1945).

36 Dobson, *Peaceful Air Warfare*, ch. 6.

37 Kolko, *Politics of War*; Block, *International Economic Disorder*; Woods, *Changing of the Guard*; David P. Calleo, *Beyond American Hegemony: The Future of the Western Alliance* (Basic Books Inc., New York, 1987); Kennedy, *Rise and Fall*; Pollard and Wells, in W. H. Becker and S. F. Wells, *Economics and World Power: An Assessment of American Diplomacy Since 1789* (Columbia University Press, New York, 1984). Figures quoted in the latter show US GNP 1945 at $220 billion compared with $91 billion in 1939; 1947 US trade amounted to 33% of world total; in 1948 the USA produced approximately 41% of the world's goods and services.

38 Alan P. Dobson, 'Labour or Conservative: Does it Matter in Anglo-American Relations?', *Journal of Contemporary History*, 25 (1990), 387–407.

39 CAB 129, CP(49)114 (memo by Dalton, 10 May 1949).

40 For help with Cold War literature, see: F. M. Carroll, 'Anglo-American Relations and the Origins of the Cold War: The New Perspective', *Canadian Journal of History*, 24(ii), (1989), 191–209; L. S. Kaplan, 'Cold War and

European Revisionism', and J. L. Gaddis *et al.* with replies in *Diplomatic History*, 2(ii) (1978) and 7(iii) (1983), respectively; Richard Crockatt, *US and the Cold War 1941–53* (BAAS pamphlet, Durham, 1989). Basic account given here is based on my research and: T. H. Anderson, *The United States, Great Britain, and the Cold War, 1944–47* (University of Missouri Press, Columbia, 1981); Alan Bullock, *Ernest Bevin: Foreign Secretary* (Oxford University Press, Oxford, 1985); Ryan, *Vision of Anglo-America*; Fraser Harbutt, *The Iron Curtain: Churchill, America, and the Origins of the Cold War* (Oxford University Press, New York, 1986); and Kimball, *The Juggler.*

41   Richelson and Ball, *Ties That Bind*; Duncan Campbell, *The Unsinkable Aircraft Carrier: American Military Power in Britain* (Michael Joseph, London, 1984).

42   CAB 128, 3(47)2, 28 Jan. 1947; CAB 129, CP(47)35, 18 Jan. 1947; CAB 128, 62(49)6, 27 Oct. 1949.

43   Harry S. Truman Library (hereafter HST Lib.), Acheson Papers, box 64 (memos of conversation, 25 Oct. (dated 3 Nov.) 1949).

44   The idea of hegemony does not seem to sit well with the compromises and accommodations that the US had to make with its allies in both the economic and the defence fields.

45   HST Lib., Acheson Papers, box 67a, folder memos of conversation 1952 (Mar., text of draft letter Acheson to Gifford, US ambassador in London); R. H. Ferrell, *The Eisenhower Diaries* (W. W. Norton, New York, 1981).

46   Library of Congress, Harriman Papers, box 271, folder Marshall Plan, Country File, UK 20 (Douglas to Secretary of State Acheson, Bruce, Harriman, Perkins and Bohlen, 7 May 1950).

47   HST Lib., PSF, box 220, folder – NSC meetings (memos for the President, 74th meeting, 12 Dec. 1950).

5   CONSERVATIVELY SPECIAL 1951–61

1   For this chapter I have drawn liberally on: Lafeber, *American Age*; Stephen E. Ambrose, *Rise to Globalism: American Foreign Policy Since 1938* (Penguin Books, Harmondsworth, 1988), and his *Eisenhower: Soldier & President* (Simon & Schuster, New York, 1990); F. S. Northedge, *Descent from Power: British Foreign Policy 1945–1973* (Allen & Unwin, London, 1974); J. W. Young (ed.), *The Foreign Policy of Churchill's Peacetime Administration 1951–55* (Leicester University Press, Leicester, 1988); Bayliss, *Defence Relations*; W. R. Louis and H. Bull, *The Special Relationship: Anglo-American Relations since 1945* (Clarendon Press, Oxford, 1986); Bartlett, *Special Relationship*; D. Acheson, *Present at the Creation* (W. W. Norton, New York, 1969), and other memoirs and biographies of leading politicians.

2   HST Lib., PSF box 115, folder – General File Churchill, Winston, 1951–53 (Fechteler to Truman, 2 Jan. 1952); ibid., folder – General File Churchill, Winston (meeting with President Truman, Jan. 1952 (1), minutes meeting 7 Jan. 1952).

3   HST Lib., Acheson Papers, box 67, folder – Jan. (minutes of 8 Jan. meeting by Acheson for L. D. Battle, 9 Jan. 1952); HST Lib., PSF, box 115, folder – General File Churchill, Winston (meeting with President Truman Jan. 1952 (1), 18 Jan. 1952).

4 Ibid.; Acheson Papers, box 67, folder – Jan. (Pearson to Acheson, 15 Jan. 1952).

5 CAB 128/24, 4(52)2 and 4, 17 Jan. 1952.

6 HST Lib., PSF, box 116, folder – General File Churchill–Truman Meetings (papers prepared for US–UK Relations, Steering Group: War Planning to Include the Re-Creation of the Combined Chiefs of Staff, R. P. Gilman, 2 Jan. 1952).

7 Eisenhower (DDE) Library, Dulles Papers Series, box 8, folder – Classified Material (memo to Eisenhower, 5 Jan. 1953).

8 DDE Lib., Ann Whitman File (AWF) box 17, folder – President–Churchill, Jan. 1–June 1954 (Churchill to Eisenhower, 21 June 1954).

9 CAB 128/18, 85(50)3, 12 Dec. 1950.

10 HST Lib., PSF, box 115, folder – General File Churchill, Winston, 1951–3, ('Brief Notes on Questions Prime Minister Churchill Might Raise', Acheson to Truman, 7 Jan. 1953).

11 Ibid. (meeting with President Truman, Jan. 1952); folder – Discussion on Atomic Matter (7 Jan. 1952).

12 Ibid. (Acheson to Pearson via ambassador Woodward, Jan. 1952).

13 Ibid. (Pearson to Acheson, 15 Jan. 1952); Dulles Papers, Subject Series box 10, Churchill–Eden Correspondence 1954 (1) (Churchill to Eisenhower 18 Sept. 1954).

14 Ibid., box 1, folder – 'Bermuda' Foreign Ministers Conference (meeting of Dulles and senior advisers, 8 June 1953).

15 CAB 128/18, 85(50)3, 12 Dec. 1950.

16 Quoted from G. C. Herring, *America's Longest War: The United States and Vietnam 1950–75* (Wiley & Son, New York, 1979), 10–11.

17 Anthony Eden, *Full Circle* (Cassell, London, 1960), 105.

18 HST Lib., PSF, box 116, folder – General File Churchill–Truman Meetings (Papers Prepared for US–UK Relations, Papers on the Middle East).

19 Ibid., box 115, folder – General File Churchill, Winston, 1951–53 (Brief Notes on Questions Prime Minister Churchill Might Raise, Acheson to Truman, 7 Jan. 1953).

20 HST Lib., Acheson Papers, box 67a, folder – August (Re Iran, memo of meeting with ambassador Franks).

21 DDE Library, C. D. Jackson Records 1953–4, box 2, folder – Bermuda Conference, 27 Nov. 1953 ('US–UK roles in Middle East').

22 Harold Macmillan, *Riding the Storm* (Macmillan, London, 1971), 122.

23 DDE Lib., CF CF, box 82, folder – Suez Canal Crisis (3) (Aldrich to Herter, 26 Nov. 1956).

24 Ibid., AWF, box 18, folder – Churchill, 8 Apr. thru Dec. 31, 1957 (1) (Churchill to Eisenhower, 23 Nov. 1956).

25 Cmnd 124, 1957, 'Defence, Outline of Future Policy'.

26 DDE Lib., CF CF, box 9, folders – Bermuda Meeting, March 21–23, 1957; For the President (1) (undated).

27 D. D. Eisenhower, *Waging Peace* (Doubleday, New York, 1965), 124.

28 For text, see Bayliss, *Defence Relations*, appendix 9.

29 For more detail, see Dobson, *Economic Special Relationship*, ch. 5.

30 Alan P. Dobson, 'The Kennedy Administration and Economic Warfare Against Communism', *International Affairs*, 64 (1988), 599–616.

31 Dobson, *Economic Special Relationship*, 147–55.

6 YEARS OF TRANSITION 1961-79

1 The early part of this chapter is drawn largely from Alan P. Dobson, 'The Years of Transition: Anglo-American Relations 1961–67', *Review of International Studies*, 16 (1990), 239–58.
2 H. Macmillan, *Pointing the Way* (Macmillan, London, 1972), 284.
3 T. Sorensen, *Kennedy* (Harper Row, New York, 1965), 558.
4 F. Costigliola, 'The Failed Design, de Gaulle and the Struggle for Europe', *Diplomatic History*, 8 (1984), 227–51.
5 John F. Kennedy Library (hereafter JFK Lib.), NSF, box 170, folder – UK General 3/1/61–5/15/61 (Ball to Kennedy, 7 Aug. 1961).
6 Ibid., folder – UK General 12/6/62–12/9/62 (White House to Rusk, 7 Dec. 1962); D. Brinkley, 'Dean Acheson and the "Special Relationship": The West Point Speech of December 1962', *Historical Journal*, 33 (1990), 599–608.
7 M. Trachtenberg, 'White House Tapes and Minutes of the Cuban Missile Crisis', *International Security*, 10 (1985), 179.
8 Sorensen, *Kennedy*, 564–5.
9 JFK Lib., NSF, box 235–8, folder – Presidential trips (Nassau Macmillan Talks 12/62, Briefing Book).
10 Sorensen, Kennedy, 566. For more detail of the Skybolt affair, see: G. Ball, *The Past Has Another Pattern* (W. W. Norton, New York, 1982); D. Nunnerly, *President Kennedy and Britain* (Bodley Head, London, 1972), and his 'Interview with Lord Thorneycroft', 18 June 1969, JFK Lib.; R. E. Neustadt, *Alliance Politics* (Columbia University Press, New York, 1970); A. Horne, 'The Macmillan Years and Afterwards', in Louis and Bull, *Special Relationship*; Bell, *Debatable Alliance*; Bayliss, *Defence Relations*.
11 Lyndon Baines Johnson Library (hereafter LBJ Lib.), NSF, boxes 18 and 19 (memo meeting with Prime Minister Wilson, 7 Dec. 1964).
12 D. Nunnerly, 'Interview with H. Brandon', 23 Feb. 1970, JFK Lib.; compare mutual references in H. Wilson, *The Labour Government 1964–70* (Penguin Book, Harmondsworth, 1974) and L. B. Johnson, *The Vantage Point* (Holt, Rinehart and Winston, New York, 1971); but see also 'Interview with James Callaghan', Feb. 1987, conducted by the author, in which, after slight hesitation, he described Wilson's relations with Johnson as good; Dimbleby and Reynolds, *An Ocean Apart*, ch. 13.
13 LBJ Lib., GEN CO, box 76, folder – CO 305 UK 1/1/65–7/1/65 (Valenti to Johnson, 26 Feb. 1965).
14 Dobson, Callaghan Interview; J. Callaghan, *Time and Chance* (Collins, London, 1987), 176; R. H. Crossman, *The Diaries of a Cabinet Minister: vol. 1, 1964–66* (Hamish Hamilton, London, 1973), entries 12 Nov. and 11 Dec. 1964, and 11 Feb. 1965; Clive Ponting, *Breach of Promise: Labour in Power 1964–70* (Hamish Hamilton, London, 1989), ch. 3.
15 Johnson, *Vantage Point*, appendix A, and pp. xi, 597–8.
16 U. Kitzinger, *Diplomacy and Persuasion: How Britain Joined the Common Market* (Thames & Hudson, London, 1973).
17 LBJ Lib., NSF Country File, box 215–16, file – UK Trendex (Francis Bator to McGeorge Bundy, 'The UK problem and thinking about the unthinkable', 29 July 1965); ibid., box 208–9, Europe, USSR, UK, folder – UK memos vol. viii 1/66–7/66 (Fowler memo. for Johnson, 14 July 1966).

18 Ibid., box 215–16, folder – Trendex (McGeorge Bundy memo for Johnson, 28 July 1965).
19 Cmnd 2901, 'The Defence Review', Feb. 1966.
20 LBJ Lib., GEN CO 305, 1963–69, folder – 7/13/66–11/3/66 (Heller to Johnson, 24 July 1966).
21 Ibid., NSF Country File, box 208–9, folder – UK memos vol. xiii 1/6–7/66 (US Embassy London to State Department); ibid., box 210–12, folder – UK memos. vol. xi 4/67–6/67 (Bruce to Rusk).
22 Cmnd. 3357, 'Supplementary Statement on Defence Policy', July 1967.
23 LBJ Lib., CF CF, box 49, folder – Financial Relations (Callaghan to Fowler, 10 Nov. 1967).
24 Wilson, *Labour Government*, 577.
25 Ibid., 579; Dobson, Callaghan Interview.
26 Nixon Project, US National Archives, Alexandria Virginia, WHCF CO, box 79, folder – CO 160 UK begin–3/5/69 (Nixon to Wilson, 11 Jan. 1969).
27 H. Kissinger, *The White House Years* (Weidenfeld & Nicolson and Michael Joseph, London, 1979), 91.
28 Ibid., 938.
29 Ibid., 937.
30 H. Brandon, 'The Private World of Richard Nixon', *New York Sunday Times Weekly Review*, 12 Nov. 1972.
31 'United States Foreign Policy for the 1970s: a New Strategy for Peace', Report by President Richard Nixon to Congress, 18 Feb. 1970.
32 Dobson, Callaghan Interview.
33 Gerald Ford Library, WHCF, box 56, CO 160, folder – 11/1/74–1/27/75 (Davis to Porter, 27 Jan. 1975: subject 'Background Information for Mrs Ford re visit of Prime Minister Harold Wilson').
34 Dobson, Callaghan Interview.
35 Ford Lib., WHCF, box 57, CO 160, folder – 11/1/75–12/31/75 (Ramsbotham to Hartman, and Scowcroft's reply, 28 Oct. and 7 Nov. 1975).
36 S. Fay and H. Young, 'How the Hard Men Took Over Britain', *Sunday Times*, 14 May 1978.
37 Dobson, Callaghan Interview.
38 Edmund Dell, *A Hard Pounding* (Clarendon Press, Oxford, 1991) and paper to staff/postgraduate seminar, Department of Political Theory and Government, University College of Swansea, 11 March 1994; Callaghan, *Time and Chance*; 'IMF Crisis Symposium', *Contemporary Record*, 3 (1989), 39–45.
39 Jimmy Carter Library, WHCF, box CA-1, folder – CA 10/1/77–8/31/78 (Eizenstat and McIntyre to Carter, 18 May 1978); interview with US Special Ambassador in charge of Bermuda 2 negotiations, Alan Boyd, 9 Apr. 1991, conducted by the author: for full account, see Alan P. Dobson, 'Regulation or Competition: Negotiating the Anglo-American Air Service Agreement of 1977', *Journal of Transport History*, 15(ii) (1994), 144–65.
40 Callaghan, *Time and Chance*, 556; C. Grayling and C. Langoon, *Just Another Star? Anglo-American Relations since 1945* (Harrap, London, 1988), 59; Bayliss, *Defence Relations*.
41 Quoted from R. Dugger, *On Reagan* (McGraw Hill, New York, 1983), 517.

7 OF INTERESTS AND SENTIMENT 1980–95, AND BEYOND

1   Available literature on Anglo-American relations becomes more journalistic and/or conceptual and analytical the nearer one gets to the present. Absence of primary sources is a major problem. This chapter is based mainly on secondary sources, memoirs and some insights gained through interviews for rather specialised research, but always with the broader relationship also in mind. Books covering the recent years of the relationship include: Campbell, *Unsinkable Aircraft Carrier*; Grayling and Langoon, *Just Another Star*; C. Hitchens, *Blood, Class and Nostalgia* (Farrar, Strauss & Giroux, New York, 1990); A. Adonis and T. Hames (eds), *A Conservative Revolution? The Thatcher and Reagan Decade in Perspective* (Manchester University Press, Manchester, 1994), ch. 6; P. Byrd (ed.), *British Foreign Policy under Thatcher* (Phillip Allan/St Martin's Press, Beddington and New York, 1988), ch. 1; D. E. Kyvig, *Reagan and the World* (Praeger, New York, 1990), ch. 3; D. Sanders, *Losing an Empire, Finding a Role* (Macmillan, Basingstoke, 1990), ch. 6; S. Gill (ed.), *Atlantic Relations beyond the Reagan Era* (Wheatsheaf, Hertfordshire, 1989); Caspar Weinberger, *Fighting for Peace: Seven Critical Years in the Pentagon* (Warner Books, New York, 1990); Margaret Thatcher, *The Downing Street Years* (HarperCollins, London, 1993); G. Warner, 'The Anglo-American Special Relationship', *Diplomatic History*, 13 (1989); D. Reynolds, 'Rethinking Anglo-American Relations', *International Affairs*, 65 (1988/9); Gregory F. Treverton, 'Britain's Role in the 1990s: An American View', ibid., 66 (1990).

2   LBJ Lib., NSF, NSC Meetings File, box 2, folder – NSC Meetings, vol. 5, Tab 69, 6/5/68, Current Issues Affecting US/UK Relations (summary of notes of 587th, 5 June 1968).

3   J. Frankel, *British Foreign Policy 1945–73* (Oxford University Press, London, 1975), 204.

4   Ibid.

5   Quoted from Lafeber, *American Age*, 665.

6   Sanders, *Losing an Empire*, 179.

7   Bayliss, *Defence Relations*, 202–5, Appendix 17, 11 March 1982 (Thatcher to Reagan, and his reply; and Weinberger to Nott, and his reply).

8   Campbell, *Unsinkable Aircraft Carrier*, 20; see also Simon Duke, *United States Bases in the United Kingdom* (Macmillan, London, 1987).

9   Weinberger, *Fighting for Peace*, 205–6; see also Shultzinger, *Diplomacy*, 340–1.

10 Weinberger, *Fighting for Peace*, 207.

11 Dimbleby and Reynolds, *An Ocean Apart*, 314–15.

12 For more detail on the impact of the EC on Anglo-American relations, see: Alan P. Dobson, 'The Special Relationship and European Integration', *Diplomacy and Statecraft*, 2 (1991); Gill, *Atlantic Relations*; L. Freedman (ed.), *The Troubled Alliance: Atlantic Relations in the 1980s* (Heinneman, London, 1983); Michael Smith, 'The Devil You Know: The US and a Changing EC', *International Affairs*, 68 (1992); D. Reynolds, 'Britain and the New Europe: the Search for Identity since 1940' [review essay], *Historical Journal*, 31 (1988); Y. Devuyst, 'European Community Integration and the United States: Toward a New Transatlantic Relationship', *Journal of European Integration*, 4 (1990).

13 Quoted from Lafeber, *American Age*, 677; Anthony Payne, 'US Hegemony and the Reconfiguration of the Caribbean', *Review of International Studies*, 20 (1994).

14 F. Pym, *The Politics of Consent* (Hamish Hamilton, London, 1984), 28–31.

15 Thatcher, *Downing Street*, 467.

16 Ibid.

17 Ibid., 783.

18 For a fuller account of this and of other troubles in Anglo-American civil-aviation affairs in the 1980s and 1990s, see Alan P. Dobson, *Flying in the Face of Competition: The Policies and Diplomacy of Airline Regulatory Reform in Britain, the USA and the European Community 1968–94* (Ashgate, Aldershot, 1995), and 'Aspects of Anglo-American Aviation Diplomacy 1976–93', *Diplomacy and Statecraft*, 4 (1993).

19 Weinberger, *Fighting for Peace*, 193.

20 Ibid., 195.

21 Anastasia Pardalis, 'European Political Co-operation and the United States', *Journal of Common Market Studies*, 4 (1987).

22 Hitchens, *Blood, Class and Nostalgia*.

23 Watt, *Succeeding*.

24 J. A. Hobson, *Imperialism* (Unwin Hyman, London, 1988); V. I. Lenin, *Imperialism the Highest Stage of Capitalism* (Progress Publishers, Moscow, 1978).

25 William Appleman Williams, probably most notable for his *The Tragedy of American Diplomacy*; but see also, *The Roots of Modern American Empire: A Study of the Growth and Shaping of Social Consciousness in a Marketplace Society* (Anthony Blond, London, 1970).

26 Payne, 'Hegemony', provides a good introduction to hegemony theory and its literature.

27 Catherine M. Kelleher, 'America Looks at Europe', in Freedman, *Troubled Alliance*, 53.

28 David Owen, 'Britain and the United States', in W. E. Leuchtenberg *et al.*, *Britain and the United States: Views to Mark the Silver Jubilee* (Heinneman, London, 1979), 76.

Bibliography

DOCUMENTARY SOURCES

British

British Public Record Office:
    Cabinet Minutes and Papers
    Foreign Office General Correspondence
Command Papers:
    Cmnd 124, 1957, 'Defence: Outline of Future Policy'
    Cmnd 2901, 1966, 'The Defence Review'
    Cmnd 3357, 1967, 'Supplementary Statement on Defence Policy'
Hansard
Interview with Lord Callaghan, 26 Nov. 1987, conducted by the author

American

US State Department publication prepared by Carlton Savage, *Policy of the United States Toward Maritime Commerce in War, vol. 1, 1776–1914* (US Government Printing Office, Washington DC, 1934)
Foreign Relations of the United States: published documents by the US State Department: various volumes
US National Archives:
    Record Group 169
    State Department Decimal Files
    Nixon Project, Central Files
Presidential Libraries:
    F. D. Roosevelt:
        President's Secretaries File
        Morgenthau Diary
    H. S. Truman:
        President's Secretaries File
        Papers of Dean Acheson
    D. D. Eisenhower:
        Ann Whitman Files
        Central Files
        Papers of John Foster Dulles
        Records of C. D. Jackson

J. F. Kennedy:
National Security Files
Interviews conducted by D. Nunnerly with Lord Thorneycroft, 18 June
1969 and with Henry Brandon, 23 Feb. 1970
L. B. Johnson:
National Security Files
Central Files
General Correspondence
Gerald Ford:
Central Files
James Carter:
Central Files
Library of Congress:
Papers of Averell Harriman

BOOKS

Acheson, D., *Present at the Creation* (W. W. Norton, New York, 1969).

Adonis, A., and Hames, T. (eds), *A Conservative Revolution? The Thatcher and Reagan Decade in Perspective* (Manchester University Press, Manchester, 1994).

Allen, H. C., *Great Britain and the United States: A History of Anglo-American Relations 1783–1952* (Odhams Press, London, 1954).

Ambrose, S. E., *Rise to Globalism: American Foreign Policy since 1938* (Penguin Books, Harmondsworth, 1988).

—— *Eisenhower: Soldier and President* (Simon & Schuster, New York, 1990).

Anderson, T. H., *The United States, Great Britain and the Cold War, 1944–47* (University of Missouri Press, Columbia, 1981).

Ball, G., *The Past Has Another Pattern* (W. W. Norton, New York, 1982).

Bartlett, C. J., *The Special Relationship: A Political History of Anglo-American Relations Since 1945* (Longman, London, 1992).

—— *The Long Retreat: A Short History of British Defence Policy* (Macmillan, London, 1972).

Bayliss, John, *Anglo-American Defence Relations 1939–84* (Macmillan, London, 1984).

Becker, W. H., and Wells, S. F. (eds), *Economics and World Power: An Assessment of American Diplomacy since 1789* (Columbia University Press, New York, 1984).

Bell, C., *The Debatable Alliance* (Oxford University Press, London, 1964).

Bergamini, David, *Japan's Imperial Conspiracy* (Heinemann, London, 1971).

Beugel, H. E. van de, *From Marshall Aid to Atlantic Partnership: European Integration as a Concern of American Foreign Policy* (Elsevier, Amsterdam, 1966).

Block, Fred, *The Origins of International Economic Disorder* (University of California Press, Berkeley, 1977).

Brandes, Joseph, *Herbert Hoover and Economic Diplomacy* (Pittsburgh University Press, Pittsburgh, 1962).

Bullock, A., *Ernest Bevin: Foreign Secretary* (Oxford University Press, Oxford, 1985).

Burk, Kathleen, *Britain, America and the Sinews of War, 1914–1918* (Allen & Unwin, Boston, 1985).

Byrd, P. (ed.), *British Foreign Policy under Thatcher* (Phillip Allan/St Martin's Press, Beddington and New York, 1988).

Cain, P. J., and Hopkins, A. G., *British Imperialism: Crisis and Reconstruction 1914–1990* (Longman, London, 1993).

Callaghan, J., *Time and Chance* (Collins, London, 1987).

Calleo, David P., *Beyond American Hegemony: The Future of the Western Alliance* (Basic Books Inc., New York, 1987).

Campbell, D., *The Unsinkable Aircraft Carrier: American Military Power in Britain* (Michael Joseph, London, 1984).

Carrington, Lord Peter, *Reflecting on Things Past* (Collins, London, 1988).

Catterall, P., and Morris, C. J. (eds), *Britain and the Threat to Stability in Europe, 1918–45* (Leicester University Press, London, 1993).

Commager, H. S., *Living Ideas in America* (Harper, New York, 1951).

Churchill, W. S., *History of the Second World War: Their Finest Hour* and *The Grand Alliance* (Cassell, London, 1949–50).

Costigliola, F., *Awkward Dominion: American Political, Economic, and Cultural Relations with Europe, 1919–33* (Cornell University Press, Ithaca, 1984).

Crockatt, R., *US and the Cold War 1941–53* (BAAS pamphlet, Durham, 1989).

Crossman, R. H., *The Diaries of a Cabinet Minister, vol. 1, 1964–66* (Hamish Hamilton, London, 1973).

Dallek, R., *Franklin D. Roosevelt and American Foreign Policy* (Oxford University Press, New York, 1979).

Danchev, A., *Very Special Relationship: Field Marshall Dill and the Anglo-American Alliance 1941–44* (Brassey's, London,1986).

—— *Oliver Franks: Founding Father* (Clarendon Press, Oxford, 1993).

Dell, E., *A Hard Pounding* (Clarendon Press, Oxford, 1991).

Dimbleby, D., and Reynolds, D., *An Ocean Apart* (Hodder & Stoughton, London, 1988).

Divine, R. A., *Roosevelt and World War Two* (Penguin Books, Harmondsworth, 1970).

Dobson, Alan P., *US Wartime Aid to Britain* (Croom Helm, London, 1986).

—— *The Politics of the Anglo-American Economic Special Relationship* (Harvester Wheatsheaf/St Martin's, Brighton and New York, 1988).

—— *Peaceful Air Warfare: The USA, Britain and the Politics of International Aviation* (Clarendon Press, Oxford, 1991).

—— *Flying in the Face of Competition: Diplomacy and Airline Policy in Britain, the USA and the European Community 1968–94* (Ashgate, Aldershot, 1995).

Dormael, A. van, *Bretton Woods: Birth of a Monetary System* (Macmillan, London, 1978).

Drummond, I. M., *Imperial Economic Policy 1917–39* (George Allen & Unwin, London, 1974).

Dugger, R., *On Reagan* (McGraw Hill, New York, 1983).

Duke, S., *United States Bases in the United Kingdom* (Macmillan, London, 1987).

Eden, A., *Full Circle* (Cassell, London, 1960).

Edmonds, Robin, *The Big Three: Churchill, Roosevelt and Stalin in Peace and War* (Norton, New York, 1991).

Eisenhower, D. D., *Mandate for Change* (Doubleday, New York, 1963).

—— *Waging Peace* (Doubleday, New York, 1965).

Ferrell, R.H., *American Diplomacy: The Twentieth Century* (W. W. Norton & Co., New York, 1988).

—— (ed.), *The Eisenhower Diaries* (W. W. Norton, New York, 1981).

Ford, G., *A Time to Heal: The Autobiography of Gerald Ford* (W.H. Allen, London, 1979).

Frankel, J., *British Foreign Policy 1945–73* (Oxford University Press, London, 1975).

Freedman, L. (ed.), *The Troubled Alliance: Atlantic Relations in the 1980s* (Heinemann, London, 1983).

Gardner, Lloyd C., *Safe For Democracy: The Anglo-American Response to Revolution 1913–23* (Oxford University Press, New York, 1984).

Gardner, R. N., *Sterling Dollar Diplomacy in Current Perspective* (Columbia University Press, New York, 1980).

Gelber, Lionel M., *The Rise of the Anglo-American Friendship* (Oxford University Press, London, 1938).

Gibbs, P. (ed.), *Bridging the Atlantic: Anglo-American Friendship as a Way to World Peace* (Hutchinson, London, 1944).

Gilbert, M., *Winston S. Churchill, vol. 5: Companion, part 1* (Heinemann, London, 1979).

Gill, S., *Atlantic Relations beyond the Reagan Era* (Wheatsheaf, Hertfordshire, 1989).

Gowing, M., *Britain and Atomic Energy 1939–45* (Macmillan, London, 1964).

Grayling, C., and Langoon, C., *Just Another Star? Anglo-American Relations since 1945* (Harrap, London, 1988).

Grey, Viscount, of Fallodon, *Twenty Five Years 1892–1916* (Hodder & Stoughton, London, 1947).

Harbutt, Fraser, *The Iron Curtain: Churchill, America, and the Origins of the Cold War* (Oxford University Press, Oxford, 1986).

Herring, G., *America's Longest War: The United States and Vietnam 1950–75* (Wiley & Son, New York, 1979).

Hinsley, F., *British Intelligence in the Second World War*, 4 vols (Cambridge University Press, Cambridge, 1979–88).

Hitchens, C., *Blood, Class and Nostalgia* (Farrar, Strauss & Giroux, New York, 1990).

Hobson, J. A., *Imperialism* (Unwin Hyman, London, 1988).

Hogan, Michael J., *Informal Entente: The Private Structure of Co-operation in Anglo-American Economic Diplomacy 1918–28* (University of Missouri Press, Columbia, 1977).

Hull, C., *The Memoirs of Cordell Hull*, 2 vols (Hodder & Stoughton, London, 1948).

Hyde, H. Montgomery, *Baldwin: The Unexpected Prime Minister* (Hart-Davis/ McGibbon, London, 1973).

Johnson, L. B., *The Vantage Point* (Holt, Rinehart & Winston, New York, 1971).

Kennedy, P., *The Rise and Fall of the Great Powers: Economic Change and Military Conflict from 1500 to 2000* (Fontana Press, London, 1989).

—— *The Realities Behind Diplomacy: Background Influences on British External Policy 1865–1980* (Fontana, London, 1981).

Keynes, J. M., *The Economic Consequences of the Peace* (Macmillan, London, 1920).

Kimball, Warren, F., *Churchill and Roosevelt: The Complete Correspondence*, 3 vols (Collins, London, 1984).
—— *America Unbound: World War 2 and the Making of a Superpower* (St Martin's, New York, 1992).
—— *The Juggler: Franklin Roosevelt as Wartime Statesman* (Princeton University Press, Princeton, 1991).
Kissinger, H., *The White House Years* (Weidenfeld & Nicolson/Michael Joseph, London, 1979).
Kitzinger, U., *Diplomacy and Persuasion: How Britain Joined the Common Market* (Thames & Hudson, London, 1973).
Kolko, G., *The Politics of War* (Weidenfeld & Nicolson, London, 1969).
Kyvig, D. E., *Reagan and the World* (Praeger, New York, 1990).
Lafeber, W., *The American Age: United States Foreign Policy at Home and Abroad Since 1750* (W. W. Norton & Co., New York, 1989).
Lenin, V. I., *Imperialism the Highest Stage of Capitalism* (Progress Publishers, Moscow, 1978).
Leuchtenberg, W. E., *et al.*, *Britain and the United States: Views to Mark the Silver Jubilee* (Heinemann, London, 1979).
Lincove, D. A., and Treadway, G. R., *The Anglo-American Relationship: An Annotated Bibliography of Scholarship, 1945–1985* (Greenwood Press, Westport, 1988).
Louis, William, R., *Imperialism at Bay: The United States and the Decolonisation of the British Empire 1941–45* (Oxford University Press, Oxford, 1978).
Louis, William R., and Bull, H., *The Special Relationship: Anglo-American Relations since 1945* (Clarendon Press, Oxford, 1986).
MacDonald, I. S., Anglo-American Relations since the Second World War (David & Charles, Newton Abbot, 1974).
Macmillan, H., *Riding the Storm* (Macmillan, London, 1971).
—— *Pointing the Way* (Macmillan, London, 1972).
Manderson-Jones, R. B., *The Special Relationship: Anglo-American Relations and Western European Union, 1947–56* (Weidenfeld & Nicolson, London, 1972).
Neustadt, R. E., *Alliance Politics* (Columbia University Press, New York, 1970).
McKenzie, F. A., *The American Invaders* (Grant Richards, London, 1902).
McMillan, J., and Harris, B., *The American Take-Over of Britain* (Hart Publishing, New York, 1968).
McNeil, W. H., *America, Britain and Russia: Their Co-operation and Conflict, 1941–46* (Oxford University Press, London, 1953).
Middlemas, K., and Barnes, J., *Baldwin: A Biography* (Weidenfeld & Nicolson, London, 1969).
Morton, H. V., *Atlantic Meeting* (Methuen, London, 1943).
Mowatt, R. B., *The Diplomatic Relations of Great Britain and the United States* (Edward Arnold, London, 1925).
Nicholas, H. G., *The United States and Britain* (University of Chicago Press, Chicago, 1975).
Nixon, R. M., *The Memoirs of Richard Nixon* (Book Club Associates, London, 1978).
Northedge, F. S., *Descent From Power: British Foreign Policy 1945–73* (Allen & Unwin, London, 1974).
Nunnerly, D., *President Kennedy and Britain* (Bodley Head, London, 1972).

Ovendale, Ritchie (ed.), *The Foreign Policy of the British Labour Government 1945–51* (Leicester University Press, Leicester, 1984).

——*Appeasement and the English Speaking World: Britain, the United States, the Dominions and the Policy of 'Appeasement', 1937–39* (University of Wales Press, Cardiff, 1975).

—— *The English Speaking Alliance: Britain, the United States, the Dominions and the Cold War 1945–51* (Allen & Unwin, London, 1985).

Parrini, Carl, *Heir to Empire: United States Economic Diplomacy 1916–23* (Pittsburgh University Press, Pittsburgh, 1969).

Pierre, A., *Nuclear Politics: The British Experience with an Independent Strategic Force, 1939–1970* (Oxford University Press, London, 1972).

Ponting, C., *Breach of Promise: Labour in Power 1964–70* (Hamish Hamilton, London, 1989).

Pym, F., *The Politics of Consent* (Hamish Hamilton, London, 1984).

Reynolds, D., *The Creation of the Anglo-American Alliance 1937–41* (Europa, London, 1981).

Richelson, J. T., and Ball, D., *The Ties that Bind: Intelligence Cooperation Between the UKUSA Countries* (Allen & Unwin, Hemel Hempstead, 1985).

Robbins, L., *Autobiography of an Economist* (Macmillan, London, 1978).

Roberts, H. L., and Wilson, P.A., *Britain and the United States: Problems in Co-operation* (Harper Bros, New York, 1953).

Ryan, Henry, B., *The Vision of Anglo-America: The US–UK Alliance and the Emerging Cold War 1943–46* (Cambridge University Press, Cambridge, 1987).

Sanders, D., *Losing an Empire, Finding a Role* (Macmillan, Basingstoke, 1990).

Schulzinger, R. D., *American Diplomacy in the Twentieth Century* (Oxford University Press, New York, 1984)

Seymour, C., *The Intimate Papers of Colonel House*, vol. 1 (Ernest Benn, London, 1926).

Sorensen, T., *Kennedy* (Harper Row, New York, 1965).

Sprout, Harold, and Sprout, Margaret, *The Rise of American Naval Power 1776–1918* (Princeton University Press, Princeton, 1914).

Stoler, M. A., *The Politics of the Second Front: American Military Planning and Diplomacy in Coalition Warfare, 1941–1943* (Greenwood Press, Westport, 1977).

Thatcher, M., *The Downing Street Years* (HarperCollins, London, 1993).

Truman, H. S., *Year of Decisions* (Doubleday, New York, 1955).

—— *Years of Trial and Hope* (Doubleday, New York, 1955).

Watt, D. C., *Succeeding John Bull: America in Britain's Place 1900–1977* (Cambridge University Press, Cambridge, 1984).

Weinberger, C., *Fighting for Peace: Seven Critical Years in the Pentagon* (Warner Books, New York, 1990).

Wheeler-Bennett, J., *The Disarmament Deadlock* (Routledge, London, 1934).

Williams, W. A., *The Roots of Modern American Empire: A Study of the Growth and Shaping of Social Consciousness in a Marketplace Society* (Anthony Blond, London, 1970).

—— *The Tragedy of American Diplomacy* (Dell Publishing Co., New York, 1972).

Wilson, H., *The Labour Government 1964–70* (Penguin Books, Harmondsworth, 1974).

Wilson, T. A., *The First Summit: Roosevelt and Churchill at Placentia Bay* (Houghton Mifflin, Boston, 1969).

Woods, R. B., *A Changing of the Guard: Anglo-American Relations 1941–45* (University of North Carolina Press, Chapel Hill, 1990).
Young, K., *Churchill and Beaverbrook: A Study in Friendship and Politics* (Eyre & Spottiswoode, London, 1966).
Young, J. W. (ed.), *The Foreign Policy of Churchill's Peacetime Administration 1951–55* (Leicester University Press, Leicester, 1988).

ARTICLES

Allen, H. C., review of D. C. Watt, *Succeeding John Bull*, in *Journal of American Studies*, 19 (1985).
Allen, R. G. D., 'Mutual Aid Between the United States and the British Empire', *Journal of the Royal Statistical Society*, 109 (1946).
Beloff, M., 'Is There an Anglo-American Political Tradition?' *History*, 36 (1951).
Brinkley, D., 'Dean Acheson and the "Special Relationship": The West Point Speech of December 1962', *Historical Journal*, 33 (1990).
Carroll, F. M., 'Anglo-American Relations and the Origins of the Cold War: The New Perspective', *Canadian Journal of History*, 24 (1989).
Contemporary Record, 3 (1989), IMF Crisis Symposium.
Costigliola, F., 'The Failed Design, de Gaulle and the Struggle for Europe', *Diplomatic History*, 8 (1984).
Devuyst, Y., 'European Community Integration and the United States: Towards a New Transatlantic Relationship', *Journal of European Integration*, 4 (1990).
Dobson, Alan P., 'A Mess of Pottage for Your Economic Birthright: The 1941–42 Wheat Negotiations and Anglo-American Economic Diplomacy', *Historical Journal*, 28 (1985).
——— 'The Export White Paper of 1941', *Economic History Review*, 39 (1986).
——— 'The Kennedy Administration and Economic Warfare against Communism', *International Affairs*, 64 (1988).
——— 'The Years of Transition: Anglo-American Relations 1961–67', *Review of International Studies*, 16 (1990).
——— 'Labour or Conservative: Does it Really Matter in Anglo-American Relations?' *Journal of Contemporary History*, 25 (1990).
——— 'The Special Relationship and European Integration', *Diplomacy and Statecraft*, 2 (1991).
——— 'Aspects of Anglo-American Aviation Diplomacy 1976–93', *Diplomacy and Statecraft*, 4 (1993).
——— 'Regulation or Competition? Negotiating the Anglo-American Air Service Agreement of 1977', *Journal of Transport History*, 15 (1994).
Gaddis, J. L., *et al.*, 'Replies', *Diplomatic History*, 7 (1983).
Hodson, H. V., 'The Anatomy of Anglo-American Relations', an inaugural lecture published by the Ditchley Foundation.
Ikenberry, G. John, 'A World Economy Restored: Expert Consensus and the Anglo-American Post-War Settlement', *International Organization*, 46 (1992).
Kaplan, L. S., 'Cold War and European Revisionism', *Diplomatic History*, 2 (1978).
Megaw, M. R., 'The Scramble for the Pacific: Anglo-American Rivalry in the 1930s', *Historical Studies*, 17 (1977).

Pardalis, A., 'European Political Co-operation and the United States', *Journal of Common Market Studies*, 4 (1987).

Payne, A., 'US Hegemony and the Reconfiguration of the Caribbean', *Review of International Studies*, 20 (1994).

Reynolds, D., Rethinking Anglo-American Relations, *International Affairs*, 65 (1988/9).

—— 'Britain and the New Europe: The Search for Identity since 1940', [review essay in], *Historical Journal*, 31 (1988).

Simpson, Michael, 'Admiral William Sims, U.S. Navy and Admiral Sir Lewis Bayly, Royal Navy: An Unlikely Friendship and Anglo-American Co-operation 1917–1919', *US Naval War College Review*, 41 (1988).

Smith, Bradley F., 'Admiral Godfrey's Mission to America June/July 1941', *Intelligence and National Security*, 1 (1986).

Smith, M., 'The Devil You Know: The US and a Changing EC', *International Affairs*, 68 (1992).

Trachtenberg, M., 'White House Tapes and Minutes of the Cuban Missile Crisis', *International Security*, 10 (1985).

Treverton, G. F., 'Britain's Role in the 1990s: An American View', *International Affairs*, 66 (1990).

Venn, F., 'A Futile Paper Chase: Anglo-American Relations and Middle East Oil 1918–34', *Diplomacy and Statecraft*, 1 (1990).

Warner, G., 'The Anglo-American Special Relationship', *Diplomatic History*, 13 (1989).

EPHEMERA

Report by President Richard M. Nixon to Congress, 18 Feb. 1970, 'United States Foreign Policy for the 1970s: A Strategy for Peace'.

Index

Printed in the United Kingdom by
Lightning Source UK Ltd., Milton Keynes
140330UK00001B/3/A